DEATH OF DR. BOTTA.

He Did Not Recover Consciousness After His Fall from a Window.

Dr. Vincenzo Botta died early yesterday morning at his home, 25 West Thirty-seventh street. He did not recover consciousness after his fall from a third-story window of his house at 3 o'clock on Tuesday morning. It is thought that the fall was due to an attack of vertigo. He had felt the attack coming on, and warned a relative, Mrs. Thomas F. Lynch, who lived with him. As he had retired feeling in good spirits he was thought to be all right for the night. His neighbor, Dr. J. S. Boyd, Jr., of 28 West Thirty-eighth street, heard Dr. Botta's fall, and, hearing groans afterward, he summoned two policemen. They found Dr. Botta unconscious. Mrs. Lynch would not allow him to be taken to a hospital.

Dr. Botta was more than six feet tall, and of impressive appearance. His culture and good fellowship made him a valued acquaintance.

Eminent in Italy, and known at European capitals, where he had pursued investigations of educational systems, Dr. Botta became equally prominent here soon after his arrival in this country in 1853. He was then 35 years old. He came to study the common school system of the United States, and liking American ways and institutions he determined to make this city his home. In two years he married Anne Charlotte Lynch, the author, and their home became a gathering place of the prominent people of the country and visitors from abroad.

Dr. Botta was born in Cavaller Maggiori, Piedmont, Nov. 11, 1818, and received his education at the University of Turin, where he afterward became professor of philosophy. He was elected to the Sardinian Parliament in 1849, and in the following year he was commissioned, with a fellow member, Dr. Parola, to examine the school system of Germany. Their report was published by the Government. The University of Berlin conferred upon Prof. Botta the degree of Doctor of Philosophy in recognition of his work in Germany. Soon after coming to this country he was made professor of languages in the University of the City of New York, and held this place until a few years ago. In 1863 he became a member of the Union League Club, and for many years and at the time of his death he was one of its Vice-Presidents.

During the Franco-Prussian war his home was the centre of a movement started by Mrs. Botta to relieve the women and children of Paris. Mrs. Botta collected the autographs of famous persons and sold the collection for $5,000. The war was ended before the collection was complete, so the sum was used to found a prize in the French Academy. Mrs. Botta died in Europe two years ago.

Dr. Botta published several works, the best known of which are "Dante as Philosopher, Patriot, and Poet," with an analysis of the "Divina Commedia;" "An Historical Account of Modern Italy," "Discourse on the Life, Character, and Policy of Cavour," "Account of the System of Education in Piedmont," and "An Introduction to Dante."

The funeral will be held on Monday, and the burial will be at Woodlawn.

PROFESSOR BOTTA'S FALL.

THE VENERABLE A[illegible] OUT OF THE THIRD-STORY WINDOW OF HIS HOME DURING AN ATTACK OF VERTIGO—IT IS FEARED HE WILL [illegible] OF HIS RIBS ARE BROKEN AND HIS HEAD BADLY INJURED.

NEW YORK, Oct. 2 (*By Direct Telephone*).—Professor Vincenza Botta, the well-known linguist and one of the Vice-Presidents of the Union League Club, fell from the third-story window of his home, No. 23 West Twenty-seventh street, early this morning, and was [illegible] it is feared he will die. It is so badly [illegible] an attack of his belief that he [illegible] vertigo.

At 3:30 o'clock this morning Mr. Boyd, who lives at No. 28 West Twenty-eighth street, directly back of the Botta residence, heard groans, and, looking out of the window, saw Professor Botta lying in the yard. Policeman Thompson, who was summoned, found the Professor unconscious. The window of his bedroom on the third floor was open.

He had evidently fallen from the window, struck an extension, and rolled off into the yard. Three physicians were called and it was found that Professor Botta had sustained fractures of four ribs. Besides severe injuries to the head was found a fracture to the right ankle.

HIS CAREER ON TWO CONTINENTS.

Vincenzo Botta was born in Cavalier Maggiore, Piedmont, on November 11, 1818, and received his education at the University of Turin. After his graduation he became Professor of Philosophy in his alma mater. In 1848 he was elected to the Sardinian Parliament, and in 1850 he was commissioned in association with Dr. Parola, another deputy, to examine the educational system of Germany. Their report on the German universities and schools was published at the expense of the Government.

Anne C. L. Botta

MEMOIRS

OF

ANNE C. L. BOTTA

WRITTEN BY HER FRIENDS

WITH SELECTIONS FROM HER
CORRESPONDENCE AND FROM HER
WRITINGS IN PROSE AND POETRY

Tanto gentile e tanto onesta pare
La donna mia!

Dante

NEW-YORK
J. SELWIN TAIT & SONS
PUBLISHERS
31 EAST 17TH STREET
MDCCCXCIV

TO MR. CHARLES BUTLER
THESE MEMOIRS ARE DEDICATED AS
A SOUVENIR OF FOUR DECADES
OF FRIENDSHIP, LOYALTY
AND DEVOTION

In Memoriam

Nata die undecima Novembris, MDCCCXV

Obiit die vigesima tertia Martii, MDCCCXCI

Introductory Note

These recollections of the late Mrs. Botta are intended for readers who take interest in the literary movement of the age, and particularly for those who, during her lifetime, were acquainted with her, and enjoyed the attraction of her sympathy and the sweetness of her friendship. They are chiefly composed of essays on her life and character, which, under the forms of letters, reminiscences, characteristics, impressions, and tributes to her memory, were written at the editor's request, by some of her most intimate and devoted friends. As a series of pen-portraits these writings reproduce to nature the beautiful personality which their authors endeavored to portray and revive.

The volume cannot be classified among biographies of the regular standard; yet it answers to the principal requirements of biographical treatment, and properly belongs to that branch of literature which, under the name of "Memoirs," has become so popular in our times.

The book opens with a biographical sketch in which the principal events of Mrs. Botta's life are recorded. This is followed by memories developing the same subject from the time she entered the Albany Female Academy to the last days of her life. Some contributions present an accurate psychological analysis of her character; some treat in a general way of her relation for the last fifty years to the historical evolution of the intellectual and social elements in American civilization. Then her poetic, literary, and artistic merits are considered, while here and there a brilliant light appears on her spiritual nature, on her moral qualities, and on the many graces with which she was so liberally endowed.

"E pluribus unum" should be inscribed on this volume; for, though written by several hands, the unity of the conception is not in any way marred by the variety of the execution,—no more so than a number of paintings of the same landscape taken from different points of view can detract from the unity of its general appearance. Indeed, the diversities in color, in light and shade, and in the perspectives aid the spectator in forming a more comprehensive and more attractive conception of the whole scenery.

To the authors of these beautiful offerings the editor presents his cordial thanks for the generous and kind devotion with which they responded to his request, thus expressing their affectionate loyalty to the memory of their departed friend.

To these contributions, selections from her letters are added. During her long and active life her correspondence was very extensive and varied; but, unfortunately, she seldom kept copies of her letters. Of those which have been collected, many are entirely of a private character; therefore only a few are introduced, as particularly expressing her personal sentiments and ideas.

Introductory Note

Letters written to her by distinguished people may be of special interest to the readers. Accordingly some of these have been culled from this part of her correspondence, limiting them, however, to letters written by friends who have already passed away. For obvious reasons, those of surviving correspondents are excluded. The volume closes with some of her writings, in prose and poetry, most of them inedited.

This introductory note may be appropriately concluded with the closing lines from her "Battle of Life":

The guardian angels are hovering near;
They have watched unseen o'er the conflict here,
And they bear her now, on their wings away,
To a realm of peace,— to a cloudless day.
Ended now is the earthly strife,
And her brow is crowned with the Crown of Life.

V. BOTTA.

Index

Index

SELECTIONS FROM HER LETTERS

Index

SELECTIONS FROM LETTERS TO HER

SELECTIONS FROM HER WRITINGS

Prose

Index

Poetry

Recollections by her Friends

Biographical Notes

By Mrs. S. M. C. Ewer, New-York.

My dear Mr. Botta:

In answer to your letter requesting me to write down my recollections of the late Mrs. Botta, whose death we all greatly deplore, I will say that I feel it to be a duty of love and gratitude to comply with your wishes. Perhaps I was more intimately connected with her in the early days than any other pupil of hers; and her influence on my character was the strongest influence of my youth. Her assistance through some of the rugged and intricate paths of my life I shall never forget, and her sweet image will forever stand before me as that of one of my best friends and benefactors.

Patrick Lynch, the father of Mrs. Botta, was born in Lucan, near Dublin, Ireland. While a student of civil engineering in the Dublin University, he took part in the Irish Rebellion of 1798. For this offense he was imprisoned for some years; then he was offered freedom on condition that he would take the oath of allegiance to the British crown. Refusing to do this, he was banished from his country at the early age of eighteen. He sailed to America with other patriots, prominent among them Thomas Addis Emmet, the eminent physician. Thomas Moore was also his friend; and when the Irish poet came to this country, Mr. Lynch traveled with him. One summer day, while they were resting under a tree, the poet improvised one of his ballads, which his companion wrote under his dictation. Later, Mr. Lynch went to Bennington, Vermont, and with a partner engaged in the dry-goods business. It is said that soon after the two men opened their store, two young ladies went in to make some purchases; after they left, the partner asked Mr. Lynch which one he liked best. He answered, "I saw only one." This one was Charlotte Gray, the daughter of Lieutenant-Colonel Ebenezer Gray, of the Connecticut line, who, under the commission of General Washington, had served through the Revolutionary War. Mr. Lynch immediately made the acquaintance of Miss Gray, and in the year 1812 they were married. They lived in Bennington some years, and had two children born there,—Thomas Rawson and Anne Charlotte; Anne was born November 11, 1815. They removed from there to Pennsylvania; and later to Windham, Connecticut. Leaving his family here, Mr. Lynch soon after went to Cuba to secure some lands which the Spanish government offered to Irish refugees. He arrived in Havana; but, in 1819, while going from there to Puerto Principe, where these lands were situated, he suddenly died at sea, leaving Mrs. Lynch with two young children,— Thomas, six years, and Anne, nearly four years, of age.

From my impressions gathered in conversations with the mother of your wife, Mr. Lynch was a gentleman of distinguished appearance, refined and elegant in manner, and a conversationist of more than ordinary culture. His letters to his wife are beautiful with expressions of love and sympathy for her and the children. He left some writings, of which "A Manual of Maxims" for guidance through life is full of practical wisdom, showing a keen insight into human character. He was an excellent draftsman. While in prison he delineated with his pen miniature maps, in color, of the several counties in Ireland, which are remarkable for their accuracy as well as fine execution. These maps are accompanied by an historical sketch of all the rebellions which had taken place in these counties for centuries, and the cruel reprisals inflicted on the people by the British power.

Soon after the death of her husband, Mrs. Lynch, with her two children, removed to Hartford, Conn., where she was able to send them to the best schools. When sixteen years of age, Anne was sent to the Albany Female Academy to complete her education. She proved to be a student of great intelligence, assiduous and zealous in the performance of her duties; she won class honors in several departments, and for two years in succession the prize for the best poem. She graduated with highest honors in 1834, and remained some time in the Academy as a teacher.

Later, she accepted a situation in the family of Mr. Gardiner, of Shelter Island, N. Y., to teach his three little daughters. Two of these afterward married, successively, Professor Horsford of Harvard College. During the two years she stayed on this island, she kept a journal which she called "The Diary of a Recluse," an interesting record giving the details of her daily life on that lonely spot, filled with solid thoughts and original ideas, although tinged with a melancholy tendency which was quite natural in one so sensitive, so eager for knowledge, and so entirely deprived of association with scholarly and sympathetic minds. She has said, however, that she considered her solitary life on that island the principal basis for the development of her mental character, as it afforded her extensive and systematic reading for a thorough self-education.

After leaving the Gardiners, she joined her mother in Providence, R. I., where she took young ladies into the family to teach and educate. It was here, in 1843, that I was placed under her charge, and soon I grew to appreciate her incomparable methods of teaching, to love her sweet disposition, and to admire her charming manners. Her acute intellectual insight into character, and her wisdom in guiding others as well as herself in the various branches of study, were remarkable. She inspired her pupils with love for intellectual occupation, strengthened their characters, and made them eager to improve in every way. Her intense interest in their advancement became to them a powerful stimulus. Her strong affection for young people was a dominant characteristic of her nature, and she delighted in promoting and watching over the gradual development of their mental and moral faculties. It was for this that, from her early days to the end, she liked to have in her house one or more young ladies to educate and prepare for the duties of life. Her ideas on education were rational and well defined. At the early age of twenty she wrote a letter to a young friend, full of practical wisdom, advising her on the best method of study. Her influence on her pupils was good and permanent, and in after years many of the young ladies who had enjoyed the privilege of her instruction, and had become wives and mothers, often expressed their gratitude for the beneficent influence of her example and advice, by which they were still inspired.

While living in Providence she occasionally wrote for reviews and magazines. In 1841 she edited "The Rhode Island Book," which contained some of the best specimens from the writers of that State, from Roger Williams down to her own time, including two of her original poems. About this time she instituted her evening receptions, which were often honored by Emerson, Dr. Brownson, Mrs. Whitman, and other eminent people. Charles T. Congdon states in his "Reminiscences of a Journalist" that the best literary society of Providence in 1843 was to be found in the parlors of Miss Lynch; and so it continued to be after she became a resident of New-York city.

In the year 1845 she was with a prominent family

in Philadelphia, superintending the studies of a young lady who desired to complete her education; and it was while here that she made the acquaintance of Fanny Kemble, who soon became strongly attached to her, presenting her to a much wider circle of literary people. In a letter which Mrs. Kemble wrote to her after having read some of her poems, she said: "I thought, on perusing your verses, This, indeed, is the work of one of God's elect." The great actress had a strong will, and resented at once the least opposition. She would raise her imperious head in disdain if anything she had said was questioned. But she has been known to submit before the sweet smile and genial manner of Anne C. Lynch, who sometimes dared to express a different opinion.

After leaving Philadelphia, she with her mother settled in New-York city. They took a house in Waverly Place, where in 1846 I again became a member of their family. Miss Lynch received every Saturday evening, wrote for periodicals, and resumed teaching, taking a position as teacher of English composition in the Brooklyn Academy for young ladies.

Soon we removed to Eighth street; then in 1849 to Ninth street. About this time she published her poems in book form; they were illustrated by distinguished artists of that time.[1] The volume elicited universal praise, and among those whose homage she received was Edgar A. Poe, who in his "Literati"

[1] The "Battle of Life" was illustrated by Duggan; "The Angel of Death," by H. K. Brown; "Teaching the Scriptures," by Huntington; "Portrait of Frederika Bremer," by Sodermark; "To the Mem-

says of her two noble poems, "The Ideal" and "The Ideal Found": "In modulation and vigor of rhythm, in dignity and elevation of sentiment, in metaphorical appositeness and accuracy, and in energy of expression, I really do not know where to point out anything American superior to them." He also commends her poem "Bones in the Desert," not forgetting some graceful and touching lines on the death of Mrs. Willis. He tells us that she wrote anonymous critical papers in the "New-York Mirror" and elsewhere, with acknowledged contributions to "The Gift," "The Diadem," and "The Democratic Review," in which she published an essay on Fanny Kemble's poems.

About this time she wrote a poem on Frederika Bremer, a copy of which was sent to that lady. This opened an interesting correspondence; and when the celebrated Norwegian made her memorable visit to America, she was the guest of our poetess for several weeks. The house in Ninth street swarmed with distinguished people, who were eager to give the popular writer their welcome to our land. It was fascinating to see the delight of this cheerful lady as she watched the hostess gliding among her guests, bestowing upon all, equally, her courtly attentions, her smiles, and an interest in their enjoyments. Miss Bremer gave her impressions of the

ory of Channing," by Durand; "The Wasted Fountains," by Winner; "The Wounded Vulture," by Cushman; "Bones in the Desert," by Darley; "The Mediterranean," by Rossiter; "Byron among the Ruins of Greece," by Rothermel.

poetess in her "Notes on American Life." There she says: "My first idea of Miss Lynch was that she led a butterfly life; but, after closer intercourse in the privacy of her home, I learned the depth of character she possessed, and now feel that I know Anne Lynch at last."

Miss Lynch visited Washington four successive seasons—from the year 1850 to 1853. In 1851 she presented a petition to Congress in behalf of her mother, who was the only living child of Lieutenant-Colonel E. Gray, claiming payment of money due for military services rendered by him in the Revolutionary War. Through her perseverance, energy, and popularity, and with the aid of prominent men in the Senate and in the House, the claim was granted.

Among her prominent friends in Washington mention may be made of Henry Clay, to whom she was for a time private secretary, Judge Berrien of Georgia, Pierre Soulè of Louisiana, and Judge Phelps of Vermont. She soon became the center of the most cultivated society in the capital, which was attracted by her intellectual qualities, genial manners, and personal magnetism.

In a speech which Daniel Webster addressed to the Senate in f850, he said: "When I and all those that hear me shall have gone to our last home, and when the mold may have gathered on our memories, as it will on our tombs, . . ." On this sentiment she wrote the following poem, which elicited from the great statesman a beautiful letter of recognition:

WEBSTER.

The mold upon thy memory! —No,
   Not while one note is rung
Of those divine, immortal songs
   Milton and Shakspere sung;
Not till the night of years enshrouds
   The Anglo-Saxon tongue.

No! let the flood of Time roll on,
   And men and empires die;
Genius enthroned on lofty heights
   Can its dread course defy,
And here on earth can claim the gift
   Of immortality;

Can save from that Lethean tide,
   That sweeps so dark along,
A people's name—a people's fame
   To future time prolong,
As Troy still lives, and only lives,
   In Homer's deathless song.

What though to buried Nineveh
   The traveler may come,
And roll away the stone that hides
   That long-forgotten tomb:
He questions its mute past in vain,
   Its oracles are dumb.

What though he stand where Baalbec stood
   Gigantic in its pride:
No voice comes o'er that silent waste,
   Lone, desolate, and wide;
They had no bard, no orator,
   No statesman,—and they died.

Anne C. L. Botta

They lived their little span of life —
  They lived and died in vain;
They sank ingloriously beneath
  Oblivion's silent reign,
As sank beneath the Dead Sea wave
  The Cities of the Plain.

But for those famed, immortal lands,
  Greece and imperial Rome,
Where Genius left its shining mark,
  And found its chosen home,
All eloquent with mind they speak,
  Wood, wave, and crumbling dome.

The honeyed words of Plato still
  Float on the echoing air;
The thunders of Demosthenes
  Ægean waters bear;
And the pilgrim to the Forum hears
  The voice of Tully there.

And thus thy memory shall live,
  And thus thy fame resound,
While far-off future ages roll
  Their solemn cycles round,
And make this wide, this fair New World
  An ancient, classic ground.

Then with our Country's glorious name
  Thine own shall be entwined;
Within the Senate's pillared hall
  Thine image shall be shrined;
And on the nation's Law shall gleam
  Light from thy giant mind.

Our proudest monuments no more
May rise to meet the sky;
The stately Capitol, o'erthrown,
Low in the dust may lie:
But mind, sublime above the wreck,
Immortal, cannot die!

The payment of her mother's claim having been received, she was quite anxious about the investment of the money. Many withheld their advice for fear of making a mistake. In this embarrassment a friend introduced Miss Lynch to Mr. Charles Butler of New-York city, who at that time was extensively engaged in railroads and lands in the West. He kindly and wisely invested the money. From that time he became her constant adviser and warm friend. His friendship for her, as hers for him, was sentimental and beautiful as it was disinterested and pure. For more than forty years he managed your affairs with skilful and generous hands; and this brought you both into constant relations with him—an intimacy which grew into a noble, ever-living affection and into an unremitting mutual devotion. She never allowed a year to pass without sending him a few original lines in commemoration of his birthday, expressing in affectionate rhymes her reverence for his generous nature, and his sympathy for all who were in need of it, and her admiration for the distinguished traits of his character as a man, as a Christian, and as a friend. The following are two of these sweet remembrances:

TO MY FRIEND,

ON HIS BIRTHDAY.

Oh, Time! deal gently with my friend,
  Who gently deals with all;
And on his loved and honored head
  Let blessings only fall

In love to God, and love to man,
  His days pass here below;
And so, to reach the home above,
  He has not far to go.

But distant be that hapless day
  That calls him from our view:
Heaven has so many souls like his,
  And Earth, alas! so few

On another anniversary she wrote to him as follows:

TO MY FRIEND,

ON HIS BIRTHDAY.

He who has walked among his fellow-men
This life's rough path for threescore years and ten,
Bearing for others, on the weary way,
The heat and burden of the toilsome day;
Sounding the silvery notes of faith and hope
Whene'er the weak or the despairing droop;
Speaking the words of sympathy and love,
Far the wild discords of the world above;
Raising the fallen, succoring the opprest —
The Holy Graal of unfound good his quest;
Holding aloft, a true and blameless Knight,
The stainless banner of the Just and Right:
He is the Christian hero of to-day,
And at his feet my tribute here I lay.

Soon after the beginning of her acquaintance with Mr. Butler, she with other guests accompanied him to the West as far as Chicago. While taking this journey she wrote many articles for the press of New-York, giving lively descriptions of the West, and prophesying a great future for that part of the country.

In 1853 she visited Europe with Mr. Butler and his family. During this visit she made the acquaintance of Thomas Carlyle and many other eminent people in England. The party then traveled to Paris, Florence, Venice, and Rome. She improved these opportunities in visiting some of the most celebrated studios, and in earnestly studying the great masterpieces of ancient art which adorn the museums and galleries of those cities. This study was afterward continued and extended in the several visits which she made to Europe with her husband.

On her return to New-York, she took up her usual occupations, and the "Saturday evenings" were resumed. To these the attention of the public was called by several writers of the time. Among them may be mentioned Catherine Sedgwick, herself a teacher and an authoress. Having attended one of these gatherings, she published an article in which she expressed much surprise that a young lady without position or fortune, and struggling for existence, should have succeeded in attracting to herself a society which in its intellectual character was far superior to any in the city.

Bayard Taylor, who became a constant guest, thus

refers to these receptions in his "John Godfrey's Fortunes": "I have been fortunate enough to obtain entrance to the 'Literary Soirées' of another lady whom I will not name, but whose tact, thorough refinement of character and admirable culture, drew around her all that was best in letters and in the arts. In her salon I saw the possessors of honored and illustrious names. I heard books and pictures discussed with the calm discrimination of intelligent criticism. The petty vanities and jealousies I had hitherto encountered might still exist, but they had no voice; and I soon perceived the difference between those who aspire and those who achieve." In a letter dated New Year's Day, 1848, he says: "Last night I attended Anne Lynch's 'Conversazione,' and met Grace Greenwood, Willis, Morris, Read, Healy, Griswold, Mrs. Ellet, Gillespie, Kate and Mary Sedgwick. We had a dance and most delightful conversations, together with recitals. Grace repeated her 'Ariadne,' Read his 'Bards,' and Kate Sedgwick Miss Barrett's 'Bertha in the Lane.'"

If I were to mention all that has been written of these popular receptions, and the names of the prominent people who attended them, it would take up too much space. I will only say that all the best writers, poets, and artists of the time, living in or passing through New-York, attended her "evenings." It was at one of these that Poe gave the first reading of "The Raven."

One of the pleasant features of these receptions consisted in several Valentine Festivals. Most of the verses were original and appropriate, written by the poets of her society. I well remember the gallant form of General Gaines as he pleasantly accepted the tribute to his fame written by our talented hostess. All the stanzas read and delivered to each visitor were spirited, but of a dignified stamp, far above the maudlin, sentimental, flippant lines that are usually circulated on the commemoration of St. Valentine. Another brilliant affair was a series of tableaux arranged by notable artists.[1] It can easily be imagined what esthetic effects were produced by such an array of genius.

The success of these gatherings was principally due to the fact that the hostess never forced her opinions on her guests. It was her policy to arouse the brilliancy of cultured minds, and keep the light burning by gentle suggestions. She never argued, and thus kept peace, and avoided hurting the feelings of her friends. Humorous and witty, she never allowed her repartee to be tinged with sarcasm.

Besides these regular evenings, she gave occasional receptions to distinguished people, whom she desired to present to her friends. I remember one given to Ole Bull — the Norwegian violinist — on his first visit to America; a friendship followed which lasted until his death. On his departure from this country after this first visit, she dedicated a poem to him, which was placed in a bouquet and presented at his Farewell Concert. These receptions

[1] Such as Darley, Church, Healy, Rossiter, Lang, Richards, May, Kensett, Elliott, and Hicks.

were more frequently given after her marriage in 1855, when the family removed to Thirty-seventh street.[1] If you will allow me, I will here allude to the perfect happiness which for an uninterrupted period of thirty-six years was enjoyed by you both in your matrimonial relations. It was consecrated by mutual love, congeniality, and a complete harmony of tastes, ideas, and aspirations. Speaking to an intimate friend of her marriage, she said that it satisfied her judgment, pleased her fancy, and, above all, filled her heart.

The moral characteristics of Mrs. Botta were preeminent and all-pervading; these were the natural growth of her strong sympathetic instinct, and strict fidelity to duty. Her sensitive conscience was quickened by her experience in early life, and by contact with those who were unfortunate. It was sustained by habitual meditation on moral sentences

[1] Among the prominent people who attended these receptions, or spent some time at her house, may be mentioned: Poe, Willis, Morris, Fanny Osgood, Emerson, Mrs. Whitman, Dr. Brownson, Cranch, Cheney, Bryant, Theodore Sedgwick, Clark, Irving, the Cary sisters, Bancroft, Halleck, Grace Greenwood, Greeley, Tuckerman, Stoddard, Dr. Holland, Bigelow, Mrs. Mary Mapes Dodge, Mrs. Kirkland, Huntington, E. Booth, Dr. Bellows, H. Giles, Bayard Taylor, H. W. Beecher, Raymond, Stedman, Helen Hunt, Mrs. Leonowens, Miss North, E. Lazarus, A. D. White, Bartholdi, R. Proctor, Froude, Charles Kingsley, Matthew Arnold, Lord Houghton, Lord Amberley, Lyulph Stanley. Madame Ristori, Salvini, Fechter, Campanini, and Madame Gerster were honored by special receptions. Special receptions were also given in honor of George P. Marsh, on the occasion of his appointment as minister to Turin, in 1861, and to the officers of the Royal Navy of Italy when they came to this country to take possession of two frigates built by an American ship-builder for the Italian Government.

from the works of Epictetus, Marcus Aurelius, Thomas à Kempis, Emerson, and others of similar type. The Christian education which she received in her youth consecrated her conscience to philanthropy as a religious duty; and charity to all became the supreme imperative of her conduct. Her sentiment in this regard is beautifully expressed in the following poem:

CHARITY.

O Thou who once on earth beneath the weight
  Of our mortality didst live and move,
  The incarnation of profoundest love;
Who on the Cross that love didst consummate,
  Whose deep and ample fullness could embrace
  The poorest, meanest of our fallen race:
How shall we e'er that boundless debt repay?
  By long, loud prayers in gorgeous temples said?
  By rich oblations on thine altars laid?
Ah, no! not thus Thou didst appoint the way:
  When Thou wast bowed our human woe beneath,
  Then as a legacy Thou didst bequeath
Earth's sorrowing children to our ministry,
Saying, As ye do to them ye do to me.

Although she never accepted any special creed, and heartily agreed with Tennyson that

There is more faith in honest doubt,
Believe me, than in half the creeds,

yet she was essentially a Christian woman: a Christian of the highest type in her sympathies, her aspirations, and her tranquil submission in all circumstances to the Supreme Power, the omnipotent, omniscient, and benevolent Father of all created things. With her friend, Margaret Fuller, she did not say that she accepted the Universe; but she willingly recognized its eternal order, and endeavored to conform her life to it: hence her never-changing, cheerful disposition, which no disappointment or even calamity could ever disturb. She used to say that "whatever may happen, it is always for the best." With these optimistic views during her life she conquered all her doubts and fears. This was the great moral quality which gave her a strength of character rarely found even in the most devoted Christians. Heartily recognizing the great results brought about by the influence of all Christian churches toward the development of civilization, she did not admit any dogmatic element in her faith, which was rather molded on the broad interpretation of Christianity as held by William Ellery Channing and his principal followers, such as Ripley, Bellows, Alger, C. T. Brooks, and Freeman Clarke, to all of whom she was united by a sincere friendship. To the memory of Channing she dedicated a poem, in which she speaks of him as follows:

Not for thy country, creed, or sect speak'st thou,
But him who bears God's image on his brow,
Thy brother, high or low.

Great teachers formed thy youth,
As thou didst stand upon thy native shore,
In the calm sunshine, in the ocean's roar;
Nature and God spoke with thee, and the truth,

That o'er thy spirit then in radiance streamed,
And in thy life so calmly, brightly beamed,
  Shall still shine on undimmed.

Her deep sentiment for Christianity she expressed in noble verses in "Teaching the Scriptures," in "Christ Betrayed," "Faith," "Hope," "Charity," and, above all, in her noble ode on

PAUL AT ATHENS.

  Greece, hear that joyful sound!
A stranger's voice upon thy sacred hill,
Whose tones shall bid the slumbering nations round
  Wake with convulsive thrill.
Athenians, gather there; he brings you words
Brighter than all your boasted lore affords.

  He brings you news of One
Above Olympian Jove. One, in whose light
Your gods shall fade like stars before the sun.
  On your bewildered night
That Unknown God of whom ye darkly dream,
In all his burning radiance shall beam.

  Behold, he bids you rise
From your dark worship at that idol shrine;
He points to Him who reared your starry skies,
  And bade your Phœbus shine.
Lift up your souls from where in dust ye bow;
That God of gods commands your homage now.

  But, brighter tidings still,
He tells of One whose precious blood was spilt
In lavish streams upon Judea's hill,
  A ransom for your guilt;
Who triumphed o'er the grave, and broke its chain;
Who conquered Death and Hell, and rose again.

Sages of Greece, come near;
Spirits of daring thought and giant mold,
Ye questioners of Time and Nature, hear
Mysteries before untold;
Immortal life revealed, light for which ye
Have tasked in vain your proud philosophy.

Searchers for some First Cause,
'Midst doubt and darkness,—lo! he points to One,
Where all your vaunted reason, lost, must pause,
Too weak to think upon,—
That was from everlasting, that shall be
To everlasting still, eternally.

Ye followers of him
Who deemed his soul a spark of Deity,
Your fancies fade, your master's dreams grow dim
To this reality.
Stoic, unbend that brow, drink in that sound;
Skeptic, dispel those doubts, the Truth is found!

Greece, though thy sculptured walls
Have with thy triumphs and thy glories rung,
And through thy temples and thy pillared halls
Immortal poets sung,—
No sounds like these have rent your startled air,
They open realms of light, and bid you enter there.

Poe, speaking of the moral character of Miss Lynch, says: "She is chivalric, self-sacrificing, equal to any fate, capable even of martyrdom, in whatever should seem to her a holy cause. She has a hobby, and this is, the idea of duty." "Do the duty that lies nearest thee, and thy next will be made plainer," was the motto she adopted when quite young; and her selection of that duty was ever judicious.

First of all was her obligation to her mother, who was often in ill health. All personal desires and favorite pursuits were sacrificed for the comfort of that dear one, whose love, as she says in the poem dedicated to her,

> Is one flower I have found still unwithered;
> Like the night-scented jasmine it gleams.

Her letters to her mother from abroad are models of filial tenderness and devotion.

She was so young when her father died that she could not remember him, yet her vivid imagination, prompted by her love, yearned for his dear memory; and one day, while looking on a miniature portrait of him, she wrote these lines:

> I strive in vain those features to restore
>   To Memory's faded tablets, which on me,
>   From the mute ivory, beam so lovingly,
> And to recall their living light once more.
>   In vain I strive to pierce that veil of years,
>   And turn away all blinded with my tears;
> But sometimes, when the garish day is passed,
> And night and sleep their spell upon me cast,
> Thou comest to me, my father, from above,
>   And then for that brief moment I am blest,
>   For I am folded to thy sheltering breast;
> And in the sacred rapture of thy love
> A holy spell is on my spirit laid:
> This mighty hunger of my heart is stayed.

Her love for her brother was very strong and tender; and after his early death she adopted his son, providing for his education and giving him most affectionate care. The same kind affection and care she bestowed on her grandnephew, Thomas Raphael Lynch, who with his mother lived in your family for several years. He died when eighteen years old, the last representative of the Lynch family.

What she was to you, what you were to her, I have already alluded to: what the loss you suffered by her death, is not for me to say. Your affliction is too deep and sacred to permit any remark.

To her friends she was always tender, sincere, and loyal; ready to sacrifice to them her time, pleasures, and feelings. Her admirable qualities of mind and heart were ever at their service. She never used her friends for her own benefit; but gave them at all times, when needed, a bountiful supply of advice, comfort, and sympathy. She never would disappoint them, although she was sometimes disappointed. She never spoke of the favors she bestowed, although kindness to her was sometimes extolled without recognition of kindness received. This ingratitude she bore with undisturbed tranquillity, regarding it not with contempt, but rather with pity.

Her sympathy was never withheld, even from those unknown to her who came for counsel or aid. Poverty, sickness, and old age were sure to find in her relief and consolation. No poor person who called at her door for assistance was sent away with empty hands. In many instances she cared, through their lives, for people who were poor and ill, making them comfortable to their last days.

Highly sensitive and refined, she was always quick to recognize mental and moral worth, always offering a helping hand with sympathy and encouragement. Thus she was able to bring forth talents which otherwise might never have come to light. "It was not so much what Mrs. Botta did for literature with her own pen," says a Boston writer, "as what she helped others to do, that will make her name a part of the literary history of the country. If she had done nothing beyond discovering Edith Thomas, she would have deserved the thanks of all lovers of real poetry. When Miss Thomas presented herself at Mrs. Botta's door, she was entirely unknown; but the portfolio of manuscripts she had under her arm made it impossible for her to remain so any longer. Mrs. Botta detected the divine spark, and passed the poet on to that other poet, Helen Jackson ('H. H.'), who set herself to work at once to make Miss Thomas known to the world. The first thing she did was to call at the 'Critic' office with a poem of Miss Thomas's in her hand, which was published in that journal just as quickly as the compositors could put it into type. Then 'The Century' published a page of the new poet's verses, and it was not long before the 'Atlantic' had her among its contributors, and the 'Atlantic's' publishers had a volume of her poems on their list. To-day, Edith Thomas is recognized as the best among the living women poets, and there are only a few men who are her superiors. So, as I said before, if Mrs. Botta had done nothing but discover Miss Thomas, she would have had a proud record."

The poems of Mrs. Botta are marked with this deep feeling of sympathy. What can be more expressive than these words from "The Wasted Fountains"?

There are aching, there are breaking,
Other hearts beside thine own.

Or these about a wounded heart in "The Battle of Life"?

In war with these phantoms that gird him round,
No limbs dissevered may strew the ground;
No blood may flow, and no mortal ear
The groans of the wounded heart may hear
As it struggles and writhes in their dread control
As the iron enters the riven soul.
But the youthful form grows wasted and weak,
And sunken and wan is the rounded cheek;
The brow is furrowed, but not with years;
The eye is dimmed with its secret tears,
And streaked with white is the raven hair;
These are the tokens of conflict there.

Mrs. Botta was naturally distinguished by modesty, delicacy, tact, refinement, simplicity, and elegance of manners; these qualities being with her the spontaneous growth of that preëminent spirituality with which she was so liberally endowed. With the cares of her household, with the duties imposed upon her by friendship and charity, and with her social distractions, she lived in the high serene region of the Ideal, far above the follies and foibles of this world. This quality shone forth in her thoughts, her actions, her voice, and her countenance. Her poetry is all alive with this spiritual, purifying touch, being a beautiful expression, under different forms, of the same lofty sentiment.[1] So it was with her works of art. She often said: "Beauty in art, in my opinion, does not consist in simply copying nature, but in retaining the true features of the subject, and breathing on them a breath of spiritual life, which should bring them up to their ideal form. There are portrait-painters who take particular care to bring forth in their pictures the imperfections of their models; a blind eye, or bad mouth,—they are sure to give prominence to these errors of nature. A true artist, I think, should try to conceal them by a proper use of light and shade; so that, without sacrificing truth, the portrait should bring forth the ideal appearance of the subject. This idea I try to realize in my portrait-busts."[2] According to this sentiment, in the selec-

1 The subjects of her poems are an evidence of the truth of this statement— "Longing," "Aspiration," "Largess," "Sweetness," "Love," "Wishes," "Endurance," "In the Library," "Music," "The Ideal," "The Ideal Found," "The Wounded Vulture," "The Heroes," "Vita Nuova," "Unrest," "Accordance," "Charity," "The Battle of Life," "Bones in the Desert," "Evening Hymn," "The Wasted Fountains," "Faith," "Hope," "To the Sun," "To the Century Plant," "The Lake and Star," etc.

2 Her principal portrait-busts are those of her husband and Mr. Charles Butler. A copy of the bust of the last named carved in marble was a few years since presented to The University of the City of New-York. She also modeled busts of Mr. Henry W. Sage, the late Mrs. A. D. White, Miss Avis Leonowens (now Mrs. Fyshe), and the Hon. Lyulph Stanley.

tion of her reading she always gave the preference to those poets and novelists who on the "wings of genius" soar high above the low realities of this life, and thus endeavor to elevate the human mind to the lofty regions of the true, the just, and the beautiful. Her favorite studies were history, literature, and art; and to these she gave all the time she could spare from her various duties. At the time of her death she was engaged in preparing a "Handbook of Universal History," which is left unfinished. This was to be a companion to her "Handbook of Universal Literature," published first in 1860, and reëdited with additions in 1890.

The following poem shows her deep reverence for the paramount influence of literature on the human mind:

IN THE LIBRARY.

Speak low, tread softly through these halls;
  Here genius lives enshrined,
Here reign, in silent majesty,
  The monarchs of the mind.

A mighty spirit-host they come
  From every age and clime;
Above the buried wrecks of years
  They breast the tide of Time.

And in their presence-chamber here
  They hold their regal state,
And round them throng a noble train,
  The gifted and the great.

O child of earth, when round thy path
The storms of life arise,
And when thy brothers pass thee by
With stern, unloving eyes—

Here shall the Poets chant for thee
Their sweetest, loftiest lays;
And Prophets wait to guide thy steps
In wisdom's pleasant ways.

Come, with these God-anointed kings,
Be thou companion here,
And in the mighty realm of mind
Thou shalt go forth a peer.

In whatever she undertook, she displayed remarkable energy and perseverance; she was endowed with indomitable courage, which enabled her to overcome many obstacles. "I am not afraid of anything," she used to say. "I feel like that great hero of whom Horace sings:

"If in fragments were shattered the world,
Him its ruins would strike undismayed."

She expressed her admiration for this virtue of moral courage, in her beautiful poem:

ENDURANCE.

Thou brave old Titan, that in chains didst lie,
Bound to the rock on the Caucasian hill,
Who by sublime endurance didst defy
Imperial Jove and all his shades of ill;
As I invoke thy spirit here to-day,—

From the old Pagan world thou speak'st to me,—
I hear thy voice across Time's echoing sea;
Bid me thus bear and conquer,—I obey.
Henceforth, like thee, I will endure and wait
(On life's black summit bound) without dismay.
Then in thine iron car roll on thy way,
Thou stern, relentless power that men call Fate,
Loose then thy bolts, thou dark and threat'ning sky—
Thou vulture at my heart, feed to satiety.

With her innate sympathy, with her tendency to long for better conditions, she could not fail to be in harmony with all movements directed toward human progress. During the civil war in America she contributed to the funds of the Sanitary Commission by the sale of an album prepared by her own hands. And again, after the Franco-German War, she disposed of another album for the establishment of a permanent prize at the French Academy for the best work on the "Education of Women." When Kossuth, the Hungarian patriot, came to America, she consecrated a poem to him. And when Italy, after a slumber of many centuries, awoke to national consciousness, she saluted her arising with "Viva Italia." She sympathized with all social and political reforms which were attempted at different times in this country; but her exquisite delicacy and modesty never allowed her to pose as a reformer. Early in her time, some of her friends—such as Ripley, Curtis, and Cranch—had joined a small agricultural and educational association, called "The Brook Farm," near Roxbury, Mass. She visited them once or twice, and saw Mr. Curtis engaged in washing dishes which had been used by "The Community." She remarked to him that perhaps he could be better employed for the progress of his fellow-men than in wasting his energy in an occupation more easily done by others. She returned from this visit fully convinced that she could accomplish more by living in the midst of humanity than by secluding herself within the narrow limits of a farm.

In the movement for the emancipation of women, she took an active part in demanding the legal rights of women to property, and to the exercise of the various professions. She did not talk much about this subject, but George P. Marsh used to say that he did not know a woman who, like Mrs. Botta, said so little on this question of woman's rights, and, when occasion arose, took so firm a grasp of her own rights as she did. As for woman's political emancipation, she thought that the conditions of society were such as to render that reform unadvisable. "The political vote given to women," she said, "would increase the quantity of the suffrage; but I doubt if it would improve its quality. Women must be educated, and then the time will come when they may claim to be a part of the political body."

With the transcendentalism of New England, which flourished at an early period of her life, she sympathized as a protest against the rigid Calvinism of the Puritan stamp. At one time she invited Bronson Alcott, one of the leaders of that movement, to preside over some *conversazioni* in her parlors, where he could elucidate his favorite subject. On one occasion, a lady in the audience, impressed by some sentiments uttered by the lecturer, inquired of him if his opinion was that we were gods. "No," answered Mr. Alcott, "we are not gods, but only godlings," an explanation which much amused Mrs. Botta, who was always quick in perceiving the funny side of a remark.

She was much interested in scientific progress, and early in her career she dedicated a poem to Science, in which she says:

Science! illumined by thy living rays,
  A brighter glory lights the dome of night;
There thou dost open to our wondering gaze
  System on system round those worlds of light
In silence winging their harmonious flight.
  And when weak sense returns to earth again,
There we behold, when thou dost guide our sight,
  Above, around, where'er our gaze hath been,
"Infinity without, Infinity within."

Her imagination was kindled by the new doctrines of Darwin and Herbert Spencer. She delighted in studying the bearing of the great natural laws of evolution, natural selection, struggle for existence, the survival of the fittest, the conservation of energy, and the prevalence of universal law, which have already conquered nearly the whole world of modern thought. She was particularly interested in these laws as applied not only to the phenomena of the physical universe, but also to history, politics, and religion. The potentiality of these discoveries was so great to her mind that she wrote to Emerson expressing her belief that they might soon become fit subjects for lyric poetry.

However, while admiring the scientific progress of her age, she maintained that modern science cannot fully explain either the mysteries of life and death, or the problem involved in the contemplation of the universe in its origin and its destiny. In her opinion there was only one possible solution, and that the one given by the Christian religion. The belief in the immanent presence of the Infinite One—as Carlyle says, "The Infinite Good One who has given to us all that is good, generous, wise, right, whatever we deliberately and forever love, in ourselves and in others"—is by itself a great light thrown on these problems. It will not make clear what is incomprehensible, nor explain what is inscrutable. But under the great canopy of a benevolent Providence we may at least possess our souls in patience, follow truth wherever it leads us, do all the good we can, trusting with Tennyson that in the long run everything will be for the best, and "every winter turn to spring."

In her youth, Mrs. Botta had a charming presence. This quality was not lost as she advanced in age, and to the time of her death she appeared much younger than she really was. Poe thus describes her when young: "She is rather above the usual height, somewhat slender, with brown hair and soft eyes—the whole countenance full of intelligent expression. Her demeanor is dignified, graceful, and noticeable for repose." N. P. Willis, in his "People I Have Met," portrays her in her youth under the name of "Jennie Eveland." "Her face is capable of most illuminative beauty, always expressive, always frank and noble, and her form is indeed the perfection of feminine symmetry. Never giving her movement a thought, she walks with a lithe grace and freedom that betray her at once as a woman of perfect make. Her head is admirably set on, and an Indian girl bred in the forest like a fawn would not be more erect, nor of more unconscious elasticity of carriage and mien. An unusually arched instep to an exquisite foot gives her the mark of high breeding, and her slender and yet roundly beautiful hand with its tapering fingers has a look of that discriminating elegance which the most careless of her friends recognize and admire. A bright blue eye, earnest and fearless; profuse brown hair, whose natural waves are controlled with difficulty by a comb; bright teeth, and one of those voices of clouded contralto which betray the tearfulness used to keeping down sadness, are other peculiarities which go to form her portrait, and which share in the delightful impressions she makes on all who have the happiness to know her."

Early in March, 1891, Mrs. Botta began to make preparations for a festival, which was to have taken place the 31st of the month, in commemoration of the thirty-sixth anniversary of her marriage. On the evening of the 15th she entertained a happy assemblage in her house; on the 17th she received the members and guests of the Nineteenth Century Club at their rooms, she being one of the directresses. On this evening she took a severe cold, which rapidly developed into pneumonia. She died suddenly, and almost painlessly, on the first hour of the 23d. This brief illness was in accordance with a wish she had often expressed.

The announcement of her death was received with universal expressions of grief, and brought many messages of sympathy and condolence to her grief-stricken husband from friends in different cities in this country and in Europe; among which may be mentioned those of King Humbert and Queen Margherita. The funeral service was held in her parlors on the 25th; and in accordance with her wish, there was no display. The closed casket, containing all that remained of this noble woman, was surrounded by a few friends,—no flowers, no music, and only a short service by the attending clergyman. Then the remains were taken to their final resting-place in Woodlawn Cemetery, accompanied by a few sorrowing ones, who saw her laid by the side of her mother under the turf among plants and flowers. A beautiful tree, the emblem of terrestrial existence, overshadows the spot, which is marked by a tall granite shaft, the symbol of that ever-ascending celestial life, of which, while here, she delighted in thinking as the possibility of the progressive future. "Ad altiora" should be inscribed on her monument as a high expression of her hope. But as a prayer from the hearts of those who loved her, I would place upon it those beautiful lines of Halleck:

Green be the turf above thee,
Friend of my better days:
None knew thee but to love thee,
Nor named thee but to praise.[1]

[1] This tribute to the memory of Mrs. Botta, and nearly all the memorials contained in this volume, were addressed in the form of letters to her husband, V. Botta, the editor of these recollections. Mrs. Ewer, *née* Sophie Congdon, was one of Mrs. Botta's first pupils and one of her dearest companions in her early life. She furnished the notes on which this biographical sketch is outlined. It has been extended so as to bring it down to the periods not included in Mrs. Ewer's notes.

Early Recollections

By Mr. Henry W. Sage, Ithaca, N. Y.

My dear Mr. Botta:

YOU ask me for some personal recollections of your wife previous to her marriage with you in 1855. I first knew Anne Charlotte Lynch in 1834. At that time I was a clerk in Albany, N. Y., and she a student at the Albany Female Academy. We boarded at the same house. Her home at that time was in Hartford, Conn., where her mother and her only brother, Thomas, were living. She earned the money for her expenses in the Academy by writing original pieces, and doing copying, which was procured for her by her brother. She was then about eighteen years of age. There were several young people in the house, and as we often met at the table, and again in the parlor for the evening, we soon became acquainted. My acquaintance with Miss Lynch ripened into a friendship which lasted to the day of her death. Hers was no ordinary character, and her friends then were the best-educated people in letters, law, and divinity. She even at that time had made a place for herself among the acknowledged leaders in literature of Albany and New-York, and, before she was aware of it, had become a star in the literary horizon. Some of her earliest poems (school compositions) had been published, and, without any other heralding, she suddenly rose to a high position. These poems were "The Mediterranean," "To the Sun," and "Byron Sleeping amid the Ruins of Greece,"—all of which were later republished in her volume of poems. The productions of her pen, and her conversation, marked by her thorough knowledge of history and literature, attracted during the next two years the attention of educated men and women; and she received the courtesy and homage of Willis, Morris, and many other eminent men of those days.

Although such attention was very flattering to one so young,—who owed nothing to position or fortune,—she was entirely free from pride or vanity. Her manners were simple and childlike. At that early age her character was as well poised as it was twenty years later. Her judgment was sound and clear; her bearing toward all, kind, cordial, sympathetic, and dignified. I think those who knew her as a school-girl, and in the full maturity of her later life, were impressed with this fact; that at the age of eighteen she had already acquired that ripeness and remarkable development of moral and intellectual character which so distinguished her at a later period of her life. But the stability and dignity of these qualities did not detract from the sweet simplicity of her manner and conversation. Wise, sympathetic, and sincere, she was always on the alert, and anxious to do for those who needed her friendship. Her ideals of life and duty were high; she never acted from an unworthy motive, but her charity for those who did was boundless. She would remark: "They lacked wisdom, and were swept by currents they could not control. I cannot blame them; God only can judge!" Her early life was among those who had strict Puritanical ideas. She adopted the essentials of Christianity, but was not partial to creeds, being deeply religious without professing to be so; and her whole life was based upon the "Golden Rule." Her purpose was to be and do all that the rule required. This developed a well-rounded Christian character, which governed her life and conduct.

Among her early friends in Albany was Amos Dean, a rising young lawyer, the founder and president of the Young Men's Association. He was at that time writing his "History of Civilization,"— an immense work of seven volumes with more than 500 pages each. The manuscript was all read and revised by Miss Lynch; she was so conscientious in this that she had to read the principal works on history, literature, art, and philosophy, with an equal attention to the work of Mr. Dean in the preparation of his book.

In 1836 she left Albany. Soon after, she went to Shelter Island to superintend the education of the young daughters of Mr. Gardiner, a prominent citizen of that place. In 1838 Miss Lynch went to live with her mother in Providence. Here Susan E. Linn, who afterward became my wife, was placed under her charge as a student in history and literature. Later our friend removed to New-York, where her literary acquaintance was largely extended. From that time we seldom met, but often corresponded, advising each other of our progress in life, and feeling equally sure of an ever-abiding friendship. We always held in vivid remembrance the first year of our acquaintance in 1834, and the discussions we then had in reference to the life before us. Our possessions at that time were few, but we had a boundless stock of faith and hope that never has failed. My Christmas gift to her in 1888, a silver pitcher with this inscription, refers to that period of her life and mine:

1834.

Two Friends look out on Life's broad sea,
And sail their Pilots, Hope and Faith;
Their hearts are strong and brave,
Prepared for calm or stormy wave!

1888.

The Friends have sailed fifty years and four,
The Pilots ever there!
Faith always at the helm,
While Hope looked out before!
And onward still they sail,
Their final Port in sight;
The open door from Earth
To God's eternal Light!

Henry W. Sage to Anne C. L. Botta, 1888.

Her later life was better known by you and others than by me. She was a rare woman. A nobler, purer, truer, never lived. She was broad and sound in her intellectual grasp, deep and tender in her sympathy, abounding in love for those nearest her, and in charity for all who needed charity.

A Loving Tribute

By Grace Greenwood, Washington, D. C.

IT is difficult to realize that more than two years have swept by since our beloved friend left us, so suddenly, with no faintest warning. Even as we walked and talked together, in the pleasant afternoon sunshine of life, she turned, and, by a covert gateway, passed into the "valley of the shadow of death," and we saw her face no more! Can it be that the violets of three springtimes and the roses of three summers have blossomed about her grave,—that the fallen leaves of two autumns and the snows of a second winter have drifted over it? To me the realization is the more difficult because of my removal from the places that once knew her—my distance from the beautiful home in which I so often saw her. It seems to me that I have only to return, to find her there—so fresh is her memory, which scarce seems a memory; for she is not only dearer, but nearer to me, than she was when in this realm of shifting shadows, delusive dreams, and mysterious longings we call life. In spirit I seem to live much in her very presence—am scarcely barred out of her pleasant, serene companionship. Yet I was quite cast down, at first, in knowing that, "in my flesh," I could see and embrace her never again. I think that the old grieve more deeply, if less passionately, than the young. When friends beloved in "the days that are no more," are taken from us, we sorrow not alone for them, but for our lost youth—its romance and light-heartedness. Countless memories of pleasant scenes and the actors therein are connected in my mind with this noble woman and loyal friend, who was intimately associated with many of the events and much of the happiness of my early life. What a help she was!—practically, mentally, and spiritually. She had always an intense desire to aid others—to minister to their happiness and well-being. It was a divine hunger of her soul. Her sympathies touched all about her, and reached far and wide; but when she could feel an intellectual or artistic as well as benevolent interest, she was most happy.

She saw pleasure through the eyes of those she loved—she had the keenest joy in their success. Though so sympathetic, she was an admirable counselor—safe, loyal, and judicious. Many came to her for advice in desperate straits, and went away stronger in resolve or patience. To the downcast, she was comfort; to the struggling, infinite encouragement.

When I first met Anne C. Lynch, she was known to me only as the writer of a few poems, whose pure and lofty spirit and exquisite artistic finish had so impressed me that when she called to see me during my first visit to New-York, I felt that in wishing to know me she did me great honor—a feeling I never lost. I was then fresh from unconventional village life, knowing little of literary or metropolitan society, while she was, for one so young, an accomplished woman of the world—yet not worldly. She was wise without guile. As I said, she was a great aid to me in many ways. Miss Lynch resided, at that time, in a modest house down-town—which was not called "down-town" then. Her home was simple in its appointments, but marked by that artistic elegance which always characterized her surroundings. With her lived her widowed mother, an old-school gentlewoman, to whom she was devoted for many years, with a filial love that almost amounted to a passion,—fond, patient, passing all praise. To me there was something pathetic in this unconscious sacrifice and unfaltering service. No ambition for intellectual or social distinction—not the strong allurements of art or brilliant society, not even the claims of a later and most dear love—had power to render her neglectful of that sacred filial duty, unfaithful to the primal cult of the heart.

The time of my first acquaintance with Miss Lynch was the time of Fanny Kemble Butler and Catherine Sedgwick; of Bryant, Halleck, Poe, and Willis,—all knowing and honoring her. Besides these friends, she had about her a goodly company of choice spirits, artistic and literary,—a delightful circle, gathered she hardly knew how; for she was far from realizing the subtle attraction, the peculiarly gentle magnetism, of her own personality. This circle widened and widened, till from it and for it she formed the most brilliant and successful *salon* I have ever known in America. They who had the *entrée* to those weekly reunions—almost uninterrupted for a score of years, and never wholly discontinued—must remember them with grateful pleasure mingled with keen regret. For all thus once favored must live in a light that can never fade, one central, living picture—the dainty yet dignified figure of a peerless hostess with an honest welcome in her soft blue eyes. The gentle pressure of her delicate hand, her frank smile, and her low, sweet voice—how real and how recent they seem!

Those evenings were *conversazioni* of an informal but most refined character—not occasions for professional talkers, nor for elocutionary display, though sometimes guests of rare histrionic talent gladly contributed to our enjoyment. I have never since seen in any young society-leader such a union of courageous truthfulness and exquisite tact as distinguished Miss Lynch; and these qualities remained with her all her life, as did a beautiful transparency of character, which revealed its purity without disguising its depth. I have heard mention made of her "repose of manner." I should rather say *poise*,—the expression of a perfect mental equilibrium. My friend's admirable feminine traits and social and intellectual equipments most impressed me during an intimate association with her in the more cosmopolitan society of Washington. This city was not then (a decade before the war) so rich in millionaires and fine mansions as it has since become; but it was passing rich in great men and in brilliant and cultivated women. Authorship was not so fashionable among Southern ladies as it now is; but the ability was by no means lacking. The wit, the taste, the poetic feeling now put to practical and profitable use in literature, were then prodigally expended in conversation, giving a peculiar charm to the society of the capital; and it was in this bright, aristocratic society that Anne C. Lynch shone by her own light—with no adventitious aids whatever. Her social success among the best people was extraordinary. At Cabinet and Presidential receptions she was seen surrounded like a queen by statesmen. One of her warmest friends in those days was Henry Clay. He had for her, he once told me, not only the admiration he always felt for a clever, witty woman, but profound respect for her scholarly attainments, her rare good sense, and, above all, her purity of character. By the way, I should hardly apply the homely term "good sense" to that marvelous instinct of our friend,—that swift and sure perception of the right thing to say and do on all occasions; what jarring topics to avoid; what sensibilities to spare; how to reach and move the noble nature, so often hidden, in those she encountered. In attempting to analyze this rare gift of hers, one might have said: It is politeness and something better,—it is tact and something finer,—the perfect ear and sight, the exquisite touch of the soul. I remember that during our first season in Washington, the ladies staying at the National Hotel gave a reception for Frederika Bremer, and unanimously appointed her friend, Miss Lynch, to do the honors. She was in her gayest mood that evening; but her manner had the same ease and simple kindliness which distinguished it always,—even to that last reception, in her own beautiful home, only a week before she died. Somewhat weary she looked then; but her smile had the old sweetness as she bade me good night. Ah, "Good night!"

Washington assemblies were in those days pleasantly unconventional, yet select—not too much thronged to be thoroughly enjoyable; and no one enjoyed them more than Miss Lynch. The polka was then fashionable, and she was very fond of it, I remember,—dancing lightly, gracefully, and untiringly, with a refined enjoyment delightful to see. She was never, even then, called beautiful; but her face was very attractive, from its bright and varying expression,—a peculiarly winsome face,—while her form was remarkable for symmetry, suppleness, and a singular lightness of movement. She always dressed with entire simplicity, but becomingly; in late years in subdued colors, mostly black, yet with a certain freshness in style,—that touch of perennial youth which to the last lingered in her voice, her smile, and her elastic step. Ideally neat in person, there was also about her an aroma of exquisite moral cleanliness, which especially endeared her to women.

The coming of good fortune and love into the life of Miss Lynch, her happy marriage to Professor Botta, her removal to a more elegant and spacious home, never had the effect of cooling her heart toward her old friends, or concentrating her generous sympathies. Having the same freedom as before, she was the same woman toward all the world; only those nearest her saw that her nature was enriched both by the giving and the receiving of the new relation. With such a helper by her side, her generous hospitality enlarged its bounds till it took in the best representatives of literature, art, and science, with the leaders and heroes of great movements for liberty and humanity of the Old World as of the New. Having always estimated very highly Mrs. Botta's literary ability — poetic and critical especially — and her artistic gifts, so modestly regarded by her, and having remarked of her in late years a steady growth in spirituality, I often felt that metropolitan society, in absorbing her so much with local social claims and even local charities, robbed the world. It was a pure, cheery light which shone from the windows of her hospitable home, and that now is quenched; but a loftier, keener, more enduring radiance might have shone from her noble intelligence, her artistic genius, untrammeled and unhindered. Yet she made much happiness in her life, and helped lesser lights to shine their brightest. Sometimes, as I recall that life of beneficent activities, and think how completely it has passed into stillness and silence, a chill of mortal doubt—a breath from the sea of eternal mystery—creeps over my heart; but only for a moment. I surely can trust that she did not cease to be, just when her great soul was ripe for being; that in one of the Father's "many mansions," in a "house called beautiful," she is at home; that the light of welcome is still on her dear face, and that her divinest joy is still in giving joy, comfort, and counsel. She labors there with her old artistic delight, she waits with her old sweet patience.

Sweet Memories

By Mrs. Cornelia G. Willis, Williamstown, Mass.

My dear Mr. Botta:

YOU have offered me a privilege in asking me to contribute to the memorial you intend publishing of your dear wife. I wish I could adequately respond to it. The spirit is very willing, but out of the long years of affectionate friendship, I find it difficult to clearly recall incidents which would give any illustration of her career, that are not too closely linked with personal experience.

As I gather up the memories, they are massed in a very vivid and clear impression of a most lovable personality—the expression of a true, high-hearted character which was rounded by the sharp discipline of life, and the deep pursuing of an affectionate and spiritual nature always to higher and higher development. Her energy was great; her common sense never failed her in practical things, and her genial kindliness kept her always in touch with the sufferings of her fellows, and enabled her to aid them in an endless variety of ways,—as illustrated by the active part she took in the organization of the Wilson

Industrial School, and other enterprises of public interest, and also in the thousand little personal and social kindnesses for which so many recipients hold her in tender memory to-day.

When I came to New-York a young woman, she was among the very first of my husband's friends to greet me. For six years we were neighbors, and saw each other daily, and that intimate intercourse wove the strong bond of affection which never weakened in all the long years, although we saw each other less often after our home was in the country. At the time I speak of, she had not been very long in New-York, and was making a brave fight to win a home for mother and herself. The effort was courageously undertaken, and cheerfully and successfully carried through. In a few years she had made for herself an enviable position, and had gathered about her a large circle of friends; and when this was attained, it was held as a vantage-ground from which still to enlarge her sphere of usefulness and helpfulness.

Her thought was always aspiring, her heart always reaching out to serve some one by deed or sympathy. Her gifts were many, and made her a most enjoyable companion as well as the steadfast friend upon whom one could rely.

I inclose a sketchy characterization which Mr. Willis wrote of her under the name of "Jennie Eveland," and published in his "People I Have Met." If he had been here to express his estimate of her when she left us, it would have sounded a deeper chord, and have been more worthy. And yet there is a thread of truth running through it, and you may care to see it. Mr. Willis loved her and valued her friendship, and no one was more welcome in our home at all times than "our dear Lynchie."

As I read this over, it seems a very poor expression of the admiration and love I bear for the friend of a lifetime; but the heart is more steadfast and eloquent than the memory, and it is the best I can offer.

If I were to sum up in two words the compelling attributes of her nature, I should say they were aspiration and good will.

Early Days

BY RICHARD STORRS WILLIS, DETROIT, MICH.

MY DEAR MR. BOTTA:

WHEN your life passed under the shadow of a great grief, our hearts went out to you; and our loving memories to her who left but those memories, severed from the winning presence which vanished from view. And when she passed to the Celestial Country, she went freighted with an affluence of varied gifts, with the benediction of all who knew her, and with a heartfelt sigh of "Peace to thee!"

In the dread silence which is one of the most terrible swift-followings of death, we can well recall the qualities of mind and heart which that silence seems to render strongly vivid to us.

As generally viewed, her nature seemed molded on a high plane of entire disinterestedness: sympathy with others rather than with and for herself, a sympathy not limited to words, but active and practical, ready with any assistance she could render in whatever was the end to be attained. While this was specially true in the literary and artistic sphere,—to which her nature was most akin,—it was equally so in the practical and often vexed problems of life. It is perhaps not so untrue that no one is more absolutely and downright practical than one naturally poetic and imaginative, if once fairly put to it—for it was true of her.

In matters literary and artistic, many a young writer and artist can attest to her helpfulness. The unwilling, if not impatient, ear, ill concealed, of so many self-absorbed strivers in these realms, was never found in her. On the contrary, she would delicately invite a confidence yearning to be imparted by those seeking a calm, clear judgment, and the advice of a cultivated, esthetic mind.

As to her own creative activity, both in poetry and her favorite branch in art,—life-modeling in plaster, to be wrought in marble,—she was silent, habitually so. In all our many years of friendly intercourse I can recall but a single instance where a voluntary allusion was made by her to her poetry, and an expression of opinion was unexpectedly sought as to what she had done; a question which revealed a sweet innate modesty in view of a literary judgment like hers.

In her dealings with the world, its affairs and its people, she showed in a marked degree two salient qualities—tact, so inestimable in worldly matters, more potent, for temporal success, than genius; and common sense, the most uncommon sense of all. How remarkably these served her purpose in the earlier, trying, struggling years of her career, few of the throngs of her acquaintances in later years were aware—and they would be surprised if they knew. These qualities gained for her at Washington a long-delayed payment due for military services rendered to the country in the Revolutionary War by the father of her mother, Colonel Ebenezer Gray; this raised her from the straitened resources with which she was supporting herself and her invalid mother—to whom she showed so tender and touching a devotion through long years of helplessness—to a luxurious, artistic, and inviting home in upper New-York.

Quite remarkable, indeed, was a personal magnetism, silent and unconscious, withal, to herself, by which she attracted kindliness, interest, and a willingness to serve, if ever service were needed. This drew to her strong, influential, and wise friends, whose counsel and assistance in the arrangement of her affairs proved so invaluable.

Why do I rehearse all these things to you, dear friend, who know them so well, unless from a feeling that what we know we like others who know it to say? Perhaps a certain indulgence also may be conceded to me, whose acquaintance with the gentle departed one antedated even your own. Her choice of acquaintances was eminently an expression of herself; in touch with all distinctive and bright classes of mind, intellectual or artistic, they were magnetically drawn to her, as she to them, and they all crystallized in her drawing-room receptions, which became so unique a feature in conventional New-York.

Not least of her attractions to a musical ear, it may be added, was her low, sweet voice,—"that excellent thing in woman,"—now silenced for all of us.

Superior in her lift of nature to aught that was demeaning,—to disparagement, envy, or resentment,—and with "charity for all and malice toward none," she passed to the land where such qualities have their source and their home. Less should we sorrow for her than for ourselves. For ourselves! yes; for such sorrow is human and irrepressible, wise as an affectional relief, to be merged later, as I trust it may be with you, into the tender after-calm of a serene resignation.

Her Personal Traits

By Parke Godwin, New-York.

I AM very glad to learn that a memorial of Mrs. Botta is about to be issued, for few persons have more richly deserved to be thus held in remembrance by their friends.

At the time I first became acquainted with her, she was already quite well known as the poetess Miss Anne C. Lynch. My attention was attracted to her then by certain poems which I had from time to time remarked in newspapers and magazines, which contained, as I thought, an unusual degree of poetic talent. There was in some of them a good deal of that pensive sadness which characterized the writings of women at that time; but others—particularly the sonnets on "Milton," "A Modern Hero," "Ristori," "Endurance," etc.—had a vigor and range of thought that lifted them quite out of the common level.

But on coming to know the person, one was soon forgetful of the poetess. She was so genial, winsome, and sympathetic, you felt at once, on knowing her, that she would be a sure, good friend in whose affection and fidelity you could confidently trust. She was always amiable, courteous, and devoted to good works. Her admiration for the goodness and the genius of others, even when these were unrecognized by the world, was spontaneous. Many is the young author, male as well as female, who found in her kind sympathy the first encouragement.

Her home, soon after her arrival in this city, became the rendezvous for nearly all that was distinguished in statesmanship, literature, and art. The receptions she gave there each week came nearer to forming a *salon* such as we read of in French and English memoirs than any we had previously had, or perhaps have had since. One was always certain to encounter there a great many interesting persons not easily to be encountered elsewhere. I shall not endeavor to recall their names (which would be to repeat the lists of fame for those days), but simply say that there was hardly a person eminent in our own history, or a foreign visitor of celebrity, whom her hospitality failed to honor. Few women known to me have had greater grace or ease in the entertainment of strangers, while in her more private intercourse, her frank, intelligent, courteous ways won her the warmest and most desirable friendships.

In her later days, her time was devoted largely to practical charities, and particularly to those which had in view the education and elevation of her own sex, and in these her labors, though most unobtrusive and modest, were highly efficient. I was never called upon, I think, to take part in any benevolent scheme in which she did not prove herself a most willing and useful assistant. Her death was almost as great a loss to society at large as it was to her more intimate friends, so much had she identified herself with the good works of her day.

A Laurel Wreath

By Mrs. Julia Ward Howe, Boston, Mass.

My dear Mr. Botta:

IT was a sad day for many of us when we heard that your beloved wife was no longer in the land of the living.

An account seemed thus to be closed in which all her friends stood as debtors, so largely had we received of her sincere kindness and hospitality.

I now still do behold her as I have so often seen her, surrounded by the excellent company which she so well knew how to gather about her, herself the much-endeared center of an appreciating circle.

The atmosphere of her household was one which it was pleasant and profitable to breathe. Intelligence, good taste, and good feeling reigned there. Filled with love for literature and the arts, Mrs. Botta had a gift more precious even than her accomplishments in those directions. She was adorned with social tact, sympathy, and discernment, and her presence and influence helped to heighten in those around her the love of high thoughts and of useful studies.

The malignant and idle gossip with which the

great world overflows was not allowed to invade the borders of her domain; where she presided, heavenly charity had at least one representative.

If this poor tribute to her many merits should appear to you to deserve a place in your memorial volume, I shall be glad to have it appear as a testimony to my affectionate remembrance of one on whose grave I would willingly place the civic wreath as well as the poet's laurel.

Recollections

By the Hon. Andrew D. White, St. Petersburg, Russia.

INTO the pleasantest recollections of my boyhood is wrought the name of Anne C. Lynch. In those days, when there was little American literature, a new poem or story brought joy to very many families throughout the country; I recall vividly the days when "Graham's Magazine" and "Godey's Lady's Book" arrived and were laid on my mother's table. Among the greatest attractions in them to her and to me were Miss Anne C. Lynch's sketches and poems. There was in them a purity, a sweetness, a kindliness which seemed to bring into the house a benediction, and in my country home, far from the city in which she lived, she became one of the objects of my especial admiration.

Many years later, on a winter evening in 1870, when lecturing in the great hall of the Cooper Institute in New-York, my attention was drawn by what seemed to me one of the most attractive faces I had ever seen, a face kindly, gentle, but at the same time with deep character in every line; it was to me very beautiful, especially as it was surrounded with flowing gray hair.

At the close of the lecture I was presented to the lady, and found that she was the object of my early admiration. I had never before seen her, and this was one of the rare cases in which an object of early admiration met later in life has come up fully to expectations.

Then began for me one of the most precious friendships of my life; one, indeed, which I have ever since regarded as one of the best things that life has given me. It came at a time most opportune, for never have I felt the need of friends more than just at that period.

It was in the earliest years of Cornell University. Into the founding and early development of that institution I had thrown myself forgetful of nearly all things else. From the first, its struggle for existence had been severe. The fact that I strove to make it a University rather than a college of the old type; the fact, too, that I had placed in its charter a clause making sectarian control of it forever impossible,—these two things brought upon it and upon me an opposition untiring and apparently overwhelming. The strong friends of every one of the twenty colleges in the State of New-York and of many other colleges in other States, their graduates, and especially those in the pulpit and press, seemed to become more and more embittered against us; many who had stood by the institution in the beginning were swept away by this storm of opposition.

Then there were hardships of various sorts arising from difficulties in organization, misunderstandings with the State officials, lack of funds, and the like—all, together, making the life of its first president for some years perhaps as unhappy as that of any man within the boundaries of the State.

The lecture at the Cooper Institute was part of the effort to breast this storm. For some time I had stood on the defensive, endeavoring to show that the University would do no harm to the religious or intellectual development of the country; but I had at last seen that this could be of no avail, and I determined to take the offensive.

In this lecture, then, at the Cooper Institute, which was entitled "The Warfare of Science," I endeavored to show how every science in all ages has had to meet theological opposition and has been bitterly opposed by ecclesiastics; I especially dwelt upon the history of education in proof of this.

The lecture brought me two friends. The first of these was Horace Greeley, editor of the "Tribune," who next day spread my lecture in its earliest form upon the pages of his great journal, and thus gave it an immense circulation among thinking men and women.

The second friend was Anne C. L. Botta, whom I then saw for the first time, and who aided me personally to make acquaintances and establish relations of the greatest use in the work then lying before me.

I became a frequent visitor at her house, where she

and her honored husband formed a center which attracted thinking people not only from their own city, but from all parts of this country and from other countries. At their table the ideas which I had most at heart were broached and discussed; thither she brought the men and women who could discuss them to the best advantage. In her parlors from time to time I met those who were best worth my knowing, and from them received inspirations to better thought and work. Time after time, almost worn out and discouraged, I sought relief from University cares in her society and in that of her husband and friends, and never failed to be revived and strengthened by it.

In her letters, too, she showed her noble characteristics; she seemed to like nothing better than discussing problems best worth thinking upon, and she always did this in a noble spirit,—bringing out thoughts and giving suggestions sure to bear useful fruit.

In this acquaintance of mine I soon found that I was but one of many to whom she was constantly giving aid. This aid was of many sorts. Her charity, both in the ordinary and higher senses of the word, was boundless; she was continually making sacrifices to it; but the aid which she took especial delight in administering, was to men and women engaged in some work which she thought good.

Young men and young women struggling to make themselves felt in science, literature, art, or the work of higher instruction, were the especial objects of her interest; to seek them out, to aid them, to encourage them, to bring them into relations with others who could inspire them,—all this was her delight; but it was all done in a way most quiet and unostentatious.

It interested me much to note her comments on her travels at home and abroad; her motto might well have been "Not things, but men." Although having a deep love for art, she found, whether in America or Europe, her main attraction in thoughtful men and women. Of these she saw very many among the best in this country, England, France, and Italy, and they were to her more than beautiful scenery or works of art. When such men and women visited New-York, her house was a place of resort for them, and one of her especial delights was found in bringing these friends of hers from various parts of her own and other countries into communication with one another. Thus was imposed upon her a great weight of social duty, which became more and more engrossing, and when to this were added the quiet works of real charity and kindness which she was constantly doing, there would seem to be little time for anything else; yet she found time, and much of it,—time enough for preparing works for instruction in literature which have proved to be widely useful, and time to give herself to studies in various directions, and to that practice in sculpture which was one of the great delights of her life. Yet with all these things pressing upon her, she steadily preserved her early sweetness and serenity. Seated in her charming rooms, surrounded by books and works of art which revealed the nobility and beauty of her tastes, she seemed, when entertaining her friends, to be one of those who have no other care than simply to be happy among the happy.

At such times one met a very wide representation of the better human effort. There were representatives of widely separate fields of activity,—clergymen, poets, essayists, editors, professors of science and of literature, artists, men of business, people who were ending their career and people who were beginning their career: all these were to be found about her,—drawn to her house by the same kindly interest in their work and welfare.

For more than twenty years, the friendship formed in the most trying period of my life, continued as an inspiration and a steady help.

During those years she was, from time to time, my guest, and I was very frequently hers; never during all that period did I know her to betray the slightest tinge of an unworthy motive in any of her words or actions; of envy, hatred, malice, uncharitableness, there was never a trace in her character; her judgments were kindly,—indeed, at times, while showing a deep love for good and a determined opposition to evil, she seemed almost too lenient toward ill-doers.

The foundation of all her judgments was the love of God and the love of man, and this love was real and deep, and it took forms ever new, ever varying, and ever beautiful.

To me—as to others—her conversation was singularly inspiring: it suggested to a man his best trains of thought; it developed in him the best he had; it made him think better of himself and of mankind; it sent him away stronger for all good work.

Her interest in affairs was exceedingly broad: religion, politics, art, literature, science, social arrangements—everything that had to do with truth, beauty, or goodness was within her province. She was a good talker, but no less good as a listener—not merely with kindly patience, but with real interest, and with the suggestive word at the right moment.

Her religion always seemed to me of the deepest and best. For dogmatic statements and differences she cared absolutely nothing; to her, indeed, they were less than nothing. To her the sources of religious inspiration were the great utterances in all the bibles of the world, but above all such as those in the Sermon on the Mount, the "first and great commandment and the second which is like unto it," and the definition of "pure religion and undefiled," as given by St. James.

She seemed to me capable of worshiping in equal fervor with Roman Catholics or with Unitarians—in a cathedral or in a hovel; and this religious spirit of hers shone out in her life and in her countenance.

Very pleasant was her optimism; she looked about her in this world without distrust, and beyond her into the next world without fear.

Among the most beautiful of her utterances were those regarding death and a future life; toward death she looked with perfect equanimity, and toward a future life with hope.

Trials came to her, trials of a kind especially fitted to break her faith in humankind, and to alloy the sweetness of her character. People whom she had befriended showed themselves ungrateful; some whom she had aided to rise from a low estate showed themselves, when arrived at higher things, forgetful and supercilious.

But she cared for none of these things. When some flagrant instances of this kind were referred to in her presence, her answer was: "What I was able to do for them I enjoyed then, and the remembrance of it I enjoy now."

Her death came unexpectedly to all her friends. Although she had lived to a ripe age, she seemed ever youthful, so that the news of her death came as a great surprise to all who had known her.

Her heart, and mind, and soul seemed so young!

Beautiful and touching was her funeral. Means had been taken to prevent any large concourse; there were gathered a few of her nearest friends—perhaps a score; they represented all classes of those whom she had befriended.

On their way to and from her grave, exchanging reminiscences of one so dear, each revealed the fact that he or she had found Mrs. Botta a friend in need —a friend when friends were few. There was no loud panegyric: there was the simple, loving recital of what each had seen and known of a most beautiful life; and there came back to me what her old friend Horace Greeley had once said to me: "Anne Lynch is the best woman that God ever made."

A Letter of Condolence

By James A. Froude, London, England.

My dear Mr. Botta:

I HAVE often thought about you in your loneliness. Your letter is sad, but not sadder than it must have been, written as it is with the fresh sense on you of your irreparable loss. To have possessed such a wife, and to have had her taken away from you, is the hardest misfortune that could possibly have befallen you. You are not a person to whom the conventional consolations can give relief, and the extraordinary charm of Mrs. Botta can only make the recollection of her more poignant. I have known many interesting women in my life, but about her there was a peculiar grace which I have never seen in any other person. She had brilliant gifts, yet she never seemed to know that she had any gifts at all. And she had that rarest of qualities—that she never thought about herself at all. Her life seemed to be spent in disinterested care and affection for others, and, while all who knew her admired her intellect, her simplicity and unvarying kindness were more admirable still. Nothing seemed to put her out or disturb her temper. I should myself be the most ungrateful of mankind if I forgot the thoughtful affection which she showed to me—who had no claim upon her—so often and in so many ways.

To you, my dear Mr. Botta, whose existence was so wrapped up in hers, all this must seem a poor, and perhaps intrusive, tribute to her worth. But there is a pleasure in telling you what I felt for her, and in letting you see that her goodness to me was not thrown away.

What you suffer I know too well from my own experience. The young, who have their work before them, find relief from time and employment. You and I have little to do but sit still and wait till we pass away ourselves and carry our memories along with us. I used to think death frightful. I think now that it has been kindly ordered. If it be alarming to die, what would it be if we were told that we were never to die? That would be worst of all.

I cannot say whether we shall ever meet again, but you will perhaps now and then think of me as one who can never cease, while he lives, to remember your lost wife.

Her Personality

BY MONCURE D. CONWAY, LONDON, ENGLAND.

MY DEAR MR. BOTTA:

I HEAR with gladness that a memorial volume of Mrs. Botta is to appear. I fear that she, with her characteristic humility, did not sufficiently appreciate the value to others of her experiences and memories, but will hope that from manuscripts and letters something of her history and intellectual growth may be made known. I used to talk with her occasionally of Edgar Allan Poe and others of the literary circle charmed by her early poetic promise and her unique personality, and felt certain that there was still visible in her the youth, the sparkle, the intellectual play, fountain-like, which delighted that generation. There were no signs of cessation; she did not repeat herself; her interest was always fresh, for the new person and the new event. So little did we dream of any failure, that my wife and I, at the time of her death, were looking forward to the formation of a Sunday-evening club for conversation, of which Mrs. Botta was to be the central figure. The "Botta Club" exists, and she exists in the spirit and aim that founded it. But, alas! we are bereft of a relation more near than is often derived from the kinship of blood.

My dear friend, it is impossible for me to write of her in any adequate way. I might tell something of her full and exact knowledge, of her artistic poetry, her skill in sculpture, of her generosity; but it would require an elaborate study to convey the impression, derived by long acquaintance, of her personality, at once so simple and complex. I have sometimes imagined its sources,—whether, along with her American genius and tact, some French vein may not have contributed to her dainty expression and taste in the use of words, or some German ancestor transmitted her touch of quaintness. Her literary and critical insight was exceedingly fine. In conversing with her about eminent contemporaries,—Emerson, Carlyle, Longfellow, Browning, Tennyson, Holmes,—I never failed to recognize her perception of the essential variety and flavor of each; and was sometimes surprised by her interpretations of familiar sentences, as if she had a private key to them. In modeling heads she never flattered, but brought out the finest quality, and it was so with her criticisms. Also with her personal estimates. She was versatile in languages, but the language of depreciation she knew not.

Surely there was nothing more unintentionally picturesque than the receptions at "the Bottas"—as we used to say. How gracious was our friend, how self-forgetting, in bringing forward the new musician, or author, or artist, without parading them! There was never a shade of ceremonious style in greetings or introductions; all was simple, sincere, genuine. In her home, so tenderly decorated by her art and taste, with her face so full of happiness, surrounded by her friends, she reminded me of the tree in fairyland which gave to each the particular fruit by each desired.

Forgive, my dear Mr. Botta, the lameness of these reflections of our dear Mrs. Botta; alas, of their feebleness I am as conscious as of their sincerity.

Sympathy

By Justin McCarthy, M. P., London, England.

My dear Mr. Botta:

I NEED hardly say how deeply I sympathized with you and sympathize with you still, on the loss of Mrs. Botta, your dear wife and my dear friend. I can sympathize with you all the more deeply because since first you and I came to know each other I too have lost a beloved companionship. Your wife was one of our earliest friends when we first visited America many years ago; she was one of the friends whom we went most eagerly to see when we returned to the States later on, and she was one of the friends whom I saw last on my latest visit to New-York not long ago. The soul of her nature—her heart of hearts—was sympathy. I never knew any one in whom the quality of sympathy was more exquisitely developed. She was a woman of rich culture and of varied attainments. She had a delightful sense of humor—so sweet, so delicate, so vivid. She had a gift of appreciation which I have never seen surpassed. What I mean is this—that whatever good in intellect or heart there might have been in any man or woman, she found it out and recognized it and cleaved to it. Other natures have the way of criticizing the defects — her genial spirit sought and found the merits that were in any one. I shall never forget the bright hours we had in her house — the talks we had, the counsel she was able to give, the broad humanity which spread out over all she said and all she did. My knowledge of her extended over more than twenty years — on my side of the ocean and on yours. My friendship and affection for her will only be limited by the length of my life; and I hope and firmly believe will not be limited by such narrow bounds. I can say of her with the utmost sincerity, in those delightful words which Steele has made immortal when writing of another woman, that "to love her was a liberal education."

My son and daughter, to whom Mrs. Botta was kind since their childhood, join with me in the profoundest sympathies and the most cordial regards.

A Tribute

By William Rounseville Alger, Boston, Mass.

THE acquaintance with Mrs. Botta, so much prized by me, began almost forty years ago with an incident characteristic of her frank and generous nature. Having read a paper of mine entitled "The Literature of Friendship," just then published in "The North American Review," she wrote me a letter expressing her enthusiastic approval of the sentiments embodied in the essay, and the delight she had experienced in its perusal. Soon after this we met in person, and at once became friends. From that hour, through the events and changes of all the ensuing years, the hearty good will and confidence uniting us have never known an interruption or a shadow, until now, alas! the undeparting shadow of her death.

I have not known a more original and interesting personality. She appears in my memory vividly distinguished from others by the spontaneity of her nature, the depth and variety of the intellectual interest she took in subjects, the readiness of attention and the magnanimity of affection with which she responded to every just claim, whether of things or of persons. It is the common complaint in our democratic time that distinctive individuality is perishing, the crowd of people growing ever more alike, wearing the stamp of a conventional average and taking their cue from the established standards of the community in which they move. Quite otherwise was it with Mrs. Botta. She drew her life direct from principles of conduct and sources of sentiment within her own soul. Her strong reason and good taste kept her free from everything eccentric or insurrectionary. But her independence, sincerity, impulsive force were always salient qualities full of attraction. They caused her to stand out in sharp contrast amidst the throng of those who have no vigorous inner life of their own, no courageous convictions or directing sympathies; but who take their guidance from fashion, accident, or caprice. Always true to herself, one always knew where to find her and what to expect from her, and was never in any danger of being deceived. She was thoroughly earnest in her appreciations, genuine and fresh in her sentiments, brave, kind, and tactful in her expressions.

Nor did advancing years and familiar intercourse with the world prevail in the least to rob her of these noble traits of spirit. Amidst all the conventionalizing influences of her social position, confronting the constant examples of stolidity and pride and fraud and mechanical routine thrust upon her attention, she remained to the last sympathetic, trustful, and generous, ever ready to forget herself in devotion to another. Such an instance is worthy of all honor, and deserves to be set before the public as a model; for nothing is more frequently seen among conspicuous members of society than a thin veneer of affected virtues over a hard polish of manner, meant to hide that utter disenchantment with others which results from a moral and esthetic deadness within themselves.

Mrs. Botta made her house for many years the constant scene of a delicate, varied, and unstinted hospitality, a virtue well deserving recognition at a date when hospitality seems fast becoming one of the lost arts. In this particular, she set a beautiful and notable example. A continual succession of celebrated people from other lands, and unnumbered strangers introduced by letter or by circumstances, in addition to her own friends and acquaintances, were her favored guests. She was an ideal hostess, looking carefully after the comfort and the wishes of each one, yet so quietly and deftly as to give him the impression that she was taking no trouble, and to make him feel completely at home and at liberty. She had in the reception and management of company a tact and charm equaled by few. She was free from every touch of pride or vanity or ostentation. Perfectly self-possessed, she never drew notice to herself, but gave unconstrained heed to everybody else. She mediated and modulated the company while not appearing to do anything except to be at ease. When conversing with any one, she gave him her undivided attention, not, as some hostesses are seen to do, distributing her glances in every direction. Nor could she ever be guilty of that other rudeness, less gross, but equally faulty—paying merely an outside attention to the outside of her interlocutor, as if her spirit were absent and his non-existent, leaving only two bodies face to face. She intuitively gave spiritual attention to the spirit, and not personal attention to the person. Beautiful manners are the revealing signals of beautiful characters. Her manners, while entirely unobtrusive, were nigh perfect, expressing sympathetic respect for others, born of self-respect and a deep and pure sensibility.

If Mrs. Botta found more in society than most persons do, it was because she carried more there. Many a one has that poverty of soul, that slowness of emotion, that sterility of fancy, which are able quickly to bankrupt the richest paradise. A few have, based on universal wealth of endowments, that great power of idealization which discovers heroes and geniuses in beggar-boys, princes in tramps, and with its own luster easily gilds even the drossiest image. This royal prerogative, so often scorned, belonged eminently to the dear friend here commemorated. She had abundance of intellect, heart, imagination, faith, romance, disinterestedness. Furnished with this magic outfit, she never wanted for objects to draw her glance, enlist her interest, and evoke her energies. In the course of her life she befriended a multitude of struggling writers, artists, adventurers, and others, bestowing on them unwearied efforts at encouragement and assistance. If in many instances they proved ungrateful or unworthy, the disappointment did not embitter or discourage her, but left her sympathies just as prompt and vivid as before, whenever a new case presented itself.

Her faculties, life, and experience were exceptionally complete on all sides. A philanthropist both by native disposition and by cultivated habitudes, so ardently patriotic that whatever affected the welfare of her country was as close and dear as any personal interest, filled with a public spirit which took intelligent and sympathizing part in the institutions and events of the community about her, while she was not in any sense a censorious reformer or agitator—she earnestly desired the improvement of our present social order, and conscientiously fulfilled those duties of citizenship incumbent on every member of a free State. But this attention to a larger circle withdrew no interest or fidelity from the domestic sphere. Her private life suffered nothing from any conflict with foreign claims. She was as devoted to the members of her household, and as punctual and efficient in the economic details of the daily round, as though not concerned with anything else. Fond as she was of social festivities, and fitted to shine in them, she was not a whit less contented with the tasks and solaces of solitude. Her literary taste and faculty, revealed in her numerous original poems and in her admirable "Handbook of Universal Literature"; her love and practice of the art of sculpture, in which she reached a high degree of excellence; her intense sensibility to all forms of beauty, whether pictorial, plastic, verbal, or musical,—supplied her, even in the loneliest retreat, with employments and satisfactions that left no vacancy.

A character so meritorious, a culture so ripe, an example so fully rounded, deserve to be embalmed in praise. Could society be replenished with specimens of the type of personality, experience, and manners she displayed, its gifted frequenters would no longer have to complain of what the sensitive Keats bewailed as "the inhuman dearth of noble natures." She exerted not merely a pleasing, but likewise an educational and uplifting influence on those around her. And the privilege of admission to her intimate friendship was a delight and an incentive never to be forgotten by its sharers. New-York is an enormous city, but to those who knew and loved her, it is appreciably poorer since she left it.

And is this the end? Remains there not, deeply hidden, some glorious sequel? Shall we never see her any more whom to see was always so pure a pleasure and so choice a benefit? It is a childish shallowness to confound with the mystic substance of her spirit the mere bodily dust which transparently veiled her and has now been laid in the grave. Spirits, impenetrably concealed from external observation, in this material state are known to others only through their bodies and through signals sent thence. But we are invincibly aware that our bodies are merely the garments of our spirits. And we both instinctively surmise and speculatively think that in other states of being, disembodied spirits may mutually recognize one another, without any material intervention, by direct sight or by perfect interpenetration. The shedding of the flesh would seem to carry no threat of annihilation for the mind which can grasp the idea of God and think everything in unbounded and incorruptible universals. Remove all limits or unessential appurtenances from the conscious personality, and its awful unity, so far from being destroyed, fills infinitude.

In some superior world where perfection makes its home, we shall know again the unique friend — not to be confounded with any other component of the race — to whom we here pay our heartfelt but halting and ineffectual tribute. It must be so; the secret instincts of our nature expect it, the prefiguring preparations of destiny prognosticate it, the intrinsic fitness of things requires it. That the grandest achievement compassed on earth and the dearest hope wrung from heaven should perish together in discordant bafflement at the low barrier of mortality, would be an incongruity which is incredible in a universe pervaded by rational purpose. It cannot be that that precious and sacred personality, long so graciously manifested to us in physical form; that chosen and honest spirit who once experienced among us such intellectual clearness, such expansive goodness, such affectional fervor, such transcendent aspiration, and through their expressive symbols awakened in others such profound and abiding responses—it cannot be that all this is now utterly extinguished, its evolution and promise as transient and unmeaning as the flash of a firefly in the night!

When we look on the large populations of metropolitan capitals, indiscriminately merged in struggling masses of sensuality and egotism, with apparently no more free distinction of persons than in so many conglomerations of vermin, it is easy to conceive them doomed to indiscriminate effacement in oblivion. But when we contemplate, as in the instance of our beloved friend, an individuality which stands apart in clear integrity, nobly differenced from the miscellaneous crowd by its self-centered originality of character and progressive determination of its own experience, all that is most intuitive in our reason, with all that is most authoritative in our conscience, confesses the seal of God, and seals the prophecy of immortality. Can such a spirit, so royal in its range of thought, so divine in its magnanimity of emotion, so immense in its dignity of will, be carelessly blotted out forever? Believe it who can and will; I cannot and will not believe it.

God is infinite, and his brood are infinites. After their mortal eclipse is over, the eternal children will see one another and the eternal Father in that Beatific Vision which, without shadow or reflection, is itself its own substantial subject, object, ground, light, eye, mediation, and fruition — every determinate distinction including the indivisible whole. That such a result is not only possible but is the actual law of creation, we already have overwhelming evidence in the experienced fact that generic unity is perfectly compatible with individual plurality. Is not the whole of a genus potentially in every individual representative of it? And may not every potentiality become actualized? God is the absolutely determined genus of free mind. All individual minds, freely determined after his pattern, are taken up into his perfection, and will thus eternally know themselves in his eternal knowledge. For whatever God knows, thereby exists, and it is inconceivable that he should ever forget anything. Therefore the chosen spirits we have known and sensibly lost, still are, and we shall find them again.

Impressions

By Charles Dudley Warner, Hartford, Conn.

IT is impossible to give in a short paper any adequate conception of Mrs. Botta. She was one of those rare natures which make us think better of the world and better of our possibilities—that is, she was an inspiration to all lives she came in contact with. It is very rare, in my experience, that a person with so many gifts as she had, holds them all in such harmony of development; very rare that genius goes to make an even-balanced character. She had, in a marked degree, the artistic temperament and the sensitiveness and intuition of the poet, and persons so gifted are apt to move in orbits more or less eccentric. But her genius was always guided by a sweet and sane spirit.

Even in her youth she was foremost in a little band of singers and students who made American letters respected, and diffused in a commercial society the liberating influence of art and of literature. Our obligation to these enthusiastic pioneers in refinement and culture should not be forgotten. The debt to Mrs. Botta is not only in that which her pen produced, but it is for the character that ennobled social life. In this generation, I do not know any one else who did more by her influence, her spiritual and intellectual force, to lift that life into a high plane of rational living.

In later years her artistic nature expressed itself in sculpture, and the talent she exhibited in this art shows that if she had been trained in it or had been able to give herself unreservedly to it, she would have attained high rank as a sculptor. This opinion does not rest upon the partiality of friends, but upon the judgment of artists who were unbiased by friendship.

She had, indeed, talents of a high order in literature and in the plastic art; but she was equally distinguished by the gifts for friendship, for sympathy, for helpfulness. And these gifts were strengthened and made effective by a native charm and graciousness which made her presence always sunshine. It seems rude to attempt coolly to analyze the attractiveness—the charm—of this noble woman. Those who had the pleasure of her friendship, however, would say, I think, that it was her love for humanity that drew so much love upon herself. She had the genius to be loved, and in return her sympathies were very wide and her friendship sincere.

It is not necessary that I shall dwell upon the fact that her home was the center of hospitality and the meeting-place of whatever was best in letters and art, native or foreign. Hospitality is a common virtue with us, but hers was especially distinguished by tact and without the least ostentation, so that her visitors looked upon her home not as a place of entertainment, but as a home. In time she came to discharge almost a public function in this sort of hospitality, and it was recognized as dictated by goodness of heart and appreciation of genius.

But this is only a small part of her claim to our affectionate remembrance and admiration. She was one of the most truly helpful persons I ever knew. Many give money and good words; she gave herself. Every young aspirant in whom she discovered talent, however unknown and friendless, had in her a friend. She spared no personal labor to give their talent a chance and a hearing. She opened her house, she used her social position to aid them, she encouraged them by her untiring sympathy. Her charity for all who needed help was as wide and deep as her enjoyment of the best in intellectual and social life. It was this rare union of sympathy with the struggling and unknown, and intense delight in the society of those whose genius had won them position in the world, that gave a unique character to her hospitality, preserved in her own soul the freshness of youth and the aspiration for beauty, and made her conspicuous among women of her generation. Her intellectual discrimination never grew dull, her sympathies never grew cool, her heart never grew old.

A Beautiful Life

By Mrs. L. G. Runkle, New-York.

To Professor V. Botta:

"A HOUSE," says Emerson, "should bear witness in all its economy that human culture is the end to which it is built and garnished. It is not for festivity. It is not for sleep. But the pine and the oak shall gladly descend from the mountains to uphold the roof of men as faithful and necessary as themselves, to be the shelter always open to the good and the true—a hall which shines with sincerity, brows ever tranquil, and a demeanor impossible to disconcert."

For more than forty years such a house has stood in this hurrying city, extending its serene welcome to poet and painter, to critic and story-teller, to sculptor and actor, to scholar and traveler, to cultivated men and women whose lives were not the lives of toys and trinkets. The pictures on the walls, the bronzes and casts and photographs, and even the books that overran the library and climbed the stairs to invade and take possession of all the undefended spaces, were, many of them, memorials of lofty friendships with gifted souls. It was the "House Beautiful," and its gracious mistress was the wife of Professor Vincenzo Botta, of the University of the City of New-York.

If, as Landor says, "that person is great who can call together the most select company when it pleases him," Mrs. Botta was entitled to this laudation. The New-York that was first tributary to her was a rich, crude, unthinking community,—not cosmopolitan, not even of an interesting heterogeneousness; a community where Mrs. Potiphar led the fashion, and Solomon Gunnybags stood for conservative worth, and the Settum-Downes for the "exclusive" set. Out of modest places she gathered the citizens of the kingdom of Mind instead of the kingdom of Mammon. Names that are hardly remembered now, represented then some achievement and much earnest endeavor—Mrs. Welby, Mrs. Brooks, Mrs. Embury, Mrs. Oakes Smith, Mrs. Kirkland, that lovely personality Mrs. Osgood, and the noble and serious Mrs. Child. In Mrs. Botta's presence people were at their best. Her sincerity was the touchstone that evoked an answering sincerity and simplicity. With her, Dr. Griswold would forego his prejudices; Poe was generous in his judgments and self-restrained; Willis forgot his affectations; and Morris ceased to be an American Tom Moore, and became an agreeable and kindly singer of pleasant songs.

To her hospitable house came Tuckerman, elegant and accomplished; the handsome young poet and painter, Cranch; George Ripley, most admirable of talkers, most faithful of friends, most genial of critics; Margaret Fuller, whom her lovers called the "Only," and her dislikers the "Terror"; Charles F. Briggs; the Carters; Grace Greenwood; the Cary sisters; Mrs. Howe; Curtis, the golden youth. Here the Stoddards, and the Stedmans, and "H. H." were familiar figures, and Bayard Taylor and Count Gurowski frequent visitors. Here came Emerson for quiet household visits, and here the sad-eyed Delia Bacon brought her sorrows and was comforted.

It is not possible even to name the friends of the house, for besides the best-known of the writers and actors and painters, there were scores and scores of delightful people who were not even well known, but simply delightful; for admission here depended on none of the accidents of life, on none of the arbitrary social discriminations, but on personal quality, on "distinction" in the finest sense. For years it seemed as if this were the one truly cosmopolitan drawing-room in the city, because it drew the best from all sources. Italy and England, France and Germany, Spain, Russia, Norway, and Hungary, Siam, China, India, and Japan, sent guests hither. Liberals and conservatives, peers and revolutionists, holders of the most ancient traditions and advocates of the most modern theories—all found their welcome, if they deserved it, and each took away a new respect for the position of his opponent.

The influence of such a social center in a commercial city cannot be exaggerated. Yet Mrs. Botta would have said that what she did anybody might do because it was so simple. Perhaps the Celtic blood in her veins gave her her unflagging youth and grace; perhaps it gave her that chivalrous spirit which led her to espouse the cause of the weak, of the struggling man, or country, or idea. She was the daughter of a gallant young Irish gentleman who spent the four years of his life from sixteen to twenty in a political prison, and, coming afterward to Vermont, married a clear-sighted, self-poised, energetic New England girl. The child of this union inherited the poetry, the imagination, and the ardor of one parent, singularly balanced by the good judgment and energy and "faculty" of the other. She was sent to the best schools, and excelled in her studies, and loved books, and wrote verses. But she also darned stockings beautifully, and knew how to make the very most of every opportunity of culture and experience, and had the rarest common sense. She was still a very young woman when she made New-York her home, but she was already known as a poet, story-writer, and essayist. So long as she lived she was a student, an insatiable reader of the best things, and a talker in whose vivid speech these garnered ideas put on new values. She was full of artistic instincts also, that made her whole house lovely. She had a great talent for sculpture, doing work so beautiful that, had not her special bent been literary, she would have made a name in art.

But with all her accomplishments, her true genius was moral. Life was the material with which she wrought. With a deep seriousness of nature, she had a frolic lightness of temperament, an unerring tact, an idealism that nothing discouraged or abated. Always earnest, she was always sunny, serene, and joyous. She saw, as she once said, in the words of her friend Emerson, that nature has laid for each the foundations of a divine building, if the soul will build thereon. And her soul built thereon, and forever showed the way to all who beheld her.

The largest mental hospitality, the simplicity that compelled simplicity, the liberal giving of her best that drew their best from all her acquaintances, the habit of living above all perturbations, all petty aims, all personal considerations—these made up the daily beauty of her life; and though that mystery which is called death has now touched her, these remain forever the possession of humanity.

An Ideal Woman

By Edmund C. Stedman, New-York.

My dear Mr. Botta:

IT is not too early now — and I trust it is not too late — for me to say how fully I have realized the change in your life resulting from a loss of which none can declare, "Thou know'st 't is common." All who remember the conditions of your former happiness feel that your trouble is the graver for the unusual term of felicity which it brought to an end. Fate is so uncompromising! The man whom it favors most is sure to be overwhelmed with sorrows in their full proportion.

Mrs. Botta was in truth no ordinary companion, no woman of a common type. It is more than thirty years since you first welcomed me to your beautiful home. During this period I too seldom availed myself of its privileges, always generously extended, and therefore I did not often meet your wife. But so vivid and helpful were the impressions made by that home and its mistress that it seems to me as if I were your frequent guest. Like every one else, I found Mrs. Botta absolutely unspoiled by her social and intellectual prominence, and so genuinely good that she suffered no peril from envy, ingratitude,—not even from the possession of everybody's honor and affection. Her grace, her personal charm, her gift of perpetual youth, were those of an ideal womanhood. She was altruism itself; at least, her only trace of selfishness was in the delight of giving aid and happiness to others.

And what a life was hers! She and you were concerned in what was active and promising throughout the slow advance of culture in this city — now the gathering-place of artists and men of letters. No newcomer can know how much she, with her tact, sympathy, aspiration, did for our intellectual life. Some years ago I begged her to write her reminiscences. This she was too modest to bring herself to do. It is a satisfaction now to learn that the preparation of a memorial volume is in progress. The production of such a volume, which cannot fail to be of importance alike to the reading public and to the writing guild, and of the deepest interest to your personal friends, will afford you consolation in your years of proud and sad remembrance.

One of the Fine Souls

By Miss Juliet Goodwin, Newport, R. I.

EMERSON says, "'T is the fine souls who serve us, and not what is called fine society." This seems peculiarly applicable to Mrs. Botta. She seemed to fill one's idea of a friend,—apprehensive, comprehensive, and sympathetic. I am glad to be able to claim a share of her regard in the past days—"days, alas! that are no more."

My first recollection of Mrs. Botta (then Miss Anne C. Lynch) is that of seeing her at a ball in Newport. She was then the private secretary of Henry Clay, and accompanied him on that occasion. Mr. Clay was a personal and political friend of my grandfather, the Hon. Asher Robbins; an introduction to him naturally brought me in contact with her whom I had known by reputation as a poetess. She had already edited the "Rhode Island Book," which held, among other contributions of local authors, her fine poem on Paul preaching at Athens—suggested by the celebrated cartoon of Raphael. I was much impressed with the force of her personality; in appearance she seemed to me to resemble Jenny Lind, partly, perhaps, from the contour of her head and the way of wearing her hair.

In subsequent visits to New-York,—she having married Professor Botta, a well-known Italian scholar, in 1855,—I often was a guest at her literary reunions, which became quite celebrated—the nearest approach New-York ever made to the French *salon*. One was sure to meet there the savants, wits, and artists of the day of both hemispheres—not only Bryant, Bancroft, and Emerson, but Froude, Herbert Spencer, Matthew Arnold, and many more. Mrs. Botta had a very quiet way of entertaining; but, endowed with a musical voice, and that sixth sense,—namely, tact,—she succeeded admirably in fusing the somewhat incongruous social elements which sometimes were found in her drawing-rooms. Her love for distinguished people was founded, I think, more upon a genuine respect and enthusiasm for talent and genius, than upon a love for ermine and purple. She did not wait for success where she thought she had found ability, but gave all the encouragement in her power to develop a latent gift. Her friends know of many such instances.

"The foundation of culture, as of character, is the moral sentiment." This was true of Mrs. Botta. She had great integrity, and her religious sympathies were broad and deep, and her intellectual efforts emanated largely from them and her humanity. A noble cause never appealed in vain to her for aid and sympathy. In these days of pinchbeck men and women who obtain in society a false prominence by a rich setting, it is pleasant to remember one who had real intellectual jewels in the pure-gold setting of a lofty character.

A Tribute

By Mrs. A. H. Leonowens, Cassel, Germany.

We have given what we ought to grief;
Now let us do our duty.

WHEN across the wide Atlantic there flashed the sad news that Anne C. Lynch Botta had passed away from among the living, there was felt a pang which, like a spell, benumbed the faculties, froze the heart, and hushed the voice. It was as if the chill and gloom of the grave, upborne from the subterranean depths that had engulfed so many and such deeply loved and venerated friends, had enveloped the clear blue sky, and had driven from it all the light and sunshine forever; as if day would never again dawn; as if no counteracting spell would ever mitigate the anguish and desolation of those almost interminable hours. When one strove to take up the thus severed thread of one's daily life, to speak, to act, to rally one's self to the immediate, the inevitable, it seemed almost a sacrilege, a profanation of one's holy grief, a forgetfulness of one's irreparable loss.

But at length the "grief-deafened ear" begins to perceive the loving voices around, and the chilled heart begins to thaw; hot tears, which blind the eyes and scorch the cheeks, bring relief; the lost friend whom we craved to see again, seems to draw near to comfort, to solace us—then what a flood of memories, recollections, and pictures come crowding in upon us! Our lips are unchained, there arises in our hearts a desire unspeakable, strong as life itself, to speak, to cry aloud, to waylay the careless, the indifferent, the stranger, if only to give some feeble voice to our tribute of love and praise; and when to this desire is added the earnest request of one whom she loved with all the strength and depth of her great soul, it becomes a labor not only of love, but an imperative call of duty, which must be obeyed—but with all fear and trembling; for what man or what woman shall dare to think that he or she has fathomed the impersonal and illimitable soul of another! And so we take up our pen with fear and trembling, and the old wound, hidden out of sight, begins again to bleed; we are pierced with the old sense of anguish, which "Time" itself cannot heal; we realize once again that we cannot part with some friends, we cannot let our angels go,—nay, not even that archangels may come in. We linger in the old familiar haunts—Long Branch, Newport, R. I., the Adirondack mountains and lakes—where we passed many a summer holiday and held such deep and joyous converse. We cannot again find another such spirit,—so dear, so sweet, so gracious; what is there then left us but to let the hot burning tears flow again, and to find no comfort anywhere beneath the great arch above us!

To strangers, perhaps, this passionate grief may seem excessive and exaggerated; but to friends—if not more intimate, with at least a clearer insight into a character so pure, generous, and elevated—it will surely seem inadequate; for the loss of such a life, and of an influence so benign and wide reaching, is truly immeasurable. It would seem as if some revelation, some inlet to a higher and loftier life, had been suddenly closed upon us, and we were left henceforth to grope our way in clouds and darkness.

My first meeting with Mrs. Botta was in the year 1868, at Hastings, on the Hudson River, and at the house of dear mutual friends. She was then in the full and perfected maturity of her noble womanhood. She had a slight graceful figure, a little above medium height, and a broad masculine brow, on which will, energy, thought, and intellect seemed to have stamped themselves; for years cannot be lived through earnestly, passionately, without leaving their marks behind, and the vast amount of reading, study, and reflection which had been forced into those early years of isolation on Shelter Island, had left a deep, thoughtful, almost sad, expression on her face, which in conversation lighted up. Her eyes were large, deeply sunk, and of a tender blue; the mouth was large, but well cut; the chin was well shaped and strong; and her smile seemed half to invite and half to restrain. Even at first sight she appeared like one who towered above her sex, at the very moment when she was quite simple, natural, and most anxious to please. Our introduction was the work of a brief moment, but there was a difference between that and every subsequent moment of my life.

She began at once to question me, her large soft eyes glowing beneath her strong intellectual brow, on the present condition of women in the East, and Siam in particular.[1] She was delighted to hear of the greater freedom allowed to Buddhist women. After discussing, with a knowledge which was surprising, the laws of the great Indian legislator, Manu, regarding women, which assert that "woman is by nature unfit for independence, and that a wife should assume the very qualities of her husband as a river loses itself in the sea," she remarked: "This is quite in contradiction to the old Vedic teachings, which everywhere upheld the sanctity of 'motherhood'; and what if the husband should happen to be a villain, a profligate, or a murderer, should the wife then submerge herself into such a sea of iniquity?" "No, no," she added; "Manu's laws may have been good enough for the childhood of the world, but for a good and loving wife to steep herself in the vices of her husband, is as abhorrent as it is inconceivable to every right-minded person." She ended, as was her wont, by pointing out the remedial forces latent in human nature itself, which tended to mitigate even those

[1] Mrs. Leonowens, the writer of this tribute, lived several years in Siam, as teacher and governess of the hereditary prince, the present king of that country. She is the author of "The English Governess at the Siamese Court," "The Romance of the Harem," and "Life and Travels in India."

very unjust laws under which women lived and suffered, admitting that much of woman's subjection to man was natural, based on her need of protection to guard her from the dangers and perils to which her higher maternal functions exposed her, and that the seclusion of women in Hindostan and other countries was due to a despotic system chiefly of Mohammedan origin, and adopted by the Hindoos merely in self-defense against the brutality of their foreign conquerors, which, like every other human institution, had passed in the course of ages into rigid etiquette.

The fact that the use of the veil by the Persian women was considered a sign of dignity and social elevation, gave her intense satisfaction. "Now," said she, "I'll wear my veil as a mark of high rank and not of shamefacedness or inferiority"; and the quaint old legend, that the beautiful Yathudara, the first cousin and wife of Buddha, rejected the veil on the occasion of her marriage, saying, "A good woman needs veiling no more than the sun or moon," was often quoted by her with a sense of real pleasure in the knowledge that women even in those ancient times possessed truer grandeur of thought and feeling than we are inclined to give them credit for. The unfeigned goodness which almost illumined her thoughtful face, the natural sympathy which shone forth in her actions, drew me instinctively to her, although I had no idea then of the joy to be experienced, the lessons to be learned, the subtle inspiring influences to be drawn from my intercourse with this one of the most remarkable of American literary women. Where on earth can one ever find such subtly mingled majesty and goodness of heart!

Not long after our first meeting, I received an invitation to come early and dine at 25 West Thirty-seventh street, and of course lost no time in accepting the same. I shall never forget the reception that awaited me. I was utterly "überrascht," as the Germans would say. There was a depth, a joy, a rapture in that brief moment which constrain me even at this distance of time to regard it as one of the most memorable epochs of my life. The slight, graceful figure of the hostess stood at the head of the staircase, on the second floor, and as I ascended the long flight of steps and approached her, she, with a sudden movement, flung her strong arms wide open, seized me, and clasped me close to her breast, as if I had been no stranger entering her house for the first time, but a long-lost friend just returned. I was utterly overcome; every barrier had been flung aside; it seemed as if something new, something divine, had descended upon me, I knew not where or whence—if not by reason of the virtue that had streamed out of this great soul into mine; enough it was to know that I no longer felt alone, friendless, and a stranger on the great American continent. "And now you must mount yet another flight of steps and make the acquaintance of my mother." Hand in hand we mounted the stairs and entered the front bedroom adjoining the guest-chamber on the third story. It was a large, bright, sunny apartment, furnished with all the comforts that love and thought could suggest.

Just by the large window, in a cozy arm-chair, sat an aged lady, her silver-gray hair gleaming under the sunlight and the folds of the daintiest of white lace caps. She was reading; when we entered, she looked up, uncertain at first, not knowing who I was; then she greeted us with a smile that seemed in itself a benediction, and the expression of sweet contentment that suffused her face gave one a sense of pleasure something like that which a fresh and beautiful flower awakens. Never before did white head seem so venerable as it then and there appeared, bending, as I saw it, over the head of a daughter almost as gray, to fold her in her arms.

That evening I met for the first time her husband, Mr. V. Botta, and, although to attempt to describe his peculiar power and influence over his gifted wife would be out of place in this brief sketch, nevertheless one could not fail to perceive that his style of thought and expression, his accurate scientific reading, his thorough knowledge of the Latin and Italian classics, and his profound insight into human nature, were aids to her of which she spoke and wrote with the deepest sense of appreciation. "He strengthened her reasoning powers, touched her spirit, enlarged her horizon by filling her with admiration for scientific thought, and, above and beyond all, by having taught her to recognize the wonderful charm of that highest and purest form of love,—as distinguished from modern romantic love, passion, or platonic friendship,—the creation of an Italian, the immortal Dante." "Here is," she says in one of her letters, "the germ of a grand future development, the unfolding of one of our dim but noblest instincts, deep sown and deathless as the soul itself, the beginning of that higher reverence for 'womanhood' which will be crystallized into the purest and highest friendship between the sexes, without any 'earthlier' admixture of personal desires, as our race goes on evolving new and higher spiritual force."

I would gladly linger on these memorable days of our first acquaintance, on the incommunicable charm of those tête-à-tête conversations, now sad, now reflective, and anon soaring and joyous as the skylark's earliest spring song, or on the quiet, restful hours we usually spent in "Ma's room," as it was called, where "everything that interests Ma" would be introduced, where memories that were growing dim and half forgotten were renewed and dwelt upon: but the limits of this paper will not permit it; suffice to say that tears have often been brought into our eyes as the loving daughter related the early trials, privations, and noble struggles of her mother, and all she had done for her personally. No one who had not witnessed time and again the happy relations which existed between these two American women could ever fully realize how tenderly they loved each the other, how breathlessly the daughter listened, when the mother was tired and weary under the weight of years and growing infirmities, even to her most unreasonable rebukes and complainings. With all her talent, her wealth of personal advantages, her boundless hospitalities, social claims and duties, amid a large literary and fashionable circle of friends and correspondents all over the world,—to her mother she was still a *little child*, obedient, loving, timid. She brought everything she did—her drawings, paintings, poems, writings, models, a pretty cap trimmed or an old bonnet made over again, and all her dearest friends too—for her mother's approval. She went and came, tripping up and down those long flights of stairs, often weary, sometimes discouraged or disappointed and grieved, but always returning fresh, bright, and cheerful to "Ma's room" to relate, like a young girl of fifteen, all that happened in her world of men and things. I have often heard them laughing merrily over some adventure or some funny incident—seemingly having what is so felicitously termed "a good time together." Mrs. Lynch lived with her gifted, loving daughter until the end, and was to the last hour of her life her daughter's beloved mother, friend, and adviser; and, in her turn, the daughter loved, cherished, and venerated her, brought her round all the sharp corners of old age and failing strength, persistently shutting her eyes to the last fact, until one day she awoke to the full realization that she must prepare to be parted from that mother who was the "sacred light" on the home altar, round whom she, her husband, and her whole household revolved, lived, moved, and had their mutual joys, sufferings, and forbearances. Here was the mother of the ancient "Zend-Avesta," the Scriptures of the Zoroastrian faith, so honored, so loved, so respected as to be almost enshrined. I know not how to describe the gentle forbearance, the unspoken tenderness, with which she guarded, tended, and nursed her mother through the last years of her life. Her mother was now rarely, if ever, seen in the drawing-room; once or twice, when some old friend from the West or from Washington happened to be present, she was, at her own request, assisted downstairs. Whenever she appeared, however, all would cluster around her; earnestly would she listen to the conversation, whatever it chanced to be,—of love, adventure, or discovery,—the narrator being always forewarned "to speak loud enough for Ma to hear." When she was tired and wished to retire, all would rise from their chairs, erect and still as one stands in a church, while "the mother," smiling and bowing, supported by her daughter, was led out and helped up to her room.

It was on one of those memorable days, after she began to feel that the parting was very near, that I called to see her. I found her with her mother, who had been washed and dressed as daintily as ever, and seated in her large arm-chair. After the usual warm embrace, she returned to her stool at her mother's feet, with her interlocked hands on her mother's knees, her strong intellectual face, full of love, turned up to the one looking down on it; they appeared quite absorbed, taking a certain pleasure in just gazing the one at the other. When this silent exchange of the holiest affection was ended, the daughter laid her head on her mother's knees, and the aged, feeble hands stroked that massive gray head, while her mother said in a trembling and almost querulous voice: "You must go now, Anne; your friend is waiting for you; you can't spend all your time with your old mother. You must—I beg of you to go; your house, your husband, your social duties, your studio up-stairs,—all claim a share of your attention."

Hard was the battle between life and death. Nursed by a heroic daughter, whose love and care knew no fatigue, the aged mother lived through that year and far into the next; but at last life yielded, and death conquered.

The loving daughter was not crushed nor annihilated, as I expected to find her, but transfigured. With Archbishop French she could say:

> O life, O death, O world, O time,
> O grave, where all things flow,
> 'T is yours to make our lot sublime
> With your great weight of woe.
>
> Though sharpest anguish hearts may wring,
> Though bosoms torn may be,
> Yet suffering is a holy thing;
> Without it, what were we?

From the bed of that lifeless mother she writes: "The majesty of death, the awe, the mystery which it awakens, are greater than I had ever conceived. My beloved mother, so necessary to me, the one being who both made me feel and kept me young, is gone—where? The strong, brave soul that inspired, encouraged, and so tenderly loved me in spite of all my faults and shortcomings!" "Now only do I realize how much she was to me, and how great a blank her absence will create in my life." "Death makes even the vilest wretch great and majestic; how much more, then, the good, noble, and brave!" "Her last conscious words were full of love and tenderness; there is in the last drop of love pressed out of a mother's dying heart, something divine and holy to the ears of an only child; my grief, inconsolable as it is, urges me on to more energetic action. I am longing to do something; but, alas! I never seem to get any further than trying to reach after the beauty which I find scattered everywhere."

After this sad event, she began to take a more lively interest than ever in, and to devote herself even more exclusively to, the training and education of little Raphael Lynch, her grandnephew, and the two interesting young girls intrusted to her care. Raphael was a pretty, fair-haired boy of about seven years of age, eager, intelligent, and running over with joy and merriment, and perpetually asking questions. He attended a good kindergarten school near by, and she might be seen any morning in the year walking up Fifth Avenue, little Raphael running along by her side, intent on studying child-nature, endeavoring to interest and draw him out, answering his innumerable questions, then putting in a little question of her own which stimulated thought and helped to awaken the boy's powers of perception, observation, reflection, and expression. The friendship which existed between the great-aunt and nephew was perfectly delightful; the ardent boy simply idolized his "Auntie," and she strove to make life brighter and happier not only for her little grandnephew, but for her young ladies, and, in fact, for the youth and age around, leading them on so wisely, firmly, yet almost unawares to themselves, teaching them how to look at things, opening their minds and ears to the wonders of art and nature, unfolding their consciences and deepening their religious aspirations. In teaching young persons, I found that she pursued a perfectly systematized plan of education, thought out and prepared by herself with the utmost care and research, beginning with universal chronology, history, geography, and literature, thence to particular epochs of the history of different nations, following these up with a prolonged reading and study of Greek history, poetry, and art, then Roman history, medieval Italy and the Elizabethan literature, ending off with the study of the best modern productions, with especial regard to science, its wonderful inventions, discoveries, and improvements. No wonder then that under such a liberal system of education she reaped "golden harvests," and that her efforts were so supremely successful. Little Raphael, however, did not live long enough to realize her dream of a noble youth and an ideal manhood; he died just as he was preparing to enter college, deeply loved and mourned by all his school-fellows, his poor mother, and his grandaunt, who, no one knows better than I, had so lovingly, so studiously sought to shape his young life after the highest ideal of self-sacrificing love and goodness.

Yet another point of interest in that delightful home in New-York city, was Mrs. Botta's studio on the fourth floor. Here one realized more fully the wonderful many-sidedness of her character. Here a long table covered with green baize stood by the window; on the wall just above it were hung crayon portraits of herself and her husband, the work of Samuel Lawrence, an eminent artist of England; both these portraits are admirable and true to life, but on the brow and large, deep eyes of Mrs. Botta, that ever-present restless yearning after the "ideal and the beautiful" which was the most striking of her characteristics, is once for all caught and portrayed. I have caught the same wistful, yearning look on her face with a thrill of wonder, and waited and longed for it to come again; for it always stirred within me something that might be called a mixture of joy and pain. Some cases containing her favorite books ran along the wall, plain, quiet, and homelike in tone and color; here there was nothing too fine, everything had the look of having been well used. On her table lay certain books, her constant companions and friends,—Emerson, Herbert Spencer, George Eliot, Longfellow, Whittier, "Light of Asia," Tennyson, Wordsworth, etc. In the drawers of her writing and study table were a series of blank books filled with choice and most exquisite extracts from all the great thinkers and teachers of the world. At some point or other of our conversation, she would dash open one of these drawers and bring forth the treasures she had gathered from all sources, and sit there brooding, questioning, pondering; these were her gems, the heirlooms of the ages—the absolute, the eternal truth, pressed out of the bibles of the world! It was worth crossing the Atlantic to spend an evening alone with her in that fourth-story studio, to catch the gleams of those wise, far-seeing eyes, to feel the touch of that soul thirsting after wisdom, the ideal, the beautiful, as the hart panteth after the water-brooks. The walls of the studio were hung with all kinds of bas-reliefs, models, busts, statues, the mantelpiece crowded with pictures, paintings, photographs. The middle of the room was generally occupied with whatever bit of sculpture she happened to be working at, which would be cast aside a dozen times, even when she had almost put the last touches to it, if she failed to embody the expression she strove to portray. If not gifted with special genius for any one of the fine arts, she certainly possessed a passionate love of abstract beauty for its own sake, and an ardent desire to express herself through several forms of art, as her paintings, sculptures, poems and other writings will show. It is easy enough to recognize, when it has been made clear to us, the work of a great genius, a world-renowned poet or famous novelist, but our blind eyes must be anointed before we can perceive all the spiritual beauty of those with whom we are brought into familiar contact. With the love and feeling of a true artist, but with a certain lack of confidence in herself, she worked unceasingly in her studio, devoting herself exclusively during the latter part of her life to modeling and sculpture; and if her works are not great and beautiful in the highest degree, they are at least noble and dignified: they seemed, if not wholly, at least in some small measure, to satisfy her intense esthetic and poetic sense, helping her to realize, even if afar off, something of the wonderful power and majesty of a great creative genius, which in all its manifestations is one and the same, differing only in degree, from the weaving of a bird's nest to the colossal works of a Michelangelo.

Another striking characteristic of Mrs. Botta was that she seemed to have a mission to teach and instruct youth, and that she proved herself almost an inspired guide to many of the youth of New-York city. Her first act was to lead them to study with her personally, or under her direction, history and literature, then gradually to lead them in some channel of art, of industry, literature, or of helping others to help themselves. How enthusiastically she was followed and obeyed by a cluster of ardent, loving young friends! It would appear that even when at school the girls of her class elected her as their teacher, and she considered it her duty to hear their tasks before they assembled in the class-room. Thus it was that she succeeded in winning all hearts from her very girlhood, not only by her kindness, but by the tact and delicacy with which she treated them. It is safe to say that no tribute so exalted was ever paid to any self-appointed teacher of American youth, if we take in consideration the age, the rank, position, character, and abilities of many of her pupils; only an overmastering personality could thus have succeeded in winning an eager obedience from youth and old age alike. One of the secrets of this overmastering personality was the good-tempered way in which she took rebuke from any one whom she knew to be sincere, and there was something really noble in her bearing when she heard herself misjudged or depreciated—she was never moved to anger, nor did she even attempt any defense or self-justification; having listened with quiet dignity, she would smile and pass on to something else. To this power we must in great measure ascribe her wonderful influence over the young; the effect of this rare tranquillity of spirit was most magical on some of her young protégés. I heard a young girl once say of her: "She is great enough to have been an inspired prophetess of olden times, and tender enough to have been the mother of our dear Saviour." Such were the words of impassioned praise that fell from the lips of a young motherless Roman Catholic girl, one of the many whom Mrs. Botta had taught and befriended.

In dealing with people too she displayed the greatest delicacy, reserve, and tact; nevertheless some there were who complained—and this complaint, with her rare candor, she admitted as perfectly just—that she was apt to idealize and then to be disappointed in them; hence arose coldness and estrangement between herself and one or more persons whom she had at first so generously helped and befriended; wounded self-love made these persons incapable of doing her justice, or even of understanding her aright. To be sure, by some sudden display of aims and motives so different from those with which she had accredited them, some persons fell from the high place in her affections to which she was wont to lift them, but the blame, if there be any, must be ascribed to where it justly belongs,—that *she* should cease to idealize is a quite natural result; for it was the whole aim of her life to live in strictest harmony with the dictates of her conscience. But for all that, in no one instance has a friend who proved worthy of that name been dropped even when she found the friend quite changed in all his former aims and views; in fact, her purely human interest in such a friend would become, if anything, deeper and stronger. She was drawn by a sort of magnetic sympathy and admiration to an individual who had gone over to a new line of thought and action from a deep sense of honest conviction; and on one occasion, when a friend expressed surprise at her intense admiration of one whose views were entirely opposed to hers, she at once quoted her favorite teacher, Emerson: "Our eyes are holden that we cannot see things that stare us in the face, until the hour arrives when the mind is ripened; then we behold them, and the time when we saw them not appears like a dream."

Those who heard her felt involuntarily that there was something even finer in the woman than anything she had ever said or done. Her memory too was wonderful, and although she always insisted that she was possessed of a "dumb spirit," and could never master but one language, it was very noticeable that few women could equal her when she was moved—which was very rarely—to speak; whatever she had to say was well expressed, lucid, terse, emphatic, and direct, without any circumlocution or repetition; and withal she had a charm of manner which was quite captivating,—so quiet, reserved, and modest that one seemed to be penetrated by the gentleness of the voice, manner, smile, bearing, as showing the utmost purity and disinterestedness of soul. She made it, in fact, a rule of her life to be most courteous and gentle to all alike. She never appeared bored when conversing with persons less gifted or less well informed than she was herself; hence her power over others, especially the young. She absolutely seemed to infuse her own individual will into them as naturally as water runs down from a higher into a lower vessel.

The richest gem, however, of all her mental and spiritual gifts was her boundless "hospitality": to all forms of thought, to every new discovery, to every spiritual idea, to all kinds of mendicants, rich and poor, Pagan and Christian, Jew and Gentile alike. Hers was by no means a lavish or prodigal hospitality, which flings its gifts and bounties to the four corners of the earth, regardless of where it falls or whom it benefits provided she herself is amused, entertained, and saved the pain and discomfort of seeing the want and suffering of her fellow-men around her. No; her hospitality was a grand sympathetic impulse which reached out to all who came to her, recommended or unrecommended, introduced or not introduced, either for friendship, help, shelter, advice, or encouragement; an impulse of love, kindliness, and pity that knew no limit; an intuitive craving of real "motherhood" to love and cherish all who needed it—an instinct which runs in the fine veins and broad arteries of all noble womanhood. It was this instinct that drew her to the least as well as to the greatest, to the rich as well as to the poor, to the unknown as much as to the famous men and women of the world. It was this instinct that rendered her more Christian than Christianity itself,—at least such forms of it as are to be found among us to-day. It was no doubt this unbounded hospitality of nature that made her the delightful hostess that she was, as well as the friendliest of friends and companions.

All kinds of people were welcomed to her hospitable mansion at 25 West Thirty-seventh street; here there was always to be found a considerable mixture of famous men and women, and not a few who would probably never be known outside of their own circle; but the slightest indication of purpose, of any one study earnestly pursued, something done or being done,—whether it was building a house, writing a book, composing a poem, making a garden, or getting a servant,—recommended itself at once to her; and it became a sort of imperative duty to her to exert all her faculties to facilitate, if possible, the object in view.

Many foreigners, like myself, retain the memory of happy days and hours spent in her beautiful drawing-room as among the brightest and most exhilarating of their New-York recollections. Who that has ever been there could forget those parlors on the second story, with their rich background of cabinets, well filled with choice books, covered with Venetian glass, mosaics, bronzes, statues (some of which were the work of her own hands), the walls hung with shields and rare pictures; the warm welcome, often with wide-extended arms, to those whom she loved best; and the delightful company of men and women eminent in art, science, religion, literature, philanthropy, that might be met there? Many distinguished Italians flocked there, sure of a hearty welcome from their graceful hostess, and of the unusual treat of hearing their beautiful language spoken faultlessly by her husband. It is characteristic of the latter, as it ever was of his matchless wife, that whatever their own individual views, opinions, and predilections, their friends were to be found in all ranks of life, all sects, all denominations, all nationalities, and every shade of political creed.

Mrs. Botta's delight in a general and animated conversation was most noticeable at some of her quiet, almost family-like, dinner-parties; it was her habit to listen with rapt attention, which so stimulated her guests that it infused into each an almost creative power of thought and expression. I heard an old gentleman, on being complimented at being so entertaining at one of these dinners, say: "I really can't account for it. I am quite surprised myself; I never before suspected that I could be so witty and amusing." All barriers seemed to be laid aside; each spoke from the heart. It was at these moments that she shone out; her broad, generous face was illuminated by those large blue eyes and with a peculiar beauty. She enforced unconsciously by her inborn nobleness of soul the rules of etiquette so laboriously framed by Catherine the Great of Russia for her *conversazioni* at the "Hermitage": "Leave your rank, your hat, and especially your sword, outside. Tell no tales out of school. Whatever goes in at one ear must go out at the other before leaving this room." But, unlike and a whole heaven above the great Catherine, her power of drawing out all that was good in others, and compelling them, while under her influence at least, to observe the one toward the other the highest rules of courtesy and good breeding, was due mainly to the fact that she herself was entirely free from self-assertion, vanity, or self-seeking, and that her sympathetic interest in each of her guests was felt to be equally deep and absorbing.

It was on one of these memorable occasions that I found myself seated beside a handsomely dressed and singularly attractive woman who was quite bright and witty: "but under *her* spell," as she afterward remarked; "for my husband finds me dreadfully dull at our own dinners!" In the course of an animated conversation some words fell from her lips which made me curious to learn her history. It was told in a few words, and with such evident joy and gratitude that she could hardly restrain her emotion. As a young girl she had run away from a home in which the light of love had never shone. From the moment she had entered it after the death of both her parents, she longed to run away. Finding herself in possession of a dollar over and above her railroad fare, she fled to New-York city to seek her fortune; but no sooner had the train started than she realized in some degree what she had done, and burst into tears. A lady on the train, observing her distress, gave her Mrs. Botta's address, and told her to be sure to go to her if she was in need of help. That night she passed in a room in the lower part of the town, which she had hired for fifty cents. No tongue, as she assured me, could describe her terror, dismay, and horror at the sounds of drunken revelry that penetrated her small attic chamber. When morning dawned she fled from it as from a plague-stricken spot, hurried to the only address which she knew in that great city, which had been given her by a mere chance, as it seemed. But it was enough to have touched that magic bell, to have stood before Mrs. Botta and poured out her tale of grief and wrong-doing. She was taken in, sheltered, protected, guided. In due time she returned to her uncle's home, and bore with patience the trials that there awaited her, and in the end became the happy wife of a distinguished lawyer. It was the great event of her life to visit her benefactress, and at the time I speak of she was on one of these visits with her two lovely girls. This was only one of the many instances where the practical earnestness and ever-ready help of this most remarkable woman did much toward bringing a strong, clear purpose into the vague yearnings and half-formed plans of life of many a young girl personally known to me.

Her New-Year receptions were also quite a feature of the social life of New-York city, and as she was a strenuous advocate for the preservation of good old-fashioned customs, she observed New-Year's Day in particular state and ceremony. A troop of pretty girls in full evening-dress generally received with her on these occasions. It was the peculiar talent of the hostess to make each of her young girls feel that in herself she was one of the loveliest of young women, that her home was the brightest and happiest spot in the world; and many a motherless young girl valued this delicious home feeling as one of the choicest privileges of her life in New-York city. It was really delightful to see the hostess with her fair bevy of young girls receiving their numerous guests, beaming a warm welcome to all. The mirth and merriment of the young people were greatly promoted by some of the eccentric persons who sometimes seized the opportunity to call on the kind hostess on this festive occasion. The more awkward and "gauche" the visitor, the more courteous and kind was the hostess, and the most popular of her young ladies would be called upon to help to entertain him. I shall never forget an amusing incident which occurred on each successive New-Year's Day, and which showed our beloved hostess to be as kindly indulgent to little human foibles and shortcomings as she was helpful and sympathetic to its greater needs and necessities. A rather portly gentleman called, as was his usual custom, on New-Year's Day, and, having delivered himself of the customary greetings and compliments, he was wont to depart in seeming haste, having on his list a hundred and one places still to call at,— but only to turn up, which he did regularly as the clock announced the dinner-hour, just at the moment when the host and hostess and their merry party were about to descend to dinner. He would enter bowing and slightly embarrassed: he had dropped his pocket-handkerchief, mislaid his umbrella, or needed some important address, he would explain; and, after some confused attempts at a search or further explanation, he would very reluctantly accept the kind hostess's proffered invitation to stay and dine with her! On one occasion, when the young ladies were making merry over this very apparent and oft-repeated ruse of the old bachelor to secure a good dinner, she mildly remarked: "My dears, it is not very wicked to wish to dine with us on such a bitter cold day as this; he is not a rich man, and I know him to be most generous and self-denying to his poor sister's family."

These are only a few out of scores of similar instances of her pure and disinterested kindliness toward her fellow-men. No one felt more keenly and lived more conscientiously up to her conviction of the interdependence and kinship of men. "We are made to work together, like feet, like hands, like eyelids, like rows of the upper and lower teeth." "It is peculiar to man to love even those who do wrong; and thou wilt love them if, when they err, thou bethink thee that they are to thee near akin." "Men exist for the sake of one another; teach them, then, or bear with them." "'Earth loves the shower, and the sacred ether loves, and the whole universe loves, the making of that which is to be.' I say then to the universe: Even I, too, love as thou." This sentiment was her favorite passage from one of her teachers, Marcus Aurelius, though she often remarked that it lacked the grandeur of the Buddhist and the Christian teaching—that is, "Like as a mother watcheth over her child, so should universal goodwill prevail toward all mankind"; and that other imperative command: "Thou shalt *love* thy neighbor as thyself."

The truth, however extravagant it may appear, was that she actually loved her neighbor better than herself, and that she tolerated in him or her, and suffered for him or her, what she never would have tolerated in, or suffered for, herself; this was the open secret of her life. But, while unsurpassed in the freedom, force, and tenderness of her conscious womanhood, she had nothing whatever of the spirit of a reformer, agitator, or even leader. As she herself says: "I can, undisturbed, witness changes and revolutions; believing, as I do, that the world is under the reign of law and not of men, I am sure that all will come right in the end. Socialism seems to me to be the slow awakening of the people to their 'right to life, liberty, and the pursuit of happiness,' as our Declaration of Independence puts it. Any system of government that forces the body of the people to labor for their daily bread, deprived of comfort, education, and bread too, often while the few live in ease and luxury, with the command of every means for intellectual and moral improvement —may be right or wrong; but, either way, the masses are beginning to think about it. But if they should rise in their strength and overthrow the civilization of to-day, I have no doubt that from the ruins would rise a higher and nobler state of things, such as followed the overthrow of Rome when the barbarians swept down upon the empire and destroyed it. I take no part in all this; I look on in wonder and awe to see what appear to me great laws in operation. So in our war against slavery—had it been left to me to destroy the institution, much as I detested it, I would not have dared to do it, not knowing what the result might be; but behold how marvelously it was wrought out!" No one so habitually realized the difficulty of forming true opinions. She insisted that many people made up their minds because they were in a hurry to act, or to decide one way or the other, or from a predisposition to one side or the other; but rarely from an honest and downright sense of conviction of the justness of one or the other opinion. "No wonder, then," she used to say, "that the wise Buddha made 'right thinking' one of the cardinal points of his means to salvation."

Few women took such real delight in the work of her sex as she did. On receiving a photograph of a lovely painting by a distinguished German lady, she wrote: "The beautiful photograph you sent to me of Fräulein Schepp lies on my table admired by every one. It is one of the most exquisite figures I have ever seen, and I am proud that a woman painted it." Her faith in her own sex led her to rejoice over any manifestation of real honest work, high resolve, or devotion to a lofty aim. She knew by heart the names of hundreds of famous women, ancient and modern, and was wont to speak of them not only with enthusiasm, but with a sort of reverent adoration; hence her oft-expressed delight in the noble Aryan and Germanic peoples, and in particular the Teutonic tribes, "because of their well-known reverence for women, because with them a queen was as sacred an object of love and homage as a king, and the perfect equality of sex which existed among them in all domestic and social relations—the wife not being bought or sold, but being accustomed to receive rather than to bring a dowry, and each, when betrothed, being obliged to invest the other with the same equipments—spear, sword, shield, dagger, and steed—in token not only of equal rights, duties, and pastimes, but of coequal physical strength and endurance."

Her sympathy for the various clubs which of late have been organized with the object of promoting the mental improvement of the society ladies of New-York was active and strong. She belonged to the Nineteenth Century Club, and took a great interest in its discussions and its liberalizing influence. She was also a member of the Wednesday Club, where ladies meet to discuss social and literary subjects.

Speaking of the importance of these institutions, in a letter to me, she says: "I am more and more convinced that it is only through women that the world is to be regenerated; and in the higher education and wider fields of action now opening to them, they seem to me to be preparing for their great mission. There has lately been established at the New-York University a professorship of 'law,' and the professor is a German lady lately come here." Eager to enlarge the sphere of her knowledge, she welcomed with all her heart the efforts to discover new laws and new phenomena in the economy of the universe, which might throw a better light on the mysteries by which the human mind is surrounded. "Hypnotism," she wrote to me, "I have believed in for many years,—long ago, when it was called 'animal magnetism,' and the learned doctors scoffed at it. I have no doubt that the race is gradually evolving newer and higher functions, and that this is one of them. The action of mind on mind, as sometimes shown in the cure of disease, is another instance of this tendency to important discoveries."

It would give us a poor idea of the intellectual grasp and insight of Mrs. Botta's mind if I should lead any one to think that she believed in the vulgar theory of Oriental metempsychosis. Often have I heard her express her admiration for Oriental and Christian mysticism—that is, so far as it does not interfere with the practical duties of life. She sympathized with the teachings of Hindoo and Christian divines, that the soul is intrinsically deathless; that it has within it the principle of life, of which you cannot predicate non-existence. You cannot say of it: "It hath been, or is about to be, or will be hereafter." It is a principle without birth, hence without death; but subject to change in its combination with matter. Matter is the true river of Lethe; immersed in it, the soul forgets much, but not everything; hence these casual gleams of memory, giving us sudden, abrupt, and momentary revelations of the past, are precisely the phenomena we would expect to meet with. These psychological facts seemed to her to warrant the belief in the preëxistence of the soul, which is preëminent in the Hindoo theology, in Plato's philosophy, and in the writings of the early fathers of the Church. Suddenly a thought is flashed into the mind, which is not only isolated in the present, but which cannot be traced back to any source in our brief experience on this side of life; we perceive an object, hear of some life, feel the touch of some fine spirit, and immediately we seem to be lifted out of the every-day circle of thoughts and feelings and plunged into a sort of vague reminiscence of some half-forgotten dream. This is one of the arguments of the "Phædo"; it is the prevailing idea of Wordsworth in his ode on the "Intimations of Immortality from Recollections of Childhood"; the joy felt in the grandeur of the sky, in the height of the mountain, in the majesty of the forest, in the murmuring of the brook, in the splendor of the grass, in the glory of the flower, and in all the wondrous beauties of this world, was to him, with his poetic nature, not only a thrill of delight—it was more: it was a half-conscious recognition—recollection—of an antenatal existence.

> Not in entire forgetfulness,
> Not in utter nakedness,
> But in trailing clouds of glory do we come
> From God—who is our home.

In answer to some of my letters from Cassel on the excellent training my grandchildren were receiving in the German schools here, she says: "I agree with you in regretting that we were born before we ought to have been in order to enjoy all the advantages of the young people of to-day. But perhaps we shall reincarnate, and, if so, I only hope we may be contemporaries."

> The soul that rises with us, our life's star,
> Hath had elsewhere its setting, and cometh from afar.

Her idea of heaven and its beatitudes was the emancipation here in this life from all the lower animal instincts,—pride, envy, hatred, malice, revenge, lust, passion, anger, greed, covetousness,—and the acquiring of transcendental virtues, which leads the soul to yearn after perfection—that haunting reminiscence of its God which the purified soul can never escape; that longing after "Nirvana"—that jewel in the lotus of the Buddhist: *Om mani padme hôm.*[1] Penetrated with these ideas, and living constantly in the ideal,

[1] O Infinite! direct my feet toward thee!

she could sweep onward and upward in ever higher and loftier circles; her duties, her pleasures, her studies, her joys, her friendships and sorrows, were all at length transformed into spiritual rather than earthly things, and full of divine beauty. "I am every day more and more impressed with the idea that I am floating in a sea of divine energy, or life, of which I am a part; a measureless ocean of living energy, which rolls its tide, as it were, into the little creek that is bounded by our senses, thus to take this form of finite life. This flowing tide ripples on the shore of the objective world; but behind is the broadening flood, which widens out beyond vision or sounding-line into the inconceivable grandeur of God." In these, almost her dying words, we can perceive something of the majesty of this great American woman, something of the living, concentrated energy and depth of her soul, something of that impersonal soul losing itself in "the inconceivable grandeur of God." We cannot fail to recognize in her a grand typical woman of the great American Republic; for there are others like unto her, working, saving, ameliorating, making the rough places smooth, and striving, ever striving, to live up to their loftiest ideals.

Mrs. Botta lived no fragmentary life measured by days, months, and years. Her life here was a continuity of a life before and a life hereafter; her life, to those who knew her, was an expression of divine energy, divine compassion, divine unity, without beginning, without end. The tangible "web" which we call birth and death is but the endless changes through which the soul, obedient to its own spiritual laws, passes on and on toward a final reunion with its own divine essence, God.

> Then, since from God those lesser lives began,
> And the eager spirits entered into man,
> To God again the enfranchised soul must tend;
> He is her Home, her Author, is her End.
> No death is hers; when earthly eyes grow dim,
> Star-like she soars, and, God-like, melts in him.

A Few Words of Love

BY MARY MAPES DODGE, NEW-YORK.

(Extract from a Letter.)

MY DEAR MR. BOTTA:

IT is beautiful to leave such a memory as hers. Even now, beyond the keen sense of loss, beyond the longing to see her dear face, to hear her voice, I rejoice in my friend for what she was to all who knew her—a beautiful presence, a brave, noble influence, a delight, an inspiration.

I had known Mrs. Botta many years, yet never did she grow a day older. A bright, earnest woman,—never trifling, never conscious of her charm,—she seemed the embodiment of perennial youth.

Never shall I forget that light, quick footstep coming down the stairs in her beautiful home—music indeed to all who loved her, or who enjoyed the privilege of her warm, uplifting friendship.

I write these words to you, to whom she was, as you have said, friend, wife, child, mother,—everything! And yet I dare not speak of your loss, your sorrow. I only can rejoice for you in her rare personality, her goodness, her sweet, beguiling wisdom, in the very grace of her existence.

Reminiscences

By the Hon. Charles A. Peabody, New-York.

IN availing myself of the opportunity to unite with other friends in paying tribute to the memory of the late Mrs. Botta, afforded me by the kindness of her sorrowing husband, I have first to select from the numerous eminent qualities of mind and heart which she possessed and illustrated in her journey through life.

The character in which she was most broadly known was that of authoress. She had written much and well. But it is not by the amount or excellence of her writings that she will be chiefly remembered by her friends and those having personal acquaintance with her. She had written sufficient to give ample evidence of ability, industry, and love of the occupation, and it was conceded on all hands that so far as she had given herself to the labors of an authoress, she had deserved, as she had received in large measure, the approbation of that part of society whose approbation is most to be desired. The intellectual character of her productions was always highly esteemed. They were always the expression of careful thought and study, of a mind amply endowed by nature, disciplined and accustomed to think and study carefully as well as industriously. There was symmetry—consistency of parts with each other—in her writings not always found in the writings of either sex, and some critics (unsympathetic perhaps) have said, less frequently found in those of the more sentimental and emotional than in those of the less delicate and susceptible branch of the family of authors.

One single product of her mind and pen has seemed to me sufficient to establish her reputation for ability, industry, and love of the acquisition of knowledge by exhaustive labor and research. I allude to the "Handbook of Universal Literature," a volume of five or six hundred pages closely printed. That volume gives a carefully prepared history of all the literatures of the world, so far as they are known in print, from the Hebrew in its earliest days—their origin and history, with the modifications and changes they have experienced from the date of their rudiments to the present time. This book, now in its twenty-third, or later, edition, and in use in colleges and universities, would seem to me to furnish almost any amount of evidence that could be desired of the highly intellectual and literary character of the authoress in the department of literary labor to which it belongs.

Other writings of hers in prose, on subjects less recondite and more in harmony with what is expected from the feminine toils and mind, might be referred to. But the "Handbook of Universal Literature" is cited as a production *sui generis*, and of a character quite unlike what is expected from the labors of her sex; and while possessing many attractions expected from the gentler and more refined sex, the work abounds with matter which is expected only of the sterner and stronger side of the human family. It is probable that she was better known and more admired for her productions in verse. It was, no doubt, in this department that she became earliest known. A volume which contained many, but by no means all, of her poems was in print several years ago. She continued to write poems to the end of her life, and many have never yet been published. They are of a grave and thoughtful character, and the pleasure they gave to her friends and appreciative readers in her lifetime is not diminished, but only hallowed, by the sad event which has taken her from their society and from this world.

In 1848, if my memory serves me, I knew her by reputation as a writer and authoress. As long ago as that, when she was Miss Lynch, and before her marriage with Professor Botta, she was a prolific writer in poetry and in prose. Her social and literary receptions, launched years before, and at that time prospering under favoring skies and breezes, were receptions of the poetess in the estimation of polite and cultured people, who knew them practically as well as by reputation. I knew, through mutual acquaintances, that they were very successful and much admired. Her literary productions even then had given her an enviable position, and enabled her to secure the approbation of the most cultured literary persons of the time.

To those who had the good fortune to be personally acquainted with Mrs. Botta, their interest in her will have far outstripped all that could be derived from familiarity with her literary works. By far the most attractive qualities of her character were sentimental and of the heart, rather than intellectual and of the head, elevated and commanding as were the latter. There was a kindliness of manner and general bearing, a readiness of sympathy and interest, which made her always accepted and welcomed as a friend. It was apparent at the first, and made one always wish for further acquaintance. She was very frank and ingenuous in manner and in fact. The feeling initiated at the first acquaintance was not discouraged or diminished, but increased by further knowledge. She was herself willing and desirous to be pleased, and showed to companions a pleasing interest in them. Her estimate of others—their acts and sayings — was always kindly, and such as gave evidence of a kindly and generous nature in herself. Her genial and affectionate nature delighted in doing good—relieving suffering and conferring happiness in every-day practical life. This was her habit, and she interested herself in any case that came to her knowledge which afforded an opportunity for the gratification of benevolent desires.

Like the rest of the world, she had to judge others

by herself, and such as her own feelings and motives were, or would have been under similar circumstances, she judged the feelings and motives of others to be; and although, judging from herself, she may have had a standard higher and more magnanimous than would give, as the result, the exact truth concerning others,—it had the effect of elevating, in her estimate and feelings, humanity and the world in which she and her companions were living.

Her actions were in accordance with her sentiments and feelings; she was always ready to embrace every opportunity for soothing and relieving the pains, sorrows, and distrusts of those about her whom her acts would affect, by attentions of kindness and sympathy. She did not decline or seek to avoid relations with the unhappy and suffering, as less affectionate natures habitually do. On the contrary, she seemed to seek such associations, and to avail herself of them as affording opportunities for kindly attentions and ministrations to the relief of her own heart, as well as the hearts on which her blessings were bestowed. It was not her habit or taste "to pass by on the other side"; moreover, such an action would not have been consistent with her character. She found her inmost satisfaction in repeating the ministrations of the good Samaritan whenever she found an object on which to bestow them.

What seems to me much more meritorious, as well as rare, in practical life, is the observance of a rule of benevolent, helpful action in the cases where no thrilling appeal is made to the sympathies—

where the actor is readily and willingly engaged in bestowing or increasing the happiness of those not having the claims arising from positive need or suffering. Her habits of hospitality were among the most remarked and admired in her character; in this, as in everything else, she attempted to confer the greatest amount of happiness possible. The happiness and enjoyment of her guests, not the brilliancy and ostentation of her entertainments, were her guide in them. They were often repeated and much more enjoyed in each instance than those conducted on the opposite principle of display. For whole decades the hospitality extended to distinguished strangers from abroad was observed and remarked by all who were acquainted with her. Hardly a foreigner of distinction in letters or refined culture visited the city who was not entertained at her house, and receptions given him or her; and no small part of them were guests residing temporarily at her house during their stay in the city. It was a common remark that few if any other houses in the city excelled or perhaps equaled it in the extent to which guests of distinction from abroad were entertained, and domestic guests and citizens were presented to them in her drawing-rooms.

She will be remembered by me as a benefactor so long as memory shall continue to serve me. There have been times in my life, as there have been in the lives of many others, when kindness of attention and sympathetic interest have been valuable above all price, and when the ministrations of a kindly nature like hers were like angelic visits.

At a time when I was suffering severe affliction, she kindly offered to render me any aid in her power, and in that connection she said that she and her husband were expecting to sail for Europe in a few days, and suggested that the change of scene which would be afforded by such a journey would perhaps be the best relief I could find under the circumstances; that if I would take passage with them, they would with pleasure do all in their power to aid and sustain me in my dejected condition. I accepted her proposal very gratefully, and the kindness of the attentions thus afforded me can never be forgotten, or the obligation discharged.

She has been kindly and beneficent by her sympathy and soothing aid to an extent that I will not attempt to describe. She was always accessible in time of need, always interested and sympathetic; but her ministrations did not end there. She had strength and the power to impart it to the depressed and suffering,—the wisdom as well as the wish which could strengthen and enliven the suffering and despondent.

As advice, she adopted the words of Emerson, and gave them to me in the following lines:

Some of your griefs you have cured,
And the sharpest you still have survived;
But what torments of pain you 've endured
From evils that never arrived!

The following poem was addressed to me by her during my affliction:

Anne C. L. Botta

UNTIL DEATH.

Make me no vows of constancy, dear friend,
To love me, though I die, thy whole life long,
And love no other till thy days shall end;
Nay, it were rash and wrong.

If thou canst love another, be it so;
I would not reach out of my quiet grave
To bind thy heart, if it should choose to go:
Love should not be a slave.

My placid ghost, I trust, will walk serene
In clearer light than gilds these earthly morns,
Above the jealousies and envies keen
Which sow this life with thorns.

Thou wouldst not feel my shadowy caress,
If after death my soul should linger here;
Men's hearts crave tangible, close tenderness,
Love's presence, warm and near.

It would not make me sleep more peacefully
That thou wert wasting all thy life in woe
For my poor sake; what love thou hast for me
Bestow it ere I go.

Carve not upon a stone when I am dead
The praises which remorseful mourners give
To women's graces,—a tardy recompense,—
But speak thou while I live.

Heap not the heavy marble on my head
To shut away the sunshine and the dew;
Let small blooms grow there and let grasses wave,
And raindrops filter through.

Reminiscences

Thou wilt meet many fairer and more gay
Than I; but, trust me, thou canst never find
One who will love and serve thee night and day
With a more single mind.

Forget me when I die!—the violets
Above my rest will blossom just as blue,
Nor miss thy tears: e'en Nature's self forgets;—
But while I live, be true!

A Noble Woman

By Kate Field, Washington, D. C.

IT is a busy, struggling world we live in, and few pause when even the greatest are borne to the grave; but sometimes the passing on of a rare soul makes us stop and think. Such a soul had the noble woman who left us suddenly on March 23, 1891, who bore the honored name of Anne Charlotte Lynch until she married Vincenzo Botta, a distinguished Italian who under the direction of his government had come to America to investigate our system of education. When he sailed for this country his future wife sailed for Europe in company with her friends Charles Butler and family.

This man and this woman passed each other on the high seas, and even when Miss Lynch returned to New-York, Professor Botta carried about for six months a letter of introduction to her, so averse was he to meeting unknown people. At last he presented it, and then—he called daily. The subject of Victor Emmanuel at once recognized the generous, sympathetic American whose quick intelligence was the least of her attractions. She had a heart; she gave it unreservedly, once and for all.

What a glorious tribute this Italian pays to his wife! "Much as I loved her in the beginning, much as I esteemed her noble qualities, I can truly say that she was far more to me at the end than at the beginning; for I knew her better and appreciated her more. She had but one fault, and it killed her—benevolence. She gave always. It was her nature. Enough that humanity needed help for her to extend her hand, whether she were well or ill. She loved her kind, and longed to benefit her generation. Her first and last thought was for others. She rarely spoke of herself, and until death itself took her from me she made light of her own suffering, and gave instructions what should be done for the doctor, the nurses, and for me. She was my rudder. I have lost all in losing her."

Better than to have written the greatest of books or modeled the best of statues, is it to have inspired such love and such respect. Mrs. Botta was a woman, and as a beautiful example of her sex I want many who never knew her, or knew her superficially, to realize the sweetness of her character; for, after all, it is character, not reputation, that makes the real human being.

"Did you ever notice how much of Christ's life was spent simply in doing kind things?" asks Drummond. Therein lay the greatness of Mrs. Botta's life. She was perpetually doing kind things for everybody, regardless of thanks or gratitude,

beaming like the sun upon the just and unjust, conscious of her own good-will—unconscious, if possible, of slight or malice. I have never known man or woman so eager for the truth, whatever it might be; so ready to receive the light, no matter whence it came; so humble in her own esteem; so ready to praise friend and foe when praise was due. The latch-string of her heart and head, as of her hospitable door, was always out. The welcome came from one who, living in the world for seventy-six years, was never spoiled by it, whose simplicity and naturalness would have graced a child.

Mrs. Botta had no fear of death. She accepted the inevitable, and often talked with her husband of that mysterious law of nature which usually seems so cruel. She believed firmly in cremation, but so dearly loved her friend and best adviser of forty years, Mr. Charles Butler, as to waive her own judgment in deference to his. "Remember," she said to her husband, "if I die before Mr. Butler, let me be buried. If I die after him, be sure that I am cremated."

She died first, and no truer mourner has this thoughtful woman than the ninety-year-old man who "longs for the touch of a vanished hand, and the sound of a voice that is still."

For many years it had been Mrs. Botta's custom to send Mr. Butler a pocket-book on Christmas wherein lay a poem inspired by her regard. The old pocket-book was always carefully laid aside for the new; the poems, intended for one eye only, were always treasured. Her last Christmas brought to Mr. Butler his eagerly expected gift, the poem almost a presage of impending fate:

As year by year adown life's stream we glide,
And see our loved ones falling at our side,
Passing like shadows to the dread unknown,
It were too drear to journey on alone
But for the friends who still our pathway cheer,
Their lessening numbers still more prized and dear;
Because the last, more precious they become,
Like the few leaves the Sibyl brought to Rome.

On one of his birthdays, Mrs. Botta remembered him with the following lines:

Life is not measured by the flow of years,
But by high deeds and noble thoughts, whereby
The soul makes its own record and uprears
A monument whereon its age appears.
If by this law we count and measure thine,
We find the record ten times eighty-nine.

At another time she sent him an illustrated Bible with these verses:

Within this Book is shrined the simple creed
Divinely given; and he who owns may read
The creed the law and prophets rest upon,
That love to God and love to man are one.
Far off in Eastern lands, and long ago,
An angel came this great truth to foreshow,—
So runs the tale,—and if to-day he came
The chosen spirits of the world to claim,
In his bright list, thy name among the blest
Like "Abou Ben Adhem's" would lead all the rest.

The woman lived up to the poet's ideal.

On March 31, 1891, Professor and Mrs. Botta would have celebrated the thirty-sixth anniversary of their wedding. The feast for them and their intimate friends did not come: there was the silence of desolation in its stead. But the happy reunion has only been postponed. I hear a gentle, kind voice whisper to those who mourn her sudden taking off: "Courage; the end is not yet. The end is never!"

An Expression of Love

By Mrs. Maria Wallace, New-York.

My dear Mr. Botta:

I AM sure you must know how gladly I avail myself of the opportunity to say my simple word in remembrance of her whom it was my happy privilege to call friend.

As a friend indeed and in truth, such as I knew her, I shall alone speak of her who has left us.

Other pens may more worthily describe her as author and artist, as the gracious hostess of her beautiful *salon*, open to all who could present any true claim upon her hospitality for themselves or their ideas. Legion must be the name of the struggling men and women to whom she proved a veritable angel of hope. These too shall rise up and call her blessed.

As a friend, her price was above rubies. The rare charm of her personality is indescribable. With her came sweetness, and light, and cheer; and when she went away the very room seemed brighter and sunnier for her coming.

Always the best in me came forth to meet her pleasant challenge. Under her vivifying influence I felt my "slimpsy," embryonic thoughts and speculations filling out and growing clearer, until the poor starveling germs bloomed into fair and individual life.

Always interested in whatsoever interested another, always claiming to have gained something, while ever giving in full measure, she touched closely the secret of losing life to find it.

In sorrow a sure stay and consoler, in joy a very echo of the joy-bells in one's heart, hers was a rarely responsive spirit, needing

> No dry discussion to unfold
> The meaning caught ere well 't was told,

but often making one's "meaning" a glad surprise to one's self.

Accept, my dear sir, this poor expression of the love and reverence I bore for her in life, and cherish still more tenderly now that she has gone from our sight.

Recollections

By Mrs. Julia Campbell Keightly, New-York.

IT is the privilege of some few private lives to become public ones in a sense generally overlooked. Such lives are not based upon organized effort; they have no fixed direction, no aim, but a continuous aspiration; their trend is toward truth only, in all departments of life. Their universal bent affords expansion to every experience; they come to dispense a calm helpfulness, to illumine the general bewilderment with an apotheosis of common sense. Like the comet, they have no known orbit, but bear light from star to star. Such sound, sweet minds are centers of power. They unify and consolidate men and thoughts. When one such life is withdrawn, it is discovered to have been a public one in the sense that it belonged to all who chose to make a claim upon it,—was a distinctive medium, a basis of free interchange. Disappearing, it leaves us confronted with a breach most wide, a chasm darkly deep. Then its vigorous cheeriness assails our memory, and dries our tears.

Such a life ended, with brief warning, at 1 A. M. of March 23, 1891, when Mrs. Botta slept—and woke not. She had achieved much in the world to which she then closed her eyes. Her sonnets and other literary works are well known. She was the friend of Poe, Willis, Emerson, Kingsley, Froude, Matthew Arnold, and so on through the long ranks of names illustrious and names shining with a milder ray. To scan the packets of letters in her writing-table was to exchange greetings with half a century of notabilities, and the roll-call of modern fame might have been read from the pages of her book of hospitality. Not alone the victors responded to her vivifying touch. Many a raw recruit received from her the first lessons in his manual. It is nowhere inscribed, not even in the unstable heart of man, how many stricken ones she uplifted and upheld. Once I said to her: "I hope they are grateful." Her eyes sparkled with amusement. "Grateful? Oh, my dear! I am the grateful one; I only rest when I am doing something"; and again she laughed in her enlivened common sense.

To applaud achievement was Mrs. Botta's delight. It was her mission, and her inspiration, to urge all, the young especially, to do some one thing well, and to evolve some special mode of usefulness. It lay, above all, in bringing the ways and means of self-help to those who had them not. This done, she expected her assistance to be returned to the community at large. She had a very passion of purpose to enlarge, to fortify, to ennoble and enrich. An ardent believer in the dignity of humanity, she longed to see its every unit self-sustained and upright, and to this end spared herself no whit. Whatever she had she gave—herself most of all. For herself she asked of others nothing but themselves; but for humanity she asked everything. Such was the spur of her incentive, that not the smallest, the most futile of lives could come within her radius and ever contract to be quite its own scant self again. With sluggish lives she had a merry discontent: "I could shake A——; she *will not* grow." Hers was a natural power, like gravitation. In such measure did she evolve it, that she, of all American women, came nearest to the formation of a *salon*. Had her interests been a shade less universal we should have had the Salon Botta, as once society had the Hôtel Rambouillet. Her friends were leaders of parties, of charities, of reforms, of social, literary, and artistic organizations. Participating in all of these, her chief pursuit was still to develop the best latent in all persons, herself included,—a universal learning, helping, doing. "Give me persons," she said. "I must have people; they are my passion; I must see them grow. I have often been deceived in them, and yet each new person intoxicates me as with wonderful possibilities."

The import of this life was great. It was true to nature. It sowed seed everywhere, without count of harvests; we know not where its hidden germs may spring. This underlying fidelity to a true type conferred its powers, confirmed its possibilities, and stamped its value as above the common estimate. For it is the want of just such characters that makes modern life, in the aggregate, the petty, personal limitation and compromise that it is. With her, we breathed a rarer air. Some one spoke to her with surprise of her having condoned the "ungrateful and treacherous conduct" of —— toward herself. "Did —— act badly toward me? I had forgotten it. He has done some excellent work." This was in consonance with a paragraph from one of her letters: "No one ever deceives us. We deceive ourselves. We lay the gilding on thickly, and are surprised when it dims and cracks, forgetting that this is the nature of gilding. Pure gold is not of our invention, but we meet it so rarely that we invent something else to take its place, in our need of ideal natures."

Mrs. Botta asked for no stage, no clique or coterie; desired neither to lead nor to be led; had no rigid compact with conventionalities; was held in no material bondage; envied no individual sway over any mind or heart; set her personal seal nowhere; offered no molds and accepted none: but challenged facts and men upon their own basis. She had no standard but truth; no rules but moral responsibility and moral freedom; no love that had the taint of selfishness; no hope that did not include the eternal well-being and doing of a perfectible humanity. Asking only to live largely and truly, she left the rest to divine justice. At an age when most persons have a cherished mental equipment,—to doubt one detail of which accumulation is an offense, because it represents the "I" to them,—Mrs. Botta's mind, on the contrary, seemed ever in flux, ever ready to re-combine, or to be held in critical suspension, precipitating anew at fresh evidence. Hers was not alone the hospitality of the roof-tree, but the hospitality of the mind as well. In her was infinite harborage. She might not accept our ideals, but she never profaned them. She understood with heart and intellect alike, even to the wrong-doing, which she took for an error of the mind, and strove to correct with nobler reasoning. As one who listens to the separate notes of that song which is the whole of life, she asked no solution of its "permitted discords," but saw that these enhanced the harmonies, and, declining to limit it, rejoiced to live it, to share its highest meaning, as she understood it, with all.

This meaning was divinely human. Hence the larger part of her good deeds escaped observation. They were the outcome of that cordial faith which ruled the sweet and secret recesses of her nature: the belief that man is here for service to his fellow-man. Yet those who came to her for partiality or emotional sentimentalism came in vain. "There is a hysteria of the heart as there is hysteria of the nerves," she said; "let us avoid both." Slow to judgment, she could indefinitely postpone the progress of "making up her mind" when her knowledge was insufficient. Capable of rashly generous impulses, she never weakened to a regret, but, accepting all consequences, lived serenely in each day. A duty wore a joyous guise. The attempt to reduce the universe to a creed or a formula had never been made by her; but she often said that the closing stanzas of "The Light of Asia" expressed her belief in sequential order and law, and once exclaimed:

"'. . . utter sure
Its measures mete, its faultless balance weighs.'

Can any one ask more or less than absolute justice?"

The writer, knowing Mrs. Botta for the last fourteen years of her life, had the good fortune to "inherit" her, as she said, from her grandfather, Chief Justice Ellis Lewis, who greatly admired Mrs. Botta in her youth, and whose maturity she in turn admired. This friendship had its afterglow in the later closer tie. Mrs. Botta's interest in those younger than herself was a benign influence unfolding her nature to the eager "heir."

She spoke of ideal friendship, and said of a friend: "She loves me for myself alone, just as I am; yet I wish to be loved also for what I might be. The ideal self alone merits the ideal friend." She was not a woman of words, but one twilight hour she said: "I must have a *little* name for you; I shall call you ——; and you will call me Bottina — the little Botta." Laughing, I replied: "You cannot disassociate love from your husband!" A delicate flush ran up among the silvered tendrils of her hair; for a moment she seemed to commune inwardly, then a light kindled in her eyes, and she said: "You have seen my portrait-bust of Botta, have n't you? It came to me like an inspiration, though I worked long over it, and now he always looks like that to me." This bust is an admirable likeness of Professor Botta in earlier life, and still it has that ideal aspect in which a man reveals himself to one beholder only.

In my note-book of those days, I find some conversations with Mrs. Botta which show at its best a certain delicate sportiveness she had, while at the same time her deeper character revealed itself. Speaking of an adventuress who exploited her kindness, she said: "I was warned not to know her. But Eve would taste for herself, you know. Besides, she could n't harm me. At my age, there is no moral contagion possible. You cannot inoculate an old woman" (here she laughed); "but she may still wish to understand a young one. One never knows whether people can be helped till one tries. But she only wanted to use me. She abused me instead, for I had to let her go. She was very beautiful, poor creature. That attracted me so much. I suppose it was the source of all her troubles, but that does n't prevent you and me from wishing we were beautiful, does it?" Here she laughed again. This little laugh of Mrs. Botta's — short, odd, and whimsical — might almost have been called her personal accent. It had a gentle satire, but somehow cheered. If a friend said some impatient or tactless thing, Mrs. Botta laughed, and lo! the tenor of the speech seemed changed. She laughed as we laugh at the clever waywardness of a beloved child, and the air was cleared of all offense. Often her wholesome humor took herself for butt.

"If you bait your line with a person, you can always catch me."

"You and I live on our nerves; it 's true we have plenty of them."

"Mr. —— always talks to me as if I were a young and beautiful woman. I do not like it—perhaps because it continually reminds me that I never was beautiful."

"I always wish I had had my photograph taken when Mr. Emerson was staying in my house. Every one felt his influence, even the servants, who would hardly leave the dining-room. I looked like a different being, and was so happy I forgot to see that he had enough to eat."

"When I look back on what I thought and wrote when I was young, I can see that I have not grown much since then. I was ahead of myself. I am now living and helping others to live what I saw clearly at that time—a long assimilation and digestion. Yes, I am much the same, but for the fact of becoming now what I then thought. I have lived all I knew, yet I feel as if I had only half lived" (laughing); "perhaps that was because I always had an imperfect circulation." Mrs. Botta then produced some of her earlier writings in confirmation of her view, and, indeed, it seemed that her mind had been luminous from a very early age. Certain it is that she took humanity as she found it; she asked no questions, passed no criticisms, proffered no condemnations.

When asked, "How can you tolerate such false characters?" she replied, "Why not? They tolerate me; yet I am their opposite." If she were wronged, a genial amusement was all she permitted herself. But if wrong were done to another she uttered a direct, kindly note of warning to the offender. In magnanimity she was entire. Hers was the triumph of character. A diligent and devoted daughter, an ideal mate, a faithful and compassionate friend, melodious in verse, careful and able in literary work, talented in modeling, vivacious and refreshing in society,—we can still put all these gifts and traits aside as pure adornment, for her real secret consisted in none of these; her real value lay beyond, at the core of her nature. It was her equipoise that made her truly great. The fountainhead of all she was is that sublime charity which thinketh no evil and hateth naught.

After a three years' separation, we met again, a few weeks before her death. Taking my arm, she walked and talked much of her latest work, a life-size bust which she was modeling in clay. Her intense interest in this occupation exhausted her. "I do not even walk any more since I began it, but meeting you has inspirited me. I can do nothing but work on that bust. It is like being in love for the first time. I am absorbed; I forget everything else. If I have succeeded, I am enraptured; I need no food; I am filled with new wine. If I fail, I am utterly broken down; it is as if the beloved one were dead." The work progressed slowly; it met with mishaps; she lost touch with it at times. Importuned to put it temporarily aside, she refused with what was almost vehemence, and betrayed a nervous exaltation. "This work is something I have," she exclaimed, "which cannot be taken away. Friends depart—we have no friends, but only befriending circumstances drawing one to another until change dissolves adhesion. Old age comes on, and the common life shrinks away from us; but art is an enchanted country where I can always lose myself. We cannot be exacting of humanity, but of art we may demand everything."

The last meeting came unknown, as it comes so often, mercifully. We walked together on Broadway, and at parting I drew her back upon a door-step to rally her upon an abstraction which continued to disquiet me. "Since coming here," I said, "I have not really come near you. You are living in a far country. No report from you of its climate, or of its conditions. You have eloped with art, your work under your arm. When will you come back from that distant land to live among mortals again?" Her eyes deepened as she pressed my hands. "Never, perhaps," she murmured, and dropped into the living stream. I watched the slight, active figure with its vivacious movement, borne onward in the crowd, and, as I watched, she slipped away from me—away into the hereafter. On the following Wednesday I kept my engagement to pass the morning with her—but it was at her funeral. That "Never, perhaps," was the last word of a friendship to me unique.

Short as was her last illness, it sufficed to make new friends through her sublime unselfishness, which manifested itself in thought for the comfort of her physicians and nurses, even to within a few hours of her passage from earthly cares. The thought of death did not visit those last hours. She slept—and passed on. But often in her lifetime she expressed a wish that no publicity, no crowd, no floral tributes should impair the quiet privacy of her funeral, and, in her exquisite modesty, she wished not to be seen after death. And so it was. Yet a tribute of which she had no conception was, and ever will be, hers, arising from all who knew her. They turn bewildered faces to a life bereft of her unswerving testimony to life's highest elements. They do not lament her loss so much as the artist and the poet, but as the woman endowed so liberally with the attributes of strength and justice. The incalculable service she rendered to her era lay in showing the beauty, the far-reaching usefulness and power of a mind devoted to lofty ideals.

A Perfect Woman

BY DR. WALLACE WOOD, NEW-YORK.

MY DEAR MR. BOTTA:

I GLADLY comply with your request. Now that time has taken off the keenest edge of our grief, it is easier to speak of her. Yet it seems but yesterday that she was with us. Alas! how will humanity ever be able to bear with equanimity the visitation of the master evil, death?

In a village churchyard, not far away, I recently read upon the tomb of an unknown these words: "Perfect wife, perfect mother, perfect friend." I repeated them over and over. Here was an ideal of the highest excellence for this "rude hamlet." My thoughts flew back to the town and the great world, and to the perfection in a wider sphere of her we mourn; for of her it must be written down that she was historian, poet, sculptor, philanthropist, as well as wife, friend, social leader; and that in none of these rôles could it be said that she was imperfect. Such versatility and power recall to the mind the record of exceptional natures and great epochs like the Renaissance. Of that strange inborn energy in her all can speak; we all know of the long outdoor walks she took, even up to the time of her death, and how she always descended the stairs with a run.

The first thing one observed in her mind, it seems to me, was its quick interest in the highest and greatest things. The atmosphere of the true, the beautiful, and the good was what she breathed; her sympathy was wide,—she seemed ever to see the universe and humanity, and to conceive of them as wholes; a mind not learned nor laborious, yet truly philosophic, in harmony with Plato and Emerson, seeing the unity amid all variety. By this faculty she conceived and executed the "Handbook of Universal Literature," one of the most useful books in any language. Literature is, simply and scientifically, the soul of humanity; this truth she saw,—this soul through that work she pictured whole and complete. She had a horror of *disjecta membra*. Universal history as at present written, she said, is pieced up of the head of one nation, the body of another, the limbs of the next, and so on; and she had already planned and begun to work out the same scheme for the philosophic unity of history that she had achieved for literature.

One might have known her for years, yet without having read her poems. When this volume is opened to such a one, it will be a revelation. Here she has pictured her own soul, complete, frank; all its wishes, all its aspirations, its loves, its longings, exactly what she thinks and feels on all the highest and grandest subjects, as well as those within the deepest and most mysterious recesses of the heart. Oliver Wendell Holmes somewhere says that there are two modes by which the soul may express itself wholly and free, may dare to be sincere. One way is prayer, the other poesie. This volume is a frank and free confession looking upward. One rises from its perusal and exclaims: "What a perfect picture of a soul!" Here is Divine Sincerity herself. If every one of our friends, each man and woman, could or would thus write himself or herself down in a hundred pages, what a new spiritual world we could create! At the moment, I think of no other volume to compare with it except the poems of Schiller. Here, too, we have confession looking upward: "The Highest," "Immortality," "The Ideal of Woman," "Love and Desire," "Virtue," "Goodness and Greatness," are some of the titles.

We turn to the titles in her works and see what subjects were of interest to her: "Nobility," "Endurance," "Aspiration," "Vita Nuova," "Wishes," "Longing," "Unrest," "Memory," "Hope," "The Ideal," "The Ideal Found," "The Hero," "To the Sun," "The Earth to the Sun," "Faith," "Love," "Sweetness," "Largess." What a perfect poem is the sonnet on "Aspiration"! One can never read it without feeling the thrill of a higher impulse.

History she loved for its grandeur and its dignity. Heroism always moved her. Prometheus and Jeanne d'Arc were her favorite subjects in art.

She was an idealist in the best sense, always moved most by the noblest and the highest. The universe, the divine, humanity, were for her real things,—existences, organism, friends; so also were literature, art, science; and so were all men and women, for she always saw the divine in them. I often asked her what she loved most, and her replies settled finally to this: "I love literature, art, science, and men and women." In fact, was it not just upon these subjects that she was always alert, eager to question, ready to listen?

In familiar acquaintance with our dear Mrs. Botta, how surely do we find the refutation of the idea that greatness of mind in woman may endanger that sacred femininity which in all society is so highly prized. She was womanly—more, she was intensely feminine: anti-masculine, so to speak,—a dainty being, a creature of rose-leaves and laces. In manner and conversation she had that beautiful combination of sentiment and naïveté which is so very rare, and having which a woman is always charming, and charming up to the utmost length of her days. In style the same quality shows itself in a perfect balance again to run between the tragic muse and the muse of comedy. She was the one without gloom, and the other without coquetry or any tinge of the common. This constituted the fascination of two remarkable actresses of our time, Mrs. Kendal and Mary Anderson. This charm showed itself in Mrs. Botta's notes. They were never waste paper. Into a note written to a friend she would put a flower like this: "Did I expect you to come up last night and read Herbert Spencer to me? Yes; I did."

How complete was her humanity, how perfect her sympathies! Men and women she loved; human intercourse was like the air she breathed, or food and drink,— she could not live a day without it. With a housekeeper she would discuss butter and gowns; with the United States minister to England she would draw out the condition of women in Europe; for the country-school mistress at a watering-place she buys Latin dictionaries, and to a crippled boy who shows signs of talent she gives lessons in sculpture. The doctor and the artist were welcome guests at her home; they had something she wished to hear and know; she was interested in both them and their work.

To church she rarely went. She once remarked in regard to it: "I came away as a sheep that was not fed." Emerson, in fact, was her pastor. With regard to immortality she once expressed herself as not one of those who wished to awaken and find themselves alive after they were dead. She was fond of reading the lines to the divine power in the last part of "The Light of Asia."

What, my dear Professor, is the nature of that quality which finding in a human being we instinctively call divine? It seems to me it is grandeur and height attained without effort: the noble and the lofty inherent. We others, common and human, toil through all the twelve labors of Heracles, and then only catch occasional celestial glimpses. How we educate and train and repress and strive and self-cultivate, and watch, fight, and pray!—and yet here is one, here is a spirit high, noble, lovely, sweet, as it were by divine right, just as easily and as naturally as a bee is a bee, and a flower is a flower.

When in the wilderness of this world it is our lot to meet with such a one, we can only express our feeling by one of two words: divine or perfect.

Perfect friend, perfect woman, perfect soul,—there need be no Purgatorio for thee!

Characteristics

By Andrew Carnegie, New-York.

As I sit down to write of my dear friend Madame Botta, who has passed away from us, the first feeling that arises is one of thankfulness that I was privileged to know such a character well. Many have the same story to tell of her, for one of her chief characteristics was that of recognizing and encouraging unknown men and women, and giving them opportunities to benefit, not only from her own stores of wisdom, and from her charming manners and conversation, but from the remarkable class she drew around her, of which she was the center and cementing bond.

It would be presumption in me, perhaps, to assert that the home of the Bottas was the nearest approach, in our country, to the *salon* of the past, for there may be others which rival it in this respect which it has not been my good fortune to enter; but, as far as my experience goes, I found there a circle of wider and more varied range than at any other. I remember well, a New-York lady of fashion once said when she heard me extol the Botta reunions, that these evenings were indeed extraordinary; one met such celebrated people, but also such "queer people," all mixed together; one never knew whom one might meet there. It can never be very much of a *salon* in which the so-called "queer people" are not found, for it is in these that talent and genius in some form is very apt to lurk. Madame Botta, the author, the sculptor, the critic, and, not least, the charming woman of the world, had naturally a wider horizon than my lady friend who was only the last of these. Society with us is far too exclusively confined to the rich and fashionable—the fault of a new civilization. In Italy, Germany, France, or England, no woman has the slightest pretension to the foremost place in society who is not able to draw to her, through congenial tastes, the literary, musical, professional, and artistic celebrities—the leading ministers, physicians, painters, musicians, and actors, and especially the coming man or coming woman in these branches. Millionaires and fashionables are poor substitutes for the real lions of a cultivated society. Madame Botta's lions could all roar, more or less; they were not compelled to chatter, or be dumb.

The position of the Bottas in the literary and artistic world enabled them to draw together not only the best-known people of this country, but to a degree greater than any, as far as I know, the most distinguished visitors from abroad, beyond the ranks of mere title or fashion. No home, I think, in all the land compared with theirs in the number and character of its foreign visitors.

Of those who contribute to this memorial, I judge that none can write from my standpoint, which is that of a young unmarried and unknown man, a stranger in the great metropolis, whose first entrance into such a circle as I have indicated came through the dear lady whose loss means so much to all of us. It pleases me to remember that I am indebted for my introduction to her to Courtlandt Palmer, a noble soul, always thinking more of others than of self. It was with equal surprise and gratification that I found myself often invited by the Bottas thereafter. Speaking, long years afterward, of the beginning of our intimacy, Madame Botta told me she invited me again because some words I had spoken the first night struck her as a genuine note, although unusual.

This shows the woman. She passed through life with open mind and listening ear, absorbing all that appeared to her to be genuine, no matter if unusual, or who uttered it,—Pagan, Christian, or Jew. I knew her well for twenty years, and so lovely was her disposition, I never remember her showing even a trace of temper but once. Upon this occasion the Professor and myself were alone with her. He had, half playfully, taken her to task for not placing the stamp of disapproval upon the conduct of certain rude but well-known people. It was a strong case, which the Professor thought justified, and even required, rebuke, while Madame had gone out of her way to show extreme courtesy. Upon being appealed to, I sided strongly with the Professor. The moral aspect of the matter was intimated, and our duty to show disapproval as well as approval was insisted upon. Something was said about her seeming indifference to the character and conduct of those honored by her. I see the lithe, gentle little woman rise and stand at the table quite near to us: "You and Botta seem to think that I do not understand and disapprove such conduct, and that I overlooked it in these people for their sake. You are mistaken; I never thought of them at all, but only what was due to myself. People can act as they please, and I am sorry it is the nature of some to act as they do: I can only act toward them as becomes myself."

I never heard her say an unkind word of a living soul. The sweet influences she exerted were as the dews which melt and enrich, never the frosty winds which blast. It never required a violation of the strictest rules of the gentlest courtesy upon the part of Madame Botta to separate the dross from the pure gold of society. Indeed, the dross fell away of its own accord, for there was no happiness near her for any but those natures touched to fine issues. Her forgiving nature rendered it impossible to retain the sense of personal wrong. One of the most serious and instructive interviews I ever had with my dear mentor and friend was as a peacemaker. Madame had felt it to be her duty to withdraw her name from a society because one of its officers had, in her opinion, spoken of the sacred beliefs of others in an unfeeling manner which had wounded deeply. It was considered desirable to induce Madame to withdraw her resignation. The interview gave me an opportunity to listen to her views upon the problems of human destiny,—the future, the supernatural, and kindred questions. To her, all religions, all forms of faith, were useful and good, and to be regarded tenderly, sacredly, by all. Matthew Arnold's lines were quoted:

Children of men! the unseen Power, whose eye
For ever doth accompany mankind,
Hath look'd on no religion scornfully
That men did ever find.

Which has not taught weak minds how much they can?
Which has not fall'n on the dry heart like rain?
Which has not cried to sunk, self-weary man:
Thou must be born again!

All that was necessary was to assure her that the offender was sorry for causing others pain, and would be more mindful of their feelings in the future. The resignation was withdrawn.

It is a pity that those who fear that the highest education, the widest range of knowledge, upon the part of women will make them less feminine, did not know Madame Botta. Everything she knew—and she knew much, and thought deeply—made her a higher type of woman. She had not a trace of anything in her whole being which was not exquisitely feminine, and this made her to many a source of refinement and strength which no less able woman could have been.

Her funeral was the sweetest and most genuine expression of sorrow I have ever seen given for any well-known character, man or woman. Only those assembled around her grave who could not force themselves to stay away. No formal invitations, no publicity, no pomp, no eulogy; only silence and tears; and not one tear from any who had not been benefited by her, and who did not mourn her loss as causing a void which could never be filled. None can ever take her place in our hearts; she occupies a niche all her own.

The tribute I pay her memory is, that I am a better man because favored with her friendship for many long years.

Her Hospitality

By Kate Sanborn, New-York.

IN sketching some of the literary women of New-York, their *salons*, their achievements, their home life, Mrs. Botta naturally headed the list. For many years she was a conspicuous and popular leader in society. When the city was smaller and life less hurried, she held weekly receptions which closely resembled the French *salon;* and although later those evenings became less frequent, they lost none of their distinctive character. In fact, she created a *salon* here, and made it a brilliant success, without the least effort or pretension, without even offering a sandwich to her happy guests; but lighting her evening lamp in her modest parlors in Ninth street, simply let it be known that she would be "at home" on Saturday evenings.

"I never made much of a point of it," she said; "it was natural, and I liked it. I was not fashionable, nor rich, and literary people were my companions." That was the open secret. She did easily what others have striven for in vain.

Mrs. Botta (Anne Charlotte Lynch) was born in Bennington, Vermont. Her grandfather was Lieutenant-Colonel Gray, of Connecticut, who served his country through the entire Revolutionary War; her father, a brave Irish lad who at sixteen was made a prisoner by the English for refusing to take the oath of allegiance to their government, and who, after four years of confinement, became an exile, banished with Emmet and other noble men who loved liberty, if need be, better than life.

Mrs. Botta was a woman of versatile talent, known as a teacher, compiler, poet, sculptor, philanthropist, and hostess. Perhaps the ease with which she could excel in such various departments prevented her gaining the high distinction she might have won if devoted to a specialty. But her life was beautifully rounded, full of good deeds, quiet charities, helpful words for the many who, needing one favor or another, crowded to her hospitable door. I have seldom made a morning call on her without finding some applicant for assistance. To be a guest in her house is a privilege never to be forgotten, and letters from Frederika Bremer, Emerson, Froude, Kingsley, Lord Amberly, and a number of great men and women show how fully her gift of entertaining genius, in a restful way, was enjoyed, appreciated, and remembered. A winter as her guest is one of the precious memories of my life. Helen Hunt wrote the following beautiful sonnet, expressing what so many have felt who have enjoyed the privilege of her hospitality.

TO A. C. L. B.

Thy house hath gracious freedom, like the air
Of open fields; its silence hath a speech
Of royal welcome to the friends who reach
Its threshold; and its upper chambers bear,
Above their doors, such spells that, entering there
And laying off the dusty garments, each
Soul whispers to herself: "'T were like a breach
Of reverence in a temple, could I dare
Here speak untruth, here wrong my inmost thought.
Here I grow strong and pure; here I may yield,
Without shamefacedness, the little brought
From out my poorer life, and stand revealed,
And glad, and trusting, in the sweet, and rare,
And tender presence which hath filled this air."

At one of her informal "breakfasts," I met Emerson, Bayard Taylor, Bryant, and "Grace Greenwood," all in their best mood. Emerson and Taylor discussed Bettina von Arnim, the child-love, or child-lover, of Goethe; and Mrs. Lippincott's stories were not a whit behind, and were told with an ease, a dash, and a climax that few possess. Those were golden hours.

Mrs. Botta's evening receptions—where everybody was "somebody," and no one was unduly lionized or neglected, while each was inspired by her graceful and sympathetic tact to do his best, and every one went away reluctantly, feeling stimulated, refreshed, and happy—are traced in many a heart in letters of gold. Her power to assimilate and magnetize amounted to genius.

In 1849 Miss Lynch published a small volume of poems. In 1860 appeared her "Handbook of Universal Literature," a laborious compilation, a comprehensive yet carefully condensed view of the literature of the world. This is largely used not only for reference but as a text-book in academies, schools, and colleges.

Those who knew Miss Lynch remember her as a graceful, animated, well-dressed woman, with a smile like sunshine, full of life and humor and hearty relish for social delights. Willis, who knew her well, speaks of her "sweet geniality and unconscious *fountainizing* of bright and pleasant things." His letters to her are full of honest admiration and the sincerest regard.

Mr. P—— brought in the last news of you. But we could only gather from him that you were as charming as ever and were going to Washington. You keep enjoying this planet. Nobody lives more while about it. I only wish you would now and then hold the burning-glass of your genius still long enough to burn a hole. Genius you have; concentration you have no time for. Tell us if that smile of yours, which you ought not to die without seeing, is as bewitching as ever.

Even while just starting for Europe, he finds time, while waiting in a banker's office, to give his friend this inspiriting advice:

Write and show the mind I see in you, and hold yourself high among the highly gifted.

The visit to Washington resulted in securing a grant of several thousand dollars for her mother. She wrote a pamphlet, stating in a powerful and convincing way, that the brave soldiers of the Revolution, who gave all to their country and saved it from humiliation, had been unjustly treated and their families left to want. This was distributed in the Senate with good effect, and, with the eloquent assistance of Henry Clay, she gained her point. It was a great triumph for a woman, and required unusual courage and persistence, tact and talent. She did not pose as a suppliant, or even ask a gratuity. It was a solemn right, and truth conquered.

In 1855 Miss Lynch was married to Vincenzo Botta, then professor of philosophy in the Royal Colleges of Piedmont, an ex-member of the Subalpine Parliament, author of a valuable book on Dante, a monograph on Cavour, and other scholarly essays, besides being a valued correspondent of the best Italian papers.

I have spoken of Mrs. Botta's compilations and poems. Her letters to newspapers were most acceptable, and her power in modeling was acknowledged by all who had seen her works. She might have distinguished herself in this direction, undoubtedly, if so many people had not almost demanded her help in various ways, and she could never refuse to help the suffering or distressed. Always appreciative of the gifts of others, quick to see talent and glad to make it known, her life was in a large sense one of self-abnegation and devotion to her friends. In all these years no one has heard her say an ill-natured word of any one, however she may have been imposed upon. Yet she was not by any means lacking in a keen sense of the ludicrous, and might have been a most witty and scathing critic if she had not been principled against paining others or shining at their expense.

What a book of recollections she could have given us, knowing intimately so many noted persons! At her early receptions were to be found Edgar Poe, Horace Greeley, the Cary sisters, pretty Fanny Osgood, Mrs. Oakes Smith, Mrs. Ellet, Mary Hewitt, Eliza Leslie, Doctor Griswold, Bayard Taylor, and Catherine Sedgwick, that bright novelist who has given us a most graphic pen-picture of a Saturday evening at Miss Lynch's:

> I passed to the drawing-room of Miss L——. It was her reception evening. I was admitted to a rather dimly lighted hall by a little portress, some ten or twelve years old, who led me to a small apartment to deposit my hat and cloak. There was no lighted staircase, no trained attendant, none of the common flourish at city parties. . . .
>
> When I entered I found two fair-sized drawing-rooms filled with guests in a high state of social enjoyment. There was music, dancing, recitation, and conversation. There were artists in every department—painting, poetry, sculpture, and music. There I saw, for the first time, that impersonation of genius, Ole Bull. Even the histrionic art asserted its right to social equality in the person of one of its most honorable professors.
>
> No one ever needed an ægis less than my lovely hostess. She has that quiet delicacy and dignity of manner that is as a glittering angel to exorcise every evil spirit that should venture to approach her. . . .
>
> Here was a young woman without "position," to use the cant

phrase,—without any relations in the fashionable world,—filling her rooms weekly with choice spirits, who came without any extraordinary expense of dress, who enjoyed high rational pleasure for two or three hours, and retired so early as to make no drafts on the health or spirits of the next day.

One bright, vivacious, lovable woman described by another! What can be better than that? Mrs. Botta was always full of life, fond of exercise, going to market every day, a perfect housekeeper, ready for any new ideas on hygiene or grace of movement from the exponents of Delsarte to the latest recipe for gingerbread. She used to be a famous pedestrian, once accomplishing seventy-two miles in four days, and one short year ago came running down two flights of stairs to greet me, as if she were in her teens. Such vitality, cheerfulness, and wise philosophy as regards the inevitable are rare endowments.

Her collection of letters from distinguished men and women is unusually precious, because her correspondents glowed in sympathy with her own heart-warmth. Those of Frederika Bremer are interesting for their simplicity, quaint foreign wording, and deep religious devotion.

In a copy of the "Neighbors" sent by Miss Bremer to her new friend, was written this poem:

TO ANNE CHARLOTTE LYNCH.

A bird of paradise I wished to see;
One of those beings more than others free,
Who soar o'er earth with colors bright and gay,
But never lower down to touch its clay;

Who, frail and delicate, yet need not cling
For rest or help but to their soaring wing.
My wish was heard; a being bright and gay
I saw; who was on earth as was not earth its stay;
Who, in this crowded world looked all alone,
With eyes that melancholy, yet serenely shone;
A being young in years, but wonderfully wise—
It is Anne Lynch, my bird of paradise.

Emerson was several times a guest of Mrs. Botta. He liked to be in her home and to be with her, saying it "rested" him—a decided compliment.

Here is one of his letters after such a visit:

CONCORD, 29th Dec., 1865.

DEAR MRS. BOTTA: You were such a good angel to me in New-York, that I have wished, every hour since I came home, to say to you that I know well how rare such goodness is, and that I prize it at its height.

To be sure, I know little or nothing of New-York, but I fancy that few people in it use it so well, have so wise possession of it as yourself. I wish that I could believe that in your miles of palaces were many houses and housekeepers as excellent as I knew at 25 West 37th street. The house is so apt to spoil the tenant, and society to brain its votary, that sense and simplicity and good-will must not be accepted as things of course, but as most exceptional splendors; and my New-Year's wish is, that where I found these, they will long, long shine for the benefit of all beholders, and to the well-being and better and best being of the luminary, and indeed the chief good is the exercise of our powers and affections. . . .

He writes after her return from Paris:

I was very glad to hear that you were safe home again to me and all of us in your house of the expanding doors. I am glad you saw Sainte-Beuve. I grieve that he is gone. He was for me the best of his nation in the late years.

And again, November 30, 1869:

Thanks for your unfailing memory and good-will. Pity me that I cannot yet use the hospitalities you offer me. I please myself, like other aging and aged men, with visions of leisure and the finer employments that shall fill it—too long delayed; the leisure that flies before is unattainable. Will it always? I am *then* to be a poet, a friend, and turn days into heaven. But to-day and to-morrow, and the year through, I find myself the drudge of tasks I cannot praise. But the taskmaster lets gleams and streams of sunshine in, and consoles us with friends and new promises.

He speaks of her invitation as "one of the happiest rainbows."

Your hospitality has an Arabian memory, to keep its kind purpose through such a long time. You were born under Hatem Yayi's[1] own star, and, like him, are the genius of hospitality.

He once more alluded to this:

The great Hindoo, Hatem Yayi, has nothing by the side of such hospitality as hers. Hatem Yayi would soon lose his reputation.

These letters, hitherto unpublished, are extremely valuable, as is, also, the following one from Mrs. Charles Kingsley, sending a copy of her life of her noble husband.

Among the first copies of my "Memoirs" I sent one to you, for I could not bear to think that you should read the book in

[1] Hatem Yayi was a celebrated Oriental whose house had sixteen doors.

any copy but one direct from me, accompanied by my grateful love. It will quite hurt me if you should have seen the book before receiving your own, dear Mrs. Botta. Oh! how often my heart has turned to you in grateful love for all your goodness to him, and how I have longed to express something of what I felt (but how little words would do it!) to you; but, while in sickness of body and sore anguish of soul I was writing, I dared not spend a breath of life on letters, lest the pen should drop from my hand before my sacred task was done. Do not think me ungrateful. You made him so happy. You gave him and my Rose such a home and such a home-feeling in the great New World—a world I shall always love for its appreciation of him and his works at a time when he was not so responded to in his own country.

To give just a glimpse of Mrs. Botta's humor, let me quote two trifles:

A draught from Helicon could once inspire
The bard to wing in song his loftiest flight;
But poets of these later days require
A draft from Wall street—payable at sight.

With you and General Lyman
To dine *alone!*—why, man!
What would dear Mrs. Grundy
Report of such a Sunday?
How think of such a dinner?
Just think of it, thou sinner!

I should like to introduce you to her home as it was—the hall, with its interesting pictures and fragrant with fresh flowers; the dining-room, the drawing-rooms, with their magnetized atmosphere of the past (you can almost feel the presence of those who have loved to linger there); her own sanctum, where a chosen few were admitted: but the limits of space forbid. The queens of Parisian *salons* have been praised and idealized till we are led to believe them unapproachable in their social altitude. But I am not afraid to place beside them an American lady, uncrowned by extravagant adulation, but fully their equal—the artist, poet, conversationist, Anne C. L. Botta.

At her last evening at home, four days before her fatal illness, she seemed in perfect health. Her sweet and gracious smile of welcome was never more kindly and attractive, her thoughtful care for each guest, without *seeming* to think, was just as of old. We looked forward to many more such reunions as we bade her good night.

Her death, distressingly sudden to her intimate friends, was after all a beautiful departure. She left earth while still young in heart, still enjoying life, her active brain showing no symptoms of declining vigor. She has joined "the choir invisible," and is still an inspiring influence, though unseen.

Her Salon

By A. J. Bloor, New-York.

I WAS just out of my teens, and at the feet of the great leaders in "high thoughts" expressed, in varying dialects, through all the literatures of previous ages, when, in a biography of Sarah Margaret Fuller d'Ossoli which came from the hands of Emerson and others, I read, in a footnote, of Miss Lynch's *salon* in the city of my residence. With that celerity of imagination which belongs to the young, I at once pictured it as an American reproduction of Lady Blessington's or of the Duchess of Sutherland's,—which had hardly yet ceased to exist,—or of Madame Récamier's, of a somewhat earlier generation; and when, some years later, and after Miss Lynch had become Mrs. Botta, I was presented to her at the house of a mutual friend, I was greatly pleased to have our conversation close with her promise, given with the quiet smile she retained to the end of her days, to send me a card to the next *conversazione* at her house. Of course I went, and as she welcomed guest after guest, some of them of great distinction in one field or another, and some of little or no mark, I first noted, extended to each, that gracious mixture of equanimity and cordiality—with just enough change in the expression of the latter as befitted the difference between an old friend and a new acquaintance—which, for more than thirty-three years thereafter, I was so often to note in her demeanor to others as well as to experience in my own person.

Two or three other women in New-York, contemporaneously with Mrs. Botta, succeeded in establishing real *salons*. Some others attempted the same, but were unsuccessful. At that time society in the city was, as it is now, divided into several sets, each having an acknowledged leader, or two or more rival leaders who tried to surround themselves with social circles of their own. But, even after allowing for the differences necessarily resulting from *bourgeois* conditions, as compared with those prevailing in communities where titular distinctions exist under the law, and where the social world is led by a Court, or the traditions of one, none of these sets included *salons* in the cosmopolitan sense of the term. One or more of them—not necessarily, by any means, consisting only of *nouveaux riches,* or of persons deficient in at least superficial culture—depended largely for prestige on the appointments which wealth enabled them to put *en evidence;* though at that time there was hardly a house in New-York that had cost, all told, as much as has since been spent on the decorative fixtures of a single room, and ceilings costing ten thousand dollars, and dinners at a hundred dollars or more a cover, were as yet unknown on this side of the Atlantic. Another set plumed itself on having grandfathers who were among the signers of the Declaration of Independence, or whose great-grandfathers had bought from the Indians—for a few hatchets and rifles piled up on a foundation of kegs of rum and topped off with some strings of beads for the squaws—a parcel of thousands of acres of wild land on which the cities and suburbs of their descendants grew up—to fill their pockets with "unearned increment"; and these good folks doubtless felt just as happy with this modicum of "ancient lineage" as a Sussex yeoman does who works with his hands, for others, on the same land that his forefathers worked for themselves, before base-born duke came in with his horde of Norman Adullamites,—or as a Parsee does, who speaks familiarly of his ancestors before the Christian era.

Still another coterie included those who had come to their position through their own or their fathers' successes in commerce and finance; while some women of fashion had built up their vogue by adding their private fortunes to the professional earnings of their husbands, and on the initials D. D. or M. D., spelt large in Latin on the latters' college parchments; and the helpmate of the successful practitioner at law serenely repeated to herself, if not to others, her worse half's quotation of De Tocqueville's dictum, that the lawyers were the real aristocrats of America. But, at their receptions, one felt that one was not in what, in the best sense of the term, could be called a *salon;* one felt that whatever pretensions might be openly or tacitly made, there was, in fact, an atmosphere more or less *borné* and provincial. The Italian proverb, *Mi date creta per cacio,* was apt to come to one's mind. Yet, none the less, an evening spent at these gatherings was always enjoyed; represented, as they were, by hospitable hosts, by friendly, intellectual, often well-read men, and by charming women who frequently were more cultured than the men.

There are women who, like Florence Nightingale, devote themselves to a higher mission than even the not unimportant one of providing an exchange for the softening and ameliorative courtesies of society; and there are others, of the best intellectual and moral grade, whose devotion to their own domestic circle and its collaterals is so absorbing as to leave them no desire or no leisure for a wider circle; while there are still others, well fitted in many respects, both interior and exterior, to be leaders, who have a horror of what they call "miscellaneous gatherings."

At all events, there were certainly ladies of the sets I have referred to who were seemingly not up to forming a real *salon,*—as often, perhaps, owing to circumstances and influences outside of their control as to deficiencies inherent in themselves. The unsuccess of others often resulted—probably not, as they themselves imagined, from lack of means and sufficiently imposing exterior appointments; but from the opposite—that is, from the too lavish display of such as they could afford, or rather from their making it appear, unconsciously perhaps to themselves, that they chiefly depended not on their own qualities, but on those of their exterior belongings, for achieving the distinction of attracting to their drawing-rooms and tables the varying, assimilative human material which forms the stock in trade of the woman who has the genius for forming and maintaining a *salon*. Their assumed standard was sometimes felt to be too artificial and assailable; the *deus ex machina* was too much in evidence to allow their guests the sense of ease which is essential to the interchange of social qualities at their best. Their preparations were so obviously elaborate as to leave no room for the comfortable impression that they were virtually impromptu—that they gave sufficient promise of recurrence and continuance. It is with mental capital as it is with financial. Its possessor does not care to waste it on experimental operations likely to lead to little or no profit; he desires, in either case, to make a permanent and profitable investment. Moreover, a simple cup of tea or bouillon is more conducive to the "high thoughts" supposed to pervade an elegant *conversazione* than are *pâtés de foie gras* and champagne, with all their indigestible congeners *à discrétion*.

It goes without saying that the woman who is the head of a distinguished *salon* in a great metropolitan center, must possess, in great degree, the propelling and administrative powers that are needed by leaders in any other walk of life. The statesman, the captain, the financier, the merchant, the man of letters, the artist, the professional man of any kind, achieves eminence, within his opportunities, by the exercise of precisely the same foresight, application, energy, and industry. And by similar forces and similar methods the woman of society forms and maintains the *salon* which gathers within its walls the cream of her *entourage*, and forms an exchange not for the coarser—if essential—commodities of the field and the mine, but for those gifts of intellect, breeding, and courtesy which, to the highly trained man or woman, are such essential elements to happiness, and which so largely contribute to refine and sweeten every-day life. But every man who leads must have some special gift from nature, without which he could not have got to the top level of his specialty. And it is so with the woman who makes and presides over a distinguished *salon.*

My observations have made it clear to my mind that the failure of not a few women who were otherwise well-endowed by nature and training, and sufficiently favored by fortune and opportunity for such a *rôle,*—and who would fain have filled it,—generally resulted, in the main, from the fact that they lacked a sufficiency of the foundational quality for fulfilling that *rôle*—that is, a sympathetic nature; or that they did not recognize the necessity for exercising it. With this must be united the gifts of intuition and amiability. The worth of simple amiability is, in fact, greatly undervalued, not alone by the great majority of men, but by many women. It is natural that men engaged in the rivalries and warfares of exchange and trade, and in the liberal professions should forget the Golden Rule and the smaller amenities of domestic life. They forget that these form the nightly balm which heals the wounds received through the day, and supply the tonic necessary for the next day's battle of life. Their wives, sisters, and daughters are apt not only to take their cue from their utterances on the subject, but to develop and foster similar sentiments in themselves through their own social rivalries with women of their own set, or more likely of those in the one immediately above it. They do so at the cost of losing the quality which lies at the bottom of the permanent success of a *salon*.

The possession of this quality in an eminent degree was the secret of Mrs. Botta's success in social life. Indeed, it would be difficult to find a lady so quietly sympathetic as was our friend. She carried this all-pervading sympathy far outside her *salon;* she was constantly engaged in acts of beneficence, and at times she quite wore herself out in the performance of such duties. If space and leisure were equal to it, I could easily produce many facts in evidence of her broad sympathy, from her correspondence with myself. I can remember her enlisting my small assistance in a scheme of her own for raising funds for the Sanitary Commission during our civil war. She made up a superb album filled with lovely little sketches done in oils and some in water-colors from the hands of many eminent artists, and then widened the scope of this conception for the benefit of sufferers in the Franco-German war. I remember helping her to dispose of some cameos in behalf of a lady friend who was an artist in Italy. I also recall to my memory long letters from her giving in careful detail every point in favor of some native or foreign protégé for whom she was seeking a position as tutor, as governess, as traveling-companion, as draftsman, or as reporter. This sympathy, however, which was the well-spring of all her actions, did not interfere with her decisiveness and self-assertion when occasion demanded. I could relate several interesting episodes connected with this independence of her character.

Having spoken of Mrs. Botta as the beneficent genius of a *salon*, I shall leave to other friends the office of describing her achievements in literature. The beauty of her poetry is well known, and her "Handbook of Universal Literature"—a *multum in parvo* of modest guise—is of the highest rank for educational purposes. Nor shall I dwell on her highly creditable work in sculpture. One or two pieces of her handiwork were to be seen in her beautiful drawing-rooms; but a further insight into her art theories was enjoyed by those who were occasionally privileged to enter her studio and talk with her an hour or two, as she sat on a high stool with her linen blouse on—the clay in one hand and the spatula in the other—before the bust which she was making.

My last conversation with Mrs. Botta would remain apart in my memory, even if it had not proved to be the last. It referred to a meeting of The Nineteenth

Century Club, at which we both were present; and after the speakers had finished, we had some conversation on their themes; she asked me to call on her and we would continue our observations. I went a few nights after. No one else was there, and we soon left the stated subject to talk about the people—so many of them shining lights in the various fields of activity—whom in olden times I had met as her guests, and of whom so many had gone to join the silent majority. This gave her occasion to state her frame of mind with reference to her own end, which she described as one altogether outside of emotion. She said "she neither desired to go nor to stay," realizing with seemingly entire apathy that her destiny in the future, as it had been in the past, was something with which her volition had nothing to do. Other remarks on this occasion reminded me that once before she told me that whatever success she had had in life she attributed to her early recognition of her own limitations,—a remark which recalled to my mind a saying of the late Professor Bache, who was a grandson of Benjamin Franklin, and for many years Chief of the Coast Survey, also the first president of the American Academy of Science. In discussing a certain case which came under our purview as officers of the Sanitary Commission, he remarked that he had long before made up his mind that the chief cause of unhappiness in this country, and of its insane asylums being so much more populous than those of most other countries, was the non-recognition among Americans of the limitations of the individual:

a lesson hard to learn in a community where universal suffrage prevails, and where one is brought up to believe that one man is as good as another.

In our conversation reference was made to the conflict between labor and capital—the rich and the poor, the well-born and the low-born, the educated and the ignorant. She thought that this conflict must come, and, indeed, was not very far off. She did not expect to live long enough to see the final clash. "But," she said, "when it comes it will much surpass alike in extent and bitterness the records of the French Revolution and the Commune, or of any previous outburst of class feeling in any age or country." She evidently thought with Ouida that "the masses"—to use Mr. Gladstone's terminology—will never forgive "the classes" for being born to, or for having conquered, the powers, pomps, and pleasures of this world.

Our conversation then fell on the relative merits of contemporary poetry. We talked of Bryant's "Flood of Years"; of some of Matthew Arnold's perfect but saddening verses; some of Tennyson's recent poems; and I reminded her that it was by her advice I read Sir Edwin Arnold's "Light of Asia" when it came out—a poem which gave her great delight. Her general view of poetry so far as I can judge from her allusions to it, was that the various elements of measured and rhythmical diction should be combined only in support of humanitarian principles.

It is with these associations that the memory of Mrs. Botta will always remain with me,—but, alas!

accompanied with saddened thoughts when in my mind's eye I see a few (the funeral being private) of the many friends, who had so often held high converse in those well-known drawing-rooms, gathered to pay their last tribute of respect and affection to the quiet form on whose marble lips the smile of welcome would never more be seen. After a short service in accordance with the Unitarian rites, her remains were taken to Woodlawn Cemetery, where, after the burial of this noble woman, her sorrowing husband and a venerable friend of many years stooped down and both placed a bunch of violets on the newly made grave. Standing there, thinking over her life, I recalled those fine lines of Wordsworth's, on the "woman nobly planned to warn, to comfort, and command"; and I could not but think that under those blossoms lay one whose exemplary and fragrant memory should be carried far beyond her immediate environment, her day and her generation.

Her Perennial Youth

By a Friend, New-York.

SOMETHING of the wondering regret that comes on the untimely taking-off of one too young to go moves those who knew Mrs. Botta best. She was so young in her sympathies, her interest in all things new and worthy was so unfailing, that one never counted up her years, and might be excused for thinking her immortal. There was about her that air of buoyancy and vigor that belongs to youth; and as she walked down the street before you, the slight figure, almost girlish in its erect poise, and the springing step flatly contradicted the story of the soft white hair and the dates in the cyclopedias. There was youth in the half-laughing eye, too, and in the dimples that heightened that ever-ready, kindly smile of hers.

It was difficult, then, to realize that this little lady's memories stretched back to the childhood of literary New-York; that she knew Poe well in his days of struggle; that Fanny Osgood and Griswold and Willis frequented her drawing-room, as have all the men and women of letters who succeeded them; and that Henry Clay was another friend of her youth. It was at her house, it is said, that Poe, some weeks before its publication, first recited "The Raven." Of the Anne C. Lynch of that period, it is remembered that she had a graceful little figure, an abundance of fine brown hair, a face winsome and lovely in expression,—though not regularly beautiful,—handsome eyes, and a delicately pretty complexion. Then, as later, she had the art to make those about her happy; and happiest of all she made her mother, who was always with her, and who lived under her care to a great age. It is pleasant to remember that, if her early youth had in it much unselfish toil for others, her after life was brightened by many good gifts of fortune—not the least of which was an ideally happy marriage.

Now and then in later years, when with those she knew best, she would recall some noted figure, some grave or merry happening of those early days; but no entreaties could persuade her to put her reminiscences on paper. No one could have sketched so vividly the writers of the first half of the century; for, though there were enmities many among them, all were agreed in their friendly regard for the sweet, bright, and sympathetic young woman whose home was neutral ground. But there was much that was grotesque and unlovely in their quarrels; and doubtless Mrs. Botta felt that if she were not to send forth half-told and therefore valueless recollections, she would be constrained to perpetuate memories of suffering, envy, and unkindness among those early friends. To her gentle heart nothing could have seemed more cruel. It will always be remembered of her that none ever heard from her lips a word of carping criticism. If she could not speak well and pleasantly of people, she spoke of them not at all. Not that she was blind to what moved to laughter or to cynicism ; a glint of humor in her bright eyes showed that she saw, if she forbore to comment.

Mrs. Botta's tact and ease as a hostess were perfect; no one was ever dull or bored in her comfortable house. She knew how to blend, without apparent effort, the most diverse social elements; and the light-hearted gaiety, simplicity, and frankness of her welcome called forth all that was best and brightest in her guests. There are probably no Americans of note as writers and artists who have not trodden her broad stairway, and no distinguished foreign traveler in this country has failed to taste her hospitality. Of these visitors in late years perhaps the most interesting was Matthew Arnold — who was his pleasantest self under that pleasant roof-tree. Never was hostess more thoughtful of the comfort and pleasure of those about her; and in talk, whether wise or witty, she was always appreciative and responsive. She was a good friend albeit she was not wont to wear her heart upon her sleeve. No one ever heard from Mrs. Botta's lips a word which might be called "gushing," but many a one will treasure utterances therefrom of the gentlest kindness.

Impressions

By Professor L. J. B. Lincoln, New-York.

So high a privilege is rarely accorded as is this opportunity to crystallize into words a deep and heart-born impression. The sweet and gracious woman whose silence is so eloquent; the kindly neighbor in a city where neighborhood is but faintly existent; the sincere and gentle adviser; the mature and ripened thinker; the sensitive poet-nature, weaving its own garlands and its own chaplet; the generous liver in the sense of living generously toward other lives; the merry humorist, whose satire was too delicate to leave a sting, and whose conversation sparkled with healthy wit,—all these and many more were side-lights in forming this impression of her daily life.

Coming to know her only within her last years, this impression, produced in our first talk together, has simply broadened and deepened, never changed. She gave herself, with all the rich argosy of her honored years, I sincerely believe, to any one upon whom her attention even rested; and in this lay, perhaps, her remarkably responsive and intelligent sympathy. It would be idle for her best and nearest friend to claim any personal and individual preferment as shown by her. Generosity, with her, seemed but the outward expression of her inmost soul-life; and who so audacious as to assert preëmption there! Nor do I think that it ever occurred to her that there was this generosity on her part. It came like the sweet breath of a child,—so natural was it, so utterly devoid of consciousness. Yet greater measure surely never came in our day, for it still lingers about her memory, and still holds us in its gentle grasp.

To art, to literature, to society, to any form of intellectual experiment, to any effort, failing and impotent howsoever it might be, toward the higher life, her inner chords of helpful sympathy responded with electric instantaneousness. Relying upon her own exquisite intuition rather than upon her experience, she piloted many a little shallop of ideal hopes and fears through the maelstrom of contending interests and social philistinism. In nothing was her generosity so unique and so courageous as in this. Where other would-be friends waited for the favoring breeze before launching an idea, she fanned its sails with her own enthusiasm and guided it to success.

Mrs. Botta, while thoroughly interested in every progressive movement, was rarely carried away from the serene and peaceful current of her own contemplative and comprehensive thoughts upon the philosophy of history and the evolution of mankind. Her literary monuments in themselves so eloquently portray the breadth and universality of her views that appreciation loses its choicest opportunity. Those of her friends who knew that until her very last hours she intended to assume the colossal task of taking up history and bringing the story of every nation of antiquity down to the present time, marveled at the exceeding mental grasp which dared to essay so enormous an effort late in life. That her theory—the strength of the historical lesson to be drawn from the study of nations after their fall—was forceful and interesting, must be apparent to any one whose reading lies in that direction. It is with the deepest regret that we realize that her mind, which had shown its ability to execute large ideas in her "Handbook of Universal Literature," conceived this nobler thought too late in her physical life to carry it to its fulfilment.

Of Mrs. Botta's poetical gifts, other and more able judges have spoken. In those rare moments when she could be induced to repeat some of her verses, her personality became indistinct compared with the spirit which her own muse evoked from herself. Delicate, fanciful, evanescent yet winning, it thrilled the tenderest emotions and dignified them as it thrilled. Deep and true and human are those sonnets; full, too, of the soaring and aspiring feeling which banishes depression. After all, *they* are her best eulogium: her own soul, speaking through her own heart, warm with her own life, and glorified with her own immortality. And perhaps it is more eloquent than other words can ever be, that since she left us, these which were impressions have become convictions, and these convictions a lasting faith in the eternal life of true generosity.

A Word about Her Poems

By Richard Watson Gilder, New-York.

My dear Mr. Botta:

I AM greatly obliged to you for the copy of Mrs. Botta's poems. They strongly bring to mind their author's modest, gentle, generous, and poetic personality. I cannot speak critically and coldly of the records of the mind of an honored friend. The feeling in the poems is not assumed; nor is the expression forced or in any way affected. I like best the sonnets; they have the charms of sincerity, thoughtfulness, and a dignified and poetic diction. They are indeed true reflections of the soul of a spiritual-minded and noble woman.

The sonnet "Longing" is, for its significance and dignity, well placed at the beginning of the book of her poems. In this the "troubled sea, that longest evermore to rise to the bright orb," is thus addressed:

Type of the soul art thou, she strives like thee,
  By time and circumstance and law bound down,
  She beats against the shores of the unknown,
Wrestles with unseen force, doubt, mystery,
  And longs forever for the goal afar
  That shines and still retreats, like a receding star.

Her Poetical Character

BY EDITH M. THOMAS, NEW-YORK.

SITTING in the study of that hospitable mansion which Helen Hunt Jackson so fittingly describes in a sonnet to A. C. L. B.,[1] the conversation between the gracious presiding spirit of the house and a guest, as yet a novice in her art, turned upon the subject of poetry. Some ultimate definition of this most indefinable and escaping element was sought. The dicta of the great masters, both in the theory and creation of the noblest verse, were cited through a wide range of authorities, from the well-known pronunciamento of Milton to our own Lowell's counsel obliquely hinted in the lines:

> Put all your beauty in your rhymes,
> Your morals in your living.

Much of this conversation, which was among the earliest of many bright hours since spent in that study, has passed from memory; but I shall never

[1] For this sonnet see page 172.

forget the glowing earnestness of her final words. "I do not think," said my hostess, "that the province of poetry is so much to idealize the real, as to help us to realize our ideals, and to make actual our highest spiritual conceptions."

Now, this desire to "help us to realize our ideals" informs every line of the true-hearted verse left us by Mrs. Botta. Regarding this bequest, an expression made by the present writer more than ten years since recurs now with an emphasized force of belief on her part.

"In these days of advanced estheticism, often with a sickly Erato as presiding muse, it is with a sense of relief and refreshment that we turn to the so-called old-fashioned school of poetry, more than ever disposed to set a high premium upon explicit motive, normal emotions, a sweet and sound morality, and good 'common sense,' in verse as well as in other departments of literature. In the volume of poems by Anne C. L. Botta, we meet with no obscurity of treatment, no ethical ambiguity; all are characterized by a winning purity and serenity of feeling, and by a lucid grace of expression."

Of her work she was wont to say in smiling deprecation, "It may not be poetry—but it is myself." In the fullest sense of the injunction she looked into her heart and wrote. And nowhere is the record of that heart's most warm, most vital and indomitable pulsations more clearly expressed than in her sonnets, from the first to the very last, which appeared in "The Century Magazine" shortly after her going hence forever. This, with its significant title, I give in full:

AB ASTRIS.

I saw the stars swept through ethereal space,
Stars, suns, and systems in infinity,—
Our earth an atom in the shoreless sea,
Where each had its appointed path and place:
And I was lost in my own nothingness.
But then I said, Dost thou not know that He
Who guides these orbs through trackless space guides thee?

No longer groveling thus, thyself abase,
For in this vast, harmonious, perfect whole,
In infinite progression moving on,
Thou hast thy place, immortal human soul,
Thy place and part not less than star and sun;
Then with this grand procession fall in line,
This rhythmic march led on by power divine.

This poem suggested the following lines:

AD ASTRA.

Unto the stars the light they lent returned!
Seer of celestial order, soother, guide,
Be still such influence, though undiscerned,
Swept onward with the white sidereal tide.

For those who knew her best, the resonant chord of her strong, purposeful, ardent, and sympathetic being still vibrates in such poems as "Aspiration," "Accordance," "Endurance," "Charity." She was indeed one with the figure of the musician, introduced into these lines:

ACCORDANCE.

He who with bold and skilful hand sweeps o'er
The organ-keys of some cathedral pile,
Flooding with music, vault, and nave, and aisle,
Though on his ear falls but a thunderous roar.
In the composer's lofty motive free,
Knows well that all that temple, vast and dim,
Thrills to its base with anthem, psalm, and hymn,
True to the changeless laws of harmony.
So he who on these clanging chords of life,
With firm, sweet touch plays the Great Master's score,
Of truth, and love, and duty, evermore,
Knows, too, that far beyond this roar and strife,
Though he may never hear, in the true time,
These notes must all accord in symphonies sublime.

To those who enjoyed the privilege of intimate association, she seems to have been the living embodiment of the virtues celebrated under the titles I have cited from her poems,—but "Greatest in the greatest of all, Charity." She has been the almoner and bestower of every noble gift of encouragement, both material and spiritual, to many whose previous road was hemmed in by obstacles. Many a tyro in letters, many a struggler in art, cannot forget whence first was reached out the helping hand, whence came the first note of approval, of timely cheer, of generous praise, and—most rare of all—of unselfish criticism; for most difficult is the part of judicious censor! The mention of gratitude for a benefit conferred by herself brought the whimsical remonstrance, almost sublimely naïve: "I deserve no credit; I only did what I liked to do."

"Greatest in the greatest of all, Charity," I have said, but I should add, "Greatest in the most refined exercise of that divine faculty"; for, were there any in whom she had invested her beautiful faith who afterward proved undeserving of the bestowal, her almost invariable summation of the case was: "It was not their fault, but mine, if they failed to reach my ideal; I expected too much." But whatever disappointment of this sort was encountered, her happy hope in the individual, as in humanity at large, was perennial and unfailing.

> But thy heart's affluence lavish uncontrolled,
> The largess of thy love give full and free,
> As monarchs in their progress scatter gold.

These words were the watchword of her from whose spirit they breathed in daily life,—creating in those around her a like liberal and loving faith in humankind.

Like Arnold's scholar, Gypsey, she was invincible to despair, and held to the soul's quest with an intrepid confidence as to its fruition.

> Thou waitest for the spark from Heaven! and we,
> Light, half-believers of our casual creeds,
>
> . . . .
>
> Who hesitate and falter life away,
> And lose to-morrow the ground won to-day,
> Ah! do not we, wanderer! await it too?

It would be but an incomplete enumeration of the qualities that met in this beloved person were no mention made of her large and genial sense of humor and of her abiding young power of participation in mirth. The quick and felicitous touch, both stimulating and contributing repartee, was as characteristic of her as were the earnestness and seriousness which the grave occasion, the philosophic consideration, evoked. As an instance of this humor the following poem addressed to the writer by Mrs. Botta from her city home in summer, may be quoted:

A SUMMER IDYL.

The city is dreary and dusty and lone,
The Smiths and the Joneses and Jenkinses gone;
The doors are all barred, and the shutters all down,
And nobody left in this desolate town—
Save the sweeper who wearily loiters and lags,
The ashman, and he who cries "Bottles and rags!"
And a hurrying crowd one knows nothing about,
Though each one of them somebody cares for, no doubt;
The streets everywhere are plowed into a rut,
For putting down pipes that never stay put.
Gazing up from my window above may be scanned
A strip of the sky as wide as my hand;
And then, looking earthward, may dimly be seen
At least a square yard once of emerald green;
But now from the heat and sewer-gas, behold!
It has taken the favorite hue of old gold.
Then the odors,—not Milton's Sabean, I own,
Nor yet those that Coleridge found at Cologne,
But here to our trained, tried olfactories known,
As the Hunter's Point perfume—from boiling old bone.
You boast of your singing birds lodged in the trees,
Of the dash of the waves, the sigh of the breeze,

The lowing of herds, the hum of the bees—
Sweet voices of Nature,—but what are all these
To our lively mosquitos' appeal to the senses,
The wail of the cats as they stray o'er the fences;
Till a friend at my side, in a rage going on,
Makes use of "cuss words" and calls for his gun.
And here comes the organ that stops at our door,
To grind out its music that makes, with the roar
Of the wagons and carts as they rumble and jolt
O'er the roughly paved streets, a prolonged thunderbolt;
And every two minutes the up-in-air train
Goes whirring along like a demon insane;
Till all thought is dispersed, like a mist in the air,
And silence is golden, we meekly declare.
Then the heat that no thoughts of the blizzard assuage,
When Phœbus and Fahrenheit start a rampage;
And when "General Humidity" joins in the tilt,
Like plucked flowers of the field the poor mortal must wilt,
Till he cries, like the wit, in disconsolate tones,
To take off his flesh and sit in his bones.
But, however, to sum up and make myself clear,
For July and August I would not be here;
But give me New-York for nine months of the year,—
With all its shortcomings there 's no place so dear;
With its life and its rush, what it does and has done,
There is no city like it under the sun.

Reverenced as a leader in all movements to confer benefit upon her fellow-creatures; appealed to for her equity of spirit and the soundness of her judicial faculty; beloved, as the woman; happy in the home whose hospitalities have made many happy; sustained by the affectionate coöperation and approval of him whose complemental qualities of mind and soul were ever her delight,—hers was the well-rounded life, attaining the fullness of years without the decadence of hope or of the impulse of her prime.

Her going forth was as she would have wished it to be, as expressed in the memorable lines of an elder spirit to whom she was kindred in nobility and power:

> Then steal away, give little warning,
> Choose thine own time;
> Say not good night, but in some brighter clime
> Bid me good morning.

It was not many weeks previous to her bidding good morning in some brighter clime, that she confided in me what perhaps was but a momentary impulse of the mind (we were speaking of leave-taking and of the Nunc Dimittis). "If any words were to be inscribed above me," she said, "I would like these," and she read from that copy of "The Light of Asia" which was the most companionable among her books:

> The Dew is on the lotus—rise, Great Sun!
> And lift my leaf, and mix me with the wave.
> Om mani padme hôm,[1] the Sunrise comes!
> The Dewdrop slips into the shining sea!

Yet though blent with the Universal (if such be the Universal) Law, so strong is the sense of her dear identity that her memory lives among us more vividly real than many a presence still clothed in mortal garb.

[1] For translation see page 127.

Her Artistic Character

By F. Edwin Elwell, New-York.

IN the first days after my return to New-York city, when the studies abroad had come to an end, and the real practical effort was to be made,—that effort so wearying both to body and soul at the beginning of an artist's career,—it was my lot to attempt to create the beautiful in art in the then rather false atmosphere of the artistic life here; in those first days, I became acquainted with this wonderful woman, Mrs. Botta.

I do not remember when first it was, or how it came about,—I only know that her sphere was one I had always loved in woman: her thought was pure and high, and in her soul burned the unquenchable fire of artistic genius; and had that flame been guided into the great flowing river of modern thought and feeling earlier in life, she would have left more public proofs of her great power in this direction.

But to us who knew her, there was little need of productions in marble or bronze to lead us to appreciate her artistic side. We had learned and felt deeply that the great mind was one with us in every throbbing emotion of our inner-soul feeling, for the art that lifts men out of the common on to that plane of ideality which is poetry, music, and all the arts combined.

Her love for art was an inward passion of the nobler kind. She saw in sculpture what would best express her inmost feelings; and when the time came that she could work in a studio, where there was perfect freedom and an absence of any small ideal of art, she covered in three weeks the same rational ground that another would have been years in accomplishing.

She loved truth,—truth in its highest sense and grandest simplicity. When she saw how great a truth the law of mass of form in art really was, she became so radiant and happy that she remarked to a friend, "I am in love again." It was the sublime simplicity of the truth that attracted her. It was seeing and loving the great simple facts in life that made her great, and her *salon* the center of the literary world of America. It was in her sphere that simple grand truth could thrive and gather to itself strength to go out from under her roof to be felt all over the country.

Indeed, few can measure her wonderful faculty of seeing the real in men and things: always lending a helping hand to any one who was sincere and aspiring, and most tenderly discarding those of mean ambition.

There was in her presence an uplifting force, a strength of soul, a lovely spiritual sphere. I have often gone in a mood to her house, and have come away filled with the holy light of higher truth. I have listened to her splendid verse, simply rendered, and I have watched that face full of tenderness and powerful thought, and have wondered what one saw most—this woman as a human being, or Mrs. Botta's spiritual self. One grew so used to this higher self of hers that the natural parting was but a momentary affliction to many of us, for soon there came into the life again the splendid song of her soul-light and truth.

It is rare enough that one finds in so gifted a literary woman as strong a genius for sculpture. Several of Mrs. Botta's busts are masculine in their touch, and have a poetical quality that if they had been fortunate enough to have been rendered in the technique of the modern French school, they would stand well with any of the modern works of the sculptors of to-day. I speak of the busts of Mr. Botta and Mr. Butler.

The fact that just before Mrs. Botta left us she was taking up the rational truths and philosophy of the French school, proves beyond a doubt that her nature was of exceptional breadth; and there can be little doubt that in a few years she would have mastered the technique enough to have given us worthy work, in which she would have expressed more clearly what her inner soul felt.

There are few women in modern society who have that quality so distinctly hers,—of inspiring one to resist the desire to succeed at once through the kind favor of over-zealous friends. Her counsel was dignified; she used to say, "It is better to succeed by one's work, and leave behind that real position that time cannot efface."

The effect of her good artistic advice and tender kindness will never be forgotten by John Ruhl, a youth of the city, who found his way out into the light through the wise assistance of Mrs. Botta and a friend. In this boy's soul burns always the sacred fire of love and veneration for the noble woman who did so much to lift others out into the light and on into the paths that lead to worldly fame. There is little need of sculptured monument to mark her departure from these our natural surroundings; for in the soul of all those who came near enough to her to feel her sublime nature, there exists now and forevermore a splendid, imperishable monument of pure affection.

An Album and the French Academy

By the Hon. John Bigelow, New-York.

THE career of the late Mrs. Botta was remarkable in many respects ; edifying and instructive in all. While yet but three years old the death of her father left her and her widowed mother dependent largely upon their own resources. With an excellent constitution, a good education, and a just appreciation of her talents, she decided to seek for them a wider sphere of activity than was offered in her quiet New England home, and, with her mother, she resolved to seek such a sphere in our great commercial metropolis. It was a bold, almost an audacious experiment; but young as she was, she had already measured her forces with some of the favorites of fortune, and the results gave her faith and courage. She had tried her prentice hand in the magazines, and some of her verses had been stamped with the *approbatur* of Bryant and Willis, at that time the aristarchy of American letters.

My acquaintance with Mrs. Botta commenced very soon after she took up her residence in New-York.

The scheme of life which, whether by instinct or deliberation, she seems thus early to have marked out for herself, was to make herself useful in some way to every one with whom she was brought into relationship. This radiance of usefulness, which helped to make her so singularly and uniformly agreeable, shone around her through life. Fortune, which is said to always favor the brave, smiled upon her. Her house soon became the favorite resort of the literary and artistic classes of our city, including not only those who had won their laurel crowns, but more especially the younger aspirants of both sexes, who were in the planting rather than in the harvesting season of their careers, and who nowhere else had such an advantageous opportunity of becoming acquainted and listening to the golden words of the masters. Many of those who in their turn have since risen to eminence, cherished through life a grateful affection for Mrs. Botta, through whose thoughtful attentions they thus received countenance and encouragement at this critical period of their lives. Her efforts to make herself useful to the world, as the surest and wisest method of making the world useful to her, flavored everything she did and said, and much of what she avoided doing and saying: surrounded her with devoted friends; made her not only a favorite, but ultimately a patroness, in our best society; caused her name to be one of the first to be sought in furtherance of any charitable, literary, or social movement; even disarmed criticism, and sent envy and jealousy away, empty and ashamed. This singleness of purpose to be of use to somebody in some way, was not with Mrs. Botta a penal servitude; it was not prosecuted reluctantly from a sense of religious duty — it was her pleasure. It gave her more satisfaction than she could get in any other way; it involved no sacrifices which she did not cheerfully make. It is not strange, therefore, that she always took the liveliest interest in whatever promised any amelioration in the material condition or the intellectual and spiritual elevation of her own sex. These were subjects upon which she frequently exercised her pen, and to which in other days she consecrated not a little of her time and best energies.

In one of her noblest schemes in behalf of womanhood, I chanced to be received into her confidence. During the War of the Rebellion she of course took an active interest in all the measures set on foot for the relief of the wounded soldiers. Among other devices for procuring the means for this charity, Mrs. Botta made a collection of autographs in 1864, which was sold and the proceeds applied to the uses of the Sanitary Commission. The gratifying success of this device prompted her to repeat it in 1870 for the benefit of the bereft families of the French soldiers wounded in the Franco-German war. Her efforts were rewarded with extraordinary success. No one made aware of her purpose could hesitate to oblige her. The result was a collection of more than a thousand autographs and photographs of the more eminent citizens of this country and Europe, and also of some hundred sketches by artists in Rome.

The album, when completed, was purchased by Mr. Henry W. Sage, of Ithaca, New-York, the founder of Sage College for the Education of Women, established in connection with Cornell University, for a sum which, after deducting the outlay, netted four thousand dollars. Meanwhile the war, happily, had terminated, and it became necessary to apply the proceeds of her benevolent endeavors to a different purpose from the one which had originally inspired it. Deliberating upon a number of different plans, she finally decided upon one which for a variety of reasons she thought would be more directly and at the same time more permanently effective of her purpose than any of the others. She offered the fund to the French Academy on condition that the interest should be given in prizes at appropriate intervals, for the best essays from any quarter of the world on the following theme: "Woman; in what way can her domestic, political, and social relations be modified in the interest of a higher civilization?"

In selecting the French Academy as her almoner for the distribution of this prize-money, she felt that she was committing it to perhaps the most august literary tribunal among nations, and one more likely than any other to attract eminent talent to the serious consideration of woman's proper place in the world. It also gave as great a promise of longevity as any other institution which could be expected to charge itself with such a duty, and whatever might be issued under its auspices was certain to receive and to merit the attention of the nations. It was a bold and noble conception, and if it has not yet borne all the fruit expected of it, it has been in no sense the fault of its large-minded proponent.

Monsieur Henri Moreau, a member of the French bar, and associated in business with M. Berryer during the later years of that distinguished barrister's professional career, kindly undertook to submit Mrs. Botta's proposal to the Academy, which he formally did through its "perpetual secretary" on the 4th of January, 1875. At the next meeting of the Academy, on the 7th of January, 1875, her proffer was formally accepted, the Academy accompanying its acceptance, however, with a request for her permission—which was conceded—to reserve to themselves the right to enlarge the scope of her theme by substituting for it "The Condition of Women." M. Patin's letter accepting the fund in the name of the Academy, and its motives for modifying the form and to some extent the import of the theme suggested by Mrs. Botta, ran as follows:

INSTITUT DE FRANCE, ACADÉMIE FRANÇAISE,
PARIS, January 14th, 1875.

The Perpetual Secretary of the Academy to M. MOREAU, *advocate.*

SIR: I communicated to the Academy at its last session, the 7th of this month, the letter which Madame Botta has been pleased to address to me and which you took the trouble to transmit to me on her behalf.

The Academy has naturally been much touched by the sentiments of esteem for itself as of sympathy for France testified in this letter and which have inspired the generous offer of Madame Botta.

Such an offer it could not hesitate to accept, which it hastens to do, with a single reservation which the maintenance of its usages, and its freedom of action, impose. It would prefer not to be restricted in accomplishing the intentions of Madame Botta by a too absolute programme, and not to engage itself to crown every five years any but the best of the works that may be addressed to it on the "Condition of Women."

Will you, sir, be our interpreter to Madame Botta, and charge yourself with the transmission to her of the homage of our sentiments of gratitude and respect, and accept for yourself the assurance of our distinguished consideration.

PATIN.

This letter shows how conservative the French Academy remains in regard to all literary or social movements which may come under its consideration, and Mrs. Botta was naturally somewhat surprised and disappointed by the change in the point of view from which the rights and interests of her sex were to be investigated under the Academy's auspices; but, taking it for granted that the gentlemen of that august body had satisfactory reasons for enlarging the scope of the inquiry for which the prize was to be given, she assented to their conditions.

At the session of the Academy on the 4th of August, 1881, the then perpetual secretary, M. Camille Doucet, announced that a competitor entitled to only a part of the prize had appeared, and that it would be competed for again two years later. The history and explanation of the action of the Academy is thus given in M. Doucet's report of the proceedings of the session. We here get a more definite—not to say amusing—view of the motives of the Academy for modifying the theme proposed by Mrs. Botta:

A portion of the prize of five thousand francs due to the generosity of Madame Botta will to-day receive an appropriate and honorable disposition, but the prize itself, as well as the prize of poetry, will be submitted to another competition and awarded two years hence.

On the 18th of December, 1874, Madame Botta wrote from New-York to the Academy proposing to place at its disposal a prize of five thousand francs to be given every five years for the best work published in France on the following subject: "How may the Domestic, Social, and Political Relations of Woman be Modified in the Interests of a Higher Civilization?"

This formula, not flattering (*assez irrespectueuse*) to our modern civilization, was of a nature to somewhat scare a pacific company, the friend of all progress but the enemy of all revolutions, especially of literary revolutions, and which is always ready to yield to its more competent brethren the honor, perilous for itself, of discussing political and social questions.

Without altogether refusing its coöperation, nor the trouble which it is its habit never to begrudge to those who ask for it, the Academy on this occasion felt compelled to show some hesitation; but soon — its entire freedom of action being reserved—the prize founded by Madame Botta by common consent was formally pledged to the best work which should be submitted on the "Condition of Women."

This prize we hoped for the first time to confer to-day. Only five competitors have responded to our appeal, and, had the subject originally proposed by Madame Botta been adopted, a little book entitled "La Femme Libre" would certainly have been entitled to a preference, but the more it responded to the programme renounced by the Academy, the more it departed from that which prevailed, from that which is a law to us, and which we are bound to respect.

In this volume, which realizes everything promised by its title, the author gives evidence of real talent, but he fails of his purpose from lack of measure and moderation. Instead of treating as a philosopher and moralist questions of morals and philosophy, it is with passion that he agitates social questions which we care not to discuss with him. His intentions are good; his methods dangerous. To ameliorate the condition of women, it is not necessary to begin by making men of them; it is not necessary to deprive them of that first merit which will always be their charm, their honor, and their right,—the merit of being women.

By its merits and by its defects this work is not one of the class which pass unnoticed. It has this advantage, and this disadvantage. The prize could not be given it; but no one has received it.

An important series of studies on the historic development of the condition of women in all countries and in all epochs had, however, attracted the attention of the Academy, which is mindful of having on two successive occasions (in 1864 and in 1872) encouraged their author, Mlle. Clarisse Badèr.

Under the several titles of "La Femme dans l'Inde Antique," "La Femme Biblique," "La Femme Grecque," and "La Femme Romaine," Mlle. Badèr undertook some twenty years ago an immense work of special information which placed her within the terms of this *concours* before it existed. She will be so much the more within it as she shall approach the completion of her task, her encyclopedic task. She raised the question; she has studied, commented, elucidated it, but, as it is still lacking a formal conclusion, she has not yet resolved it.

Desiring to honor persistent effort; to recompense literary labors animated throughout by a moral purpose—to use the expression of M. Villemain in conferring the prize on "La Femme dans l'Inde Antique"; wishing also to testify to the utmost its desire to respond without delay to the wishes of the donor, the Academy has appropriated from the Botta fund the sum of two thousand francs to Mlle. Clarisse Badèr, awaiting the completion of a work so full of promise.

Two years hence, gentlemen, I have said,—and I will repeat it,—this prize, which is now again submitted to competition by the Academy,—this prize of five thousand francs will be awarded to the best work which, before the 1st of January, 1883, shall be presented on the "Condition of Women."

Unhappily and curiously enough, the "Condition of Women" had not proved an inspiration to French genius. Neither in the *concours* of 1883 nor of 1887 did any competitors for this prize appear. The reason why is not obvious. There are very few even among the most eminent writers in France who can afford to make light of such an opportunity of earning five thousand francs. Perhaps it was not generally known that the Academy had such a prize to bestow; it may be that those who would have inclined to discuss the theme knew or feared that the Academy would not allow them a sufficient latitude for its proper treatment from their point of view; and it may be—though this view we hope is entitled to no respect—that the Academy did not think the "Condition of Women" admitted of any improvement. Whatever the reason, the learned assembly deemed it advisable to leave the gentler sex to their fate and to recommend the adoption of a more comprehensive programme. This view was communicated to Mrs. Botta in the following letter from the perpetual secretary:

INSTITUT DE FRANCE, ACADÉMIE FRANÇAISE,
PARIS, 7th May, 1887.

The Perpetual Secretary of the Academy to MADAME BOTTA.

MADAME: For the past twelve years it has been the duty of the Academy to respond to your confidence, and it has neglected nothing to insure to the prize so generously founded by you the destination indicated by you for it.

Never, Madame, has this result been completely realized, and this year it has not received a single work which conformed to the prescribed conditions.

Greatly regretting its inability to fulfil your intentions, it has charged me to explain to you the situation and to ask what it would be agreeable to you that it should do to secure a good use for the sum hitherto consecrated by you to the best work on the "Condition of Women."

This subject, Madame, has not inspired a single author, and, after several renewals, it seems certain now that a like result will continue always to subject the Academy to the like embarrassment.

Will you not then consider, Madame, whether it will not be agreeable to modify your too restricted or too arbitrary programme? There are other orders of literary labor worthy of your interest and of your generosity which would better attain your end through the Academy, which has only good ends in view, if you would give it a larger latitude for the employment of the revenue from your foundation "in the interest of letters," as has already been done by our illustrious colleague, M. Vitet. I beg you, Madame, to accept my respectful homage.

CAMILLE DOUCET.

To this letter Mrs. Botta, upon due reflection, sent the following reply:

NEW-YORK, 29th May, 1887.

To Mr. Camille Doucet, etc.

SIR: I regret to learn by your letter of May 7th that the prize offered by the Academy for the best book on the "Condition of Women" failed to awaken the interest that the subject seemed to have demanded. The object in founding this prize was not only to express the sympathy and admiration of a great nation, but also to encourage the production of such works as would tend to the elevation of women, who, it cannot be denied, form a very important element in the advancement of the human race and in the development of civilization. Since this object seems to have failed, I cheerfully accept the suggestion of the illustrious gentlemen who constitute the Academy, communicated to me in your letter, and request that the fund be appropriated to such objects and in such a manner as they may think best. Should any form be necessary in order to utilize this change, my husband and myself will be in Paris some time during the summer, when it can be satisfactorily arranged. With great regard, etc.,

A. C. L. Botta.

To this Mrs. Botta received the following answer:

Institut de France, Académie Française,
Paris, 17th June, 1887.

The Perpetual Secretary of the Academy to Madame Botta.

Madame: I have received the letter you did me the honor to write me, and I lost no time in communicating it to the Academy at its session yesterday.

The gracious manner in which you have received the proposition which I had occasion to submit to you has been highly appreciated by the company, and I am charged to thank you on its behalf.

Believe me, Madame, that before asking you to modify your first intentions it was necessary that the impossibility of satisfying them should be absolutely demonstrated, so earnestly does the Academy always desire to comform to the wishes of the generous persons who honor it with their confidence.

Feeling fully authorized by your last letter, the Academy yesterday made the following disposition of your prize, with which I hasten to acquaint you:

"In future the Botta prize shall be bestowed every three years. It shall be 3000 francs, and the Academy, inspired by the testamentary dispositions of M. Vitet, will apply this sum in the way it shall deem best 'in the interest of letters.' For the next year, and for that year only, the Botta prize will amount to 6000 francs in consequence of the unappropriated income which will have accumulated at that time.[1]

"This prize will thereafter alternate with the two triennial prizes of 3000 francs founded respectively by M. Thiers and by M. Guizot."

You will see, Madame, that your prize, assimilated as it is to the Guizot, Thiers and Vitet prizes, will be in all respects constituted under the most honorable conditions, and the Academy in future will have no difficulty in making a good use of it and in a way to afford you entire satisfaction.

With the thanks of the Academy, please accept, Madame, my respectful homage.

CAMILLE DOUCET.

The official record of the action of the Academy in reference to the Botta prize at its annual session on the 24th of November, 1887, runs as follows:

As modified by the will, by the good will, of its founder, the prize, at first destined by Madame Botta as a recompense for some moral and philosophical work on the "Condition of Women," has received a different destination. In future this prize of three thousand francs will be bestowed every three years, and, as in the case of the Vitet prize, the Academy will appropriate this sum in the way that shall seem best to it "in the interest of letters." In announcing this good news to all those who may soon be called to profit by it, I have pleasure in publicly thanking, in their name as in our own, the kind benefactress, the generous American lady who for the second time manifests her sympathy for French writers and her confidence in the Academy, by charging us with one of those commissions which it is not always easy, but always agreeable, to have to discharge.

[1] At the next sitting the Academy decided to offer out of the Botta Fund a Gold Medal of Honor to the author of "Pensées d'une Reine," Carmen Sylva (the nom de plume of the Queen of Roumania); and two prizes of 2500 francs each to two other women writers.

The fate of this effort of Mrs. Botta to encourage a more profound and careful study of the interests of her sex is calculated to provoke reflections which this is scarcely an appropriate place to record, but the effort itself, though it failed to be crowned with the kind of success she had hoped for it, was a shining illustration of one of the noblest traits of her character and constitutes a substantial title to the respect and gratitude of her sex. It may also ultimately prove more useful to mankind than if her original limitations had been insisted upon.

Mrs. Botta was not only a poet — though never making any pretensions to fame as a poet — she was also an artist. Her busts of some of our well-known country people are justly esteemed for their merit, and bear evidence of a talent for which a little more ambition would have insured distinction. She was the author of several books, all designed to instruct rather than to amuse, some of which, though published more than thirty years ago, are still in general use in schools and colleges, and are perpetuating her influence in the community of which she was *decus et tutamen*. Fortune smiled upon her labors, and she lived to verify the soundness of the theory with which she began, and to which she adhered through life, that making herself useful to the world was the best way of making the world useful to her.

Our city has had to mourn the loss of few women who had more friends, and none perhaps who was more universally respected.

A Paper

READ BEFORE THE NINETEENTH CENTURY CLUB

By Mrs. Katherine L. Youmans.

I GLADLY fulfil the request of my associates of The Nineteenth Century Club to say a few words in memory of my old and cherished friend, Mrs. Vincenzo Botta, though in the brief and crowded time allotted me I fear my tribute will prove most meager and inadequate.

Mrs. Botta's history has been for so long a time an open book to New-Yorkers that its details are probably familiar to most of us; still a whole generation has come upon the scene since she took her place on it, and the story is certainly full enough of interest to bear repetition. Miss Lynch was the daughter, on one side, of an able and brilliant young Irish patriot who was imprisoned for four years for the part he took in the uprising of "United Irishmen" in 1798 (during which he was offered not only liberty, but a commission in the English army, if he would swear allegiance to its government), and then banished to this country; and, on the other, of a bright, brainy executive New England mother of choicest Revolutionary blood. Thus equipped by inheritance with a capacity for independent thinking, she improved it to the utmost by a girlhood of earnest study under the ablest teachers of the land. Even as a school-girl her poems and essays elicited much admiring comment.

Coming to New-York in the year 1845 with quite a reputation as a writer in varied lines as well as that of an able and successful teacher, she engaged in her favorite employment of instruction of young ladies. Endowed with a personality of great magnetism and graceful charm, she soon gathered around her the choicest spirits of her new home and of neighboring towns, as well as of visiting strangers of distinction from beyond the sea. Her rooms became a favorite rallying-point for persons eminent in every line of successful achievement,—the leading writers, artists, scientists, and dramatists both of the Old World and the New,—as well as a home where the disappointed and hard-pressed found solace and rest.

The educating, refining influence of such a social center in this then crude, uncultured mercantile metropolis can scarcely be overestimated. It was emphatically a triumph of "high thinking and plain living"; for Mrs. Botta always retained the French simplicity of *salon* entertainment, even when the ample means of later days would have warranted a more lavish expenditure, and when the practice was universal of luxurious table-cheer. It was, moreover, a triumph of broad and liberal thinking; for the largest mental hospitality was a marked feature of these reunions. As in our own club, no one was ever made uncomfortable by his belief or his unbelief. Jew and Gentile, Buddhist and Romanist, the orthodox enthusiast and the cool-headed Agnostic, were welcomed alike, so long as they were honest and earnest, so long as they were gentle in spirit and courteous in utterance. Indeed, the spirit of the hostess was too elevated and serene, too far removed from the petty rivalries, jealousies, and animosities of lesser natures not to impress itself powerfully upon the character of the gatherings under her roof. The environment was irresistibly tranquilizing. Fraternization and good-comradeship were in the air. How many struggling young aspirants for fruitful recognition, how many defeated and sore-hearted toilers for the success which eternally eluded their grasp, have found here emphatically a "helping hand" and a "sheltering arm"? How many successful ones in the prosperity of their after lives have gratefully acknowledged their indebtedness to the encouragement and stimulation given by this wise-judging, generous-hearted woman?

In 1855 she was happily married to Vincenzo Botta, a professor of philosophy in the Royal Colleges of the University of Turin. Mr. Botta in his early life had become identified with the liberal party in the political movement of the years 1847 and 1848 having for its object the securing a constitutional government in Piedmont and through it the independence and the unification of Italy as a nation. In 1849 he was elected member of the Piedmontese Parliament, and later he was sent with a colleague to

Germany to investigate the system of education prevailing in various parts of that country. In 1853 he was charged with the same mission to the United States, where he finally decided to remain. He was soon appointed professor in the University of the City of New-York. He is the author of several valuable works, among which may be mentioned "A Monograph of the Life and Policy of Count Cavour," and "An Introduction to the Study of Dante." Being in this country at the time of our civil war, he was able, through his connection with the press of Italy, to promote and to strengthen the sympathy of his countrymen for the abolition of slavery and the restoration of the Union. He is a correspondent-member of the Royal Academy of the Lincei, in Rome, which is to Italy what the Institute is to France. In recognition of services rendered to the Italian Government in this country, he received from Victor Emmanuel the Cross of Commendatore in the Royal Order of the Cross of Italy, of which the King is the First Master. Later, he was presented by King Humbert with a beautiful gold medal bearing this inscription: "To VINCENZO BOTTA, in every fortune of his country a wise interpreter of Italian thought to the great and friendly people of the United States.—UMBERTO."

In 1849 Miss Lynch published a volume of short, graceful poems, beautifully illustrated by her artist-friends.

In 1860 appeared Mrs. Botta's "Handbook of Universal Literature" (revised and brought down to 1890 three years ago), a work evincing great industry of research, delicacy of literary insight, and well-poised judgment. She was rewarded for this laborious work by its wide acceptance as a volume of reference and an educational text-book. Mrs. Botta was unremitting in her services to the cause of education. To her own sex she was especially helpful, and, though she had small sympathy with what is popularly termed the emancipation of women, no one could be more deeply sympathetic with their aspirations for a higher and nobler life. Her aim was to fit them to use worthily the large liberty they craved.

Her own life, in its rare symmetry, was a beautiful example of her teachings: the devoted daughter and wife; the faithful friend, who counted no sacrifice too great in behalf of those she loved; the earnest lover of humanity, who saw good in all, and from whose gentle lips came never a word of censure for the shortcomings of others, though her self-criticism was severe and her standard of right living exactingly high; the wise, intelligent ruler of her household, whose working seemed to be that of delicate machinery, so quiet was it and frictionless; and the gracious hostess who was always swift to welcome both friend and wayfarer to what Emerson used to call "The house of expanding doors." Her industry was tireless. Besides an extensive range of choice reading, which brought her in close touch with the leading interests of the day, she had always in hand some task requiring either activity of brain or skill of manipulation; and at the time of her death she was employed in writing a historical work for the use of schools, and was giving the finishing touches to a portrait bust of an English friend. Indeed, so successful were her efforts in sculpture that it was evident that if she had not so early chosen a literary and educational career, she might have won a distinguished reputation as an artist.

The pathetic circumstances attending the sudden taking-off of our friend were especially painful to her associates of this club, for it was in the exposure incident to her attendance upon its social duties that she received her death-blow; but this swift translation without the ordeal of a painful illness was what she earnestly longed for. For her it was a blessed gain that she passed away with no thought that her last hour was close at hand.

The sharpness of the sudden blow was for us who loved her, and who feel that such a loss will make the world seem infinitely poorer for evermore. Like its distinguished founder, she strongly impressed her own personality upon the spirit of our club, and has left us a legacy in the society whose interests she had so near at heart; and it seems to me we can further the prosperity we are so earnestly laboring to secure in no surer way than by shaping our councils in fullest accord with the teachings of her own broad-lined, vari-sided, forceful and beneficent life.

Resolutions

OF THE "WEDNESDAY AFTERNOON CLUB," NEW-YORK.

BY THE SECRETARY OF THE CLUB.

AT a meeting of the "Wednesday Afternoon Club" the following resolutions were offered:

Whereas, In the orderly and beautiful sequence of life, that great experience which we call death has befallen one of our number; therefore

Resolved, That in the passing away of Mrs. Botta, the "Wednesday Afternoon Club" recognizes the loss of its most honored member.

Resolved, That her rare mind, her broad culture, her pleasure in the prosperity of the club, and her constant friendliness to what was best in its intention, have been, since its foundation, among the most helpful and inspiring of its influences.

Resolved, That while no tribute of so formal a nature as this can express our sense of that radiant energy and sincerity of soul which demanded a like high-heartedness in others, yet we wish to put on record even so inadequate a recognition of her many-sided capacity, her intellectual distinction, her spiritual loveliness, and her belief in the evidence of things unseen.

The resolutions were spoken to as follows by the secretary:

Some one has truly said of Mrs. Botta that a sense of her untimely taking off, as if she were too young to go, moves those who knew her best. Perhaps this wonderful youthfulness of hers, which was never levity, was her most remarkable characteristic. Her nature was profoundly serious. Always she had considered life as a trust, an experience, an agency; never as a personal possession, to be used according to her wish or momentary need. She felt the woes and wants of this world of confusion and uncertainty, and did her best to better them. Yet, withal, over this earnestness of her character flickered ever an almost frolic gaiety of spirit, as if she knew that more than for its needed food and fire, so to speak, the soul asked for light. She came of a Celtic father, gay, humorous, full of impulsive chivalry, and of a practical New England mother, herself of Revolutionary stock, clear of judgment, careful of the household economy, upright, exemplary, and "facultied." In the daughter these inherited qualities blended into a most harmonious whole. Years ago, when she had classes in an unremembered New-York—the New-York "before the war"—and was overworked, and had many persons to provide for, her modest lodgings were beautiful with refinement, were attractive to the best people, and constituted, perhaps, the one literary center in that crude commercial city where Mrs. Potiphar was a leader of fashion and Mr. Solomon Gunnybags the prototype of the honored citizen.

Afterward, when the beautiful house in Thirty-seventh street opened its doors, everybody who by attainment or quality deserved a welcome received one. Mrs. Botta was the most delightful of hostesses because she never remembered herself. The sincerity of her welcome, and her conviction of the agreeableness of her guests, made them always agreeable. Or perhaps some large part of the perpetual pleasantness of the house was due to the pleasantness of the domestic life within its walls. It is not often that two people of like culture, of like interests, of like pursuits, have the good fortune to live together for half a lifetime, and thus to develop that delicate intimacy of mind and heart that makes them ideal comrades, as were the master and mistress of this abode. If her charm of manner were her father's legacy, the New England side of Mrs. Botta had its full expression. She was a finished housekeeper, her domestic administration being orderly, careful, and regular. But she never sacrificed her home to her house. The housekeeping was dainty that the home might exist, and she said that she had long ago learned the wisdom of being deaf, dumb, and blind when the exigencies of household management required it. She was an exquisite needlewoman. making the most artistic and elegant of trifles, and even sewing seams, if need were. But of late years she used laughingly to declare it a kind of irreligion for those women to sew who could afford to hire sewing, because, in every case, it defrauded two persons of their rights. She had a great talent for cookery, composed an occasional dish with the delicacy of a *cordon bleu,* and was not at a loss if her cook departed without notice. Her artistic side is better known to most of us perhaps. She used to draw and paint in earlier days, and for sculpture it may be said with all restraint that she had genius. When a portrait bust of her modeling was lately sent to Rome to be put into marble, the foremost of Italian sculptors, not knowing its maker, declared that nothing would be beyond the reach of the artist if he would come to Rome and study *technique* for a year.

These things should be spoken of here, because Mrs. Botta was so modest that nobody would ever have learned from her that she had any special gift or grace. To praise her literary work is superfluous, but it should, perhaps, be added that her literary taste was perfect, and that she proved herself an able critic by not being hypercritical. She felt the author's intention and endeavor, and she recognized the success of that which is often called failure.

But, after all, her true genius was a moral genius. Her life is the one finished and perfect work which is left to us. She saw, as she once said, that for each of us nature lays broad the foundations of a divine building, if the soul will build thereon — and her soul did build. In one respect she seemed almost unique among women. Her judgments had no personal bias. If you were unjust to her, or indifferent, or misrepresented her, that made no difference in her attitude toward you. She still praised your excellencies. If she thought you had defects, she never mentioned them; she never even dwelt upon them in her thought. The core and center of her being was love. She asked nothing; she gave all things. And perhaps the fittest that can be said of her creed and deed is what she herself has said in a little poem called

LARGESS.

Go forth in life, O friend, not seeking love;
  A mendicant that with imploring eye
  And outstretched hand asks of the passers-by
The alms his strong necessities may move.

For such poor love, to pity near allied,
  Thy generous spirit should not stoop and wait,
A suppliant, whose prayer may be denied,
  Like a spurned beggar's at a palace gate!

But thy heart's affluence lavish, uncontrolled,
  The largess of thy love give full and free,
As monarchs in their progress scatter gold.
  And be thy heart like the exhaustless sea,
That must its wealth of cloud and dew bestow,
Though tributary streams or ebb or flow.

Selections from Her Letters

Selections from Her Letters

TO MISS ANNA PLATT.

HARTFORD, CONN., November 11, 1835.

My dear Anna: . . . This is my birthday, and I am twenty years old. Who that knows me would not rather say sixty? I believe I have had every variety of feeling humanity is capable of, and there remains nothing for me now, not even a disappointment. My mind, too early matured, has reached at this period the limit it should only have attained at threescore; and now, like some plant, blossoming prematurely, it droops and withers, while all around it is verdant.

But you will call me an egotist, and I shall deserve it; so let me turn to some more agreeable topic.

I have been reading Sismondi's "Literature of the South of Europe" in connection with "The History." It is exceedingly interesting. Do let me give you a hint or two about study; it may tire you, but, indeed, I cannot avoid it. It is the strongest proof of my friendship, for I assure you there are not many that I think are worth teaching. I have had some thought of writing a work on education, but I get so disheartened at seeing people so ignorant of the difference between good and bad, that I think they may go to their " wallowing in the mire."

You will say that you go to school and get all your lessons well. I grant it. You may do this until you are nineteen,—then you leave, and you know, perhaps, ten or twelve books perfectly. But, my dear Anna, this is not knowledge; it is drudgery, and you go to it as a task. It is the mere stowing away of a few isolated facts that you have no command over, and are as likely to bewilder as to benefit. It is like being in a dim recess and looking out at the landscape: everything is indistinct and mutilated, but go on some high tower and you comprehend the whole in all its beauty.

The great defect in education is this: you see only parts of beautiful pictures, the moral or design of which you cannot comprehend without the whole. One word of advice, and I am done. Read an epitome of the history of the whole world,—I mean of every country, beginning with the oldest,—and get the skeleton firmly marked out in your mind. Then take up the distinguished individuals, the literature, arts, sciences, and religions in their order. In this way you would acquire more in three months than in ten years at an ordinary school. I could amplify to infinity, but I forbear. . . . You may think this too superficial a method; but by no means must you stop at the end of three months—nor will you wish to do so, for you will have comprehended the whole, and the minute details could not fail to interest you. . . .

Affectionately yours, ANNE C. LYNCH.

TO HENRY GILES.

NEW-YORK, February 16, 1845.

Dear Friend: . . . I have been thinking over our talk about poetry and trying to account to myself for the faith that is in me. The poets of antiquity do not satisfy me (shall I say such a thing and yet live?), and for this reason they can not, they do not give us the *possible* of humanity, but only its actual. The Dutch painters may rival nature in their cabbages, but you do not place them on a level with the ideal artists of Italy, or compare their works with the sublime productions of Michelangelo or Raphael. Yet there is nothing monstrous or unnatural in their works; if there were, we should not recognize beauty or sublimity in them; they represent the *possible* of nature. So I conceive a great poet should do; not content with merely reproducing nature, he should so idealize it as to fill entirely the capacity we have to apprehend perfection, and till this is done, it appears to me that the greatest poet has not spoken. The office of poetry, I think, is not merely to express beauty or passion (the highest office, I mean), but some of the great facts and possibilities of our natures, because in them lie the highest interests of humanity.

We are in a world of sorrow, wretchedness, selfishness, and crime; the ways of men are bowed to the earth with one or all of these burdens, unconscious even of their power to stand erect and survey the beauteous earth around and the heavens above them.

The poet, or the man of genius, is born to aspire where others grovel; and not only that, but he alone has the power of stirring this dull mass, and elevating it to his own region, or at least to the contemplation of it. With this immense lump to be leavened, then, how can the true poet rest satisfied to sing only for his own amusement? Do tell me if you think this is all wrong, or any part of it. I did not intend to say so much; yet it is in me, and if it is wrong, I wish to correct it. I inclose a poem, which please show to the Rev. Dr. Furness, and let me know if he likes it. I am very grateful for his kindness in the past. . . .

Believe me ever truly yours,

ANNE C. LYNCH.

NEW-YORK, March 11, 1845.

. . . I am mentally in the condition of a bottle of champagne which has been well shaken and is all ready to rush out with a great noise and effervescence, a sound and fury, which signifies nothing. But my great consolation is that things will go on, destinies be accomplished, and my own among all others, active or passive, *nolens volens*. Yours will, too; and why should we fret and make ourselves miserable over this little space of time, that every moment makes shorter? Life is not worth the care and anxiety we give to it. If we would only think for a few minutes every morning: My life will last but for a few years,—this, even, may be the last,—and I shall go "where all have gone, where all must go," and the world will go on just the same; wisdom will not die with me, and truth, goodness, and beauty are alone immortal. If we would do this, it seems to me we should live more in the absolute and less in the actual. We should become like the great principles we worship—almost "impersonal." Do work up this thought into a sermon for me; for my own preaching has but little effect.

Yours, A. C. L.

TO N. P. WILLIS.

NEW-YORK, December, 1851.

Dear Friend: . . . Perhaps it is because I know that you, like myself, are not known and are not happy. Your heart is over-burdened with its love; mine is empty. You love like a poet, and one moment of such a love is worth ages of this commonplace sentiment that goes by that name. One is the vivid and glowing fire; the other is the painted semblance of fire. I could love so, and I would rather have this power of loving, though it should, as it has, "run to waste, or watered but the desert," than to have all that I see others have, call it by what name you will.

> Love! to that pale uncertain flame
> The fervent God denies his name,

says Mrs. Norton. Nothing great was ever achieved without passion. Appetite is a quality of the senses, but passion belongs to the soul, and is the source of all enthusiasm and of whatever lifts us above the level of that mediocrity where the mass of men are destined to live.

Love, which would be to me the sun of my existence, has not dawned on me, and I dwell in the dreariness of a polar night. Do not think this a figure; it is literally true. The bloom and perfume of my existence has never been called forth, and I feel that I shall die without having lived. But do not think that I complain. "To bear is to conquer our fate." I have struggled bravely with mine; I have borne and conquered. Those who live in the polar regions build themselves huts, kindle their fires, and light their torches—ineffectual substitutes for the sun. One single ray shines on my polar night; this is the love of what is beautiful in sentiment, in action, or in outward form or manifestation. The passion of my soul that should have been given to love beams on the altar of the beautiful. The light that it gives me, it is true, is cold as the beams of the Aurora Borealis; but it is constant and increasing, and if I could forget the sun, it would be more sufficing.

Without any vulgar ambition for distinction, I have

yet the strongest desire to give expression to some of the feelings and sentiments that make me "the cannibal of my own thoughts." I would like to exercise my faculties as a strong man would exercise his muscles. . . .

Sincerely yours, A. C. L.

TO LOUIS KOSSUTH.

NEW-YORK, December 18, 1851.

Sir: When, two or three years since, the news reached us of the disaster that overwhelmed you in Hungary, inspired by your character and your heroism, I wrote the accompanying poem. I hope you will forgive my muse if, at the tomb of Hungary in contemplating her future resurrection, she for a moment lost sight of her champion; and now that he comes to our shores, not a released captive, but a conqueror enchaining all hearts,—a conqueror such as the world has never before seen,—I know that he will again forgive my muse if, dazzled and overpowered, she as yet finds no language for her inspiration, and has no ideas, but only feelings.

It is common to speak of the age of poetry as passed by; to me it has always appeared as yet to come. While the literature of the past has tended only to idealize the actual, I have thought that the new and higher literature should aim to elevate the actual into the ideal; that the sublime truths of Christianity were yet to be uttered in the trumpet-tones of eloquence and poetry, that should vibrate through the universal heart of humanity. I have thought that this was to come, but in another generation than mine.

Yet I have listened to the words of the new evangel as they fell from the lips touched by a coal from the altar of God, and even now, as I hear them echo from continent to continent, kindling the benumbed hearts of the nations, they are to me the sublime prelude of a golden age yet to come, as well as a new literature, of which I recognize in you the first hero, orator, and poet.

I have the honor of signing myself, with great admiration and reverence, truly yours,

A. C. Lynch.

EXTRACTS FROM LETTERS TO MR. CHARLES BUTLER.

New-York, November 3, 1851.

. . . I must sing the old song, and confess that the last week has gone the same way with its numerous, I cannot add "illustrious," predecessors.

The mystery as to "what becomes of the pins" is nothing in comparison to the wonder—what becomes of the time.

Then again we can replace pins lost—but not lost time. . . .

I am truly yours, A. C. L.

New-York, November 24, 1851.

. . . I was reading last night a beautiful passage from Wordsworth, which, it was said, Smith O'Brien had copied over his chimney-piece in Richmond prison. "One adequate support for the calamities of mortal life exists—one only; an assured belief that the procession of our fate, however sad or disturbed, is ordered by a Being of infinite benevolence and power, whose everlasting purposes embrace all accidents, converting them to good."

What a consoling and tranquilizing thought, and what a truth! . . .

Sincerely yours, A. C. L.

NEW-YORK, May 19, 1852.

Dear Mr. Butler: . . . This day is the anniversary of our first acquaintance, and I cannot let it pass by without at least one line in commemoration of what to me is one of the most pleasant incidents of my life, and which I am certain you do not regard with indifference, for you have given me too many kind assurances to the contrary.

It was my destiny, perhaps my misfortune, to be born with some peculiarities—I might perhaps say *romantic* peculiarities—of character. My standard was high, and I have used the word *misfortune* because it seems to express faintly the unhappiness I have felt almost all my life in finding most every one fall short of it. I demanded something more benevolent, more disinterested, more magnanimous, more Christian than I found; and my unsatisfied, disappointed sympathies and affections came back to my wounded heart and brought desolation and almost despair.

It was in such a state of mind as this that one

year ago to-day, as it seemed by chance, and yet as I believe was guided by an all-wise Providence, I started on the journey we made together—I may say that we are still making; for I take it for granted that this journey, though we did not know it then, was the "Voyage of Life," and was to continue as we travel on toward that West, where the sun sets never to rise again here.

You cannot understand, my dear Mr. Butler, how much you have been to me. You never can because you can never know; God alone can know how much I have needed such a friend. It is not that you are kind to me, for I have had kindness and affection bestowed upon me often before. It is more, perhaps, because your ideas of duty, of life, of goodness, and of responsibility correspond with mine; because you are one of those I have always been seeking for and never have found before. I thank God that I have met you, for it has made me happier and better; and it has awakened in me the desire to be worthy of the regard that I feel you entertain for me. I must now close this brief and imperfect expression of my sentiments on this occasion, and in the mean time believe me most truly yours, ANNE C. LYNCH.

WASHINGTON, D. C., November 1, 1852.

Dear Friend: I send you a line to tell of my safe arrival. I feel always a peculiar gratitude after I, or those I love, have escaped the perils by land or sea that encompass us while traveling. Yet I do not see why this should be so, unless it is because I am not grateful enough at other times. It seems to me that our whole lives should be one perpetual hymn of gratitude and praise; that as the flower constantly sends forth its perfume, so the incense of love and adoration should rise constantly from our hearts. And thus it would be if we lived always in the sun of God's presence; if the cares of earth did not come like dark clouds between us and him and intercept the light of his smile, leaving us to the darkness and gloom of our own hearts. Is it not strange that, when the "Peace of God" has once descended upon us, we should ever after distrust it, and drive it away? That Peace that passes all understanding, that chastens our joys, and sanctifies our sorrows, prepares us alike for adversity and prosperity. Yet so we, or I at least, do constantly; and so I often dwell in the mists and shadows of the valley, rather than in the eternal sunshine of the mountain-top. To mount upward we must toil and struggle. Ole Bull's motto is certainly a true one: "By Life, battle—by battle, Life."

The sun is shining beautifully, and the air is like summer. Hoping this will find you well, and enjoying the blessings of this world, I am ever truly yours,

A. C. L.

NEW-YORK, November 16, 1852.

Dear Friend: . . . The great event (to me) of the past week has been the recurrence of my birthday. Oh, if these years had been differently improved, I should have less cause to regret that they are so many. But of all useless and idle things *regrets* are the most so, unless they stimulate to something better in the future. Let us then in all things forget those that are passed, and press forward toward whatever good there is to be found in the future. This only is ours; the past is irrecoverable, irretrievable. Let us then rightly improve the days to come. I am speaking for myself; but then these resolutions are equally good for you and for every one.

What occurred yesterday, nothing can change; but to-day, to-morrow, the future is ours, and to a great extent we can control it. Why not then

> Let the dead Past bury its dead!
> Act,—act in the living Present!
> Heart within, and God o'erhead!
>
> Lives of great men all remind us
> We can make our lives sublime,
> And, departing, leave behind us
> Foot-prints on the sands of time.
>
> Foot-prints, that perhaps another,
> Sailing o'er life's solemn main,
> A forlorn and shipwrecked brother,
> Seeing, shall take heart again.

Believe me ever sincerely yours,

A. C. L.

New-York, December 1, 1852.

My dear Friend: . . . I was very glad to hear of your safe arrival, and trust that by this time you are safely anchored, where you will find many friends.

The troubles and trials which beset you on the

way are past; and I am not sure but such a journey might be safely recommended as a moral discipline, and a wholesome corrective of any impatience of temper. Please write to me always very freely of the disagreeable things you encounter. I assure you it will be a positive kindness; for while I have nothing to think of but my own annoyances, I am quite miserable; but I forget them in thinking of those of others. This I am convinced is the true secret of happiness — the forgetfulness of ourselves in others.

When we can lose this intense self-consciousness in love for the suffering humanity around us, and the all-good, all-wise God above us, we have attained the highest happiness within our reach here in this life.

I think we see the truth of this even in art. An actor cannot touch his audience until he has lost himself in the conception of his part. And the true inspiration as applied to art seems only to indicate how far a man has forgotten himself. . . .

With kindest wishes, I am sincerely yours,

A. C. L.

NEW-YORK, January 2, 1853.

My dear Friend: . . . What a kind Providence watches over you everywhere, and over me, too. If I could only trust it in my every-day life, in action or inaction as I do in my hours of reflection, I should be borne aloft over much that often depresses and distracts me.

How good and how happy we ought to be! But how impossible it seems for a human being to be really happy. Every new possession seems to bring a new want. This utter insufficiency of everything human and earthly, to satisfy the soul, seems one of the strongest proofs of its immortality.

I once thought of writing a kind of fairy tale, in which the hero should by some supernatural aid have all his wishes gratified. He should desire wealth, fame, love, power, and each in turn should fail to satisfy. At last, in despair, he should resign his supernatural power of accomplishing his wishes, and seek from the guardian spirit who attended him the secret of that happiness he had failed to secure. He now learns for the first time that "the Kingdom of Heaven is within him." That he carries it with him and diffuses it around. That it is in seeking the happiness and good of *others* that he is to find his own, rather than in the pursuit of selfish ends. How do you like the plot? . . .

I am sincerely yours, A. C. L.

GREENWICH, CONN., June 19, 1853.

My dear Friend: . . . The weather has been so warm in the city the past week, that I proposed to Ma that we come here and spend Sunday. . . .

We had a pleasant ride of an hour in the cars, and when we reached this town found very pleasant accommodations. I rose very early this morning, intending to see the sun rise; but he was ahead of me. However, I had a most delightful walk of two hours.

The country about here is beautiful. On one side is the sound with Long Island in the distance, and on the other a varied and most picturesque landscape. Two hours of such tranquil enjoyment as I had in my solitary walk this morning, and of such sweet and pleasant thoughts, are enough to last one for a week, if they are not too exacting, and certainly more than most people have. I came home devoutly thankful to God that he permitted me to exist in a world of so much beauty, and asking nothing more than I possess. If one could always feel so! But then, it is well doubtless to have some drawback, some alloy to the happiness we are capable of enjoying, or it would make "this life of ours too fair for aught so fieet."

I have been reading to-day the gospel of John; and the more I read the New Testament, the less it seems to me is the spirit of modern Christianity in harmony with it: its simple and sublime precepts seem so often lost in an empty formalism, in sectarian bitterness, and Pharisaical goodness. But do not think, I pray you, that I would condemn others, or judge them, only so far as I necessarily must to make my own decisions of conduct and life.

What a beautiful example we have in those memorable words, "Let him who is without sin among you, cast the first stone." If we only followed this one principle, what a change there would be in our society. But at some future time we will argue those points on which we differ, if you choose. I am not fond of argument at any time; but to-day, especially, it is out of place. God, nature, and my own soul seem to be in such harmony that I would not be disturbed by a question or a doubt.

Trusting you have enjoyed this day to its fullest measure, believe me always truly yours,

A. C. L.

NEW-YORK, January 1, 1854.

My dear Friend: The first time I take my pen in this new year, or the first use I make of it, is to wish you the happiest of New Year's and all the blessings of this beautiful life. It is not well, I suppose, to wish to be too happy, or to wish too much for our friends; so if you can be, during the next year, as kindly watched over and protected as you have been in the years that have passed, we ought perhaps to consider the measure full. I think I can fully understand how, in the earlier ages, this sense of the goodness and mercy of the Creator should have expressed itself in literal or material offerings. Though these are no longer required, is there not still in the hearts of all of us a sacrificial altar whereon our offerings of gratitude should be laid? And have we not all a Mount Moriah whereon we may test our obedience and resignation?

Ma joins me in kindest wishes to you for the new year. And believe me sincerely yours,

A. C. L.

WINDHAM, CONN., April 21, 1854.

My dear Friend: My beloved mother is very ill. She has lain in a sort of stupor all day, moaning with every breath. The doctors are doing all they can for her, and the people are all very kind. . . .

April 22d.—I have more hope of Ma than I had

yesterday, but all is extremely doubtful. Whatever it may be, my only prayer is that I may have the strength to say to my Heavenly Father, "Not my will, but thine, be done." If I can only rest on this Rock,—the "Rock of Ages,"—though the waters of affliction sweep over me, I shall stand firm. I make a great struggle to suppress my emotions. I dread to, and dare not, think of the loneliness that awaits me if this, my only tie, is severed. But I trust that strength will be given me. . . .

April 26th.—My dear mother is much better, and continues to improve hourly. It is very pleasant and spring-like to-day, and I am so happy. The farmers are turning out to plow and plant. What a beautiful emblem of the resurrection is this revival of the suspended life of nature,—this springing forth of the seed "sown in corruption, raised in incorruption; sown in weakness, raised in power!" It is only in the country that we can truly feel, or most truly feel, that "God is everywhere" present. In the human heart only there seems to be something antagonistic—something that creates a discord in the divine harmony of the universe. Nature seems to me the mirror where "the Almighty's form glasses itself"; as heaven is reflected in the waters of a tranquil lake, and man is the spirit that troubles the waters and obscures the heavenly vision. There is a beautiful passage of Scripture that I promised a friend some time ago to write a poem on,—"He shall sit as a refiner of silver." It is, or was, the custom of the refiner to test the purity of this metal by melting it until he could see his face reflected in it. A beautiful comparison, is it not?

April 27th.—I regret so much that Ma is not fully recovered so we might return home again; and yet I am so devoutly thankful for her restoration that I feel that I shall never be needlessly unhappy again. The events of the past weeks seem to me like a sorrowful dream or nightmare, from which I am but too happy to awake; and my gratitude to that kind Providence that overrules all things so wisely and so well, either for our joy or our sorrow, is deeper than I have language to express.

With my best wishes and remembrances for you and yours, and all who are united to you by the ties of kindred and affection, I am most truly yours,

A. C. L.

WINDHAM, CONN., August 16, 1854.

My dear Friend: We reached this ancient and venerable town about nine o'clock. This is the scene of my early experiences, and every tree and stone is a familiar object. No other place has ever made such an impression on me as this. I have never seen a room that looked as large as the old hall when I learned to dance at the tavern across the way; and the distances about the town were really magnificent to my little eyes.

Children who are born and spend their early lives in the city really lose a great charm in life,—the charm of realizing these early impressions, as well as the advantages of the impressions themselves.

It is quite warm here to-day; but the country, the trees, the landscape,—everything,—is beautiful. The earth is everywhere radiant with the beauties and teeming with the abundance which our Heavenly Father lavishes upon us with such profusion. Why are we not all happy? Why are we not all good? Why are we not in harmony with nature and with God? Why is not life, as it should be, one continued hymn of thanksgiving and of love? We all know that it is not; but do we know that we could not make it so? To-day it seems to me easy to be good, and therefore to be happy; but this is in the country. It is much more difficult amid other surroundings. But we may continue to try.

Ever most truly yours, A. C. L.

BENNINGTON, VT., Oct. 8, 1854.

My dear Friend: This morning I saw the sun rise over these beautiful hills and shine into the valleys, glorious with their autumnal hues; and my heart and soul were filled with reverence, joy, and gratitude, such as in cities it is impossible to feel; and, naturally enough, this is so, for nature is always in harmony with God, while men and society are at war with him. All the discord in the universe comes from us. Here in this old town all is rest and quiet, and here one can enjoy all the harmonies of nature.

How much you would enjoy this beautiful scenery! And I wish you might have the rest; for you are always moving about like the veritable "Wandering Jew." I hope the time will come when you may enjoy something of the repose and pleasure of domestic and private life.

Your absent ones are now fairly at sea, and if this lovely weather extends eastward, they will have a pleasant passage. God grant that it may, and that they may be restored to you in safety and health.

I am, with best wishes, very truly yours,

A. C. L.

CHARLESTON, S. C., April 9, 1855.

My dear Friend: . . . It is pleasant to have seen this country, for we all want to see and experience for ourselves; and, so far, it is really most interesting. Botta is very well, very happy, very kind, very good. I feel great pleasure in knowing that all my friends will love him when they know him. I think that we cannot fail to be happy, because we consider the happiness of each other, rather than our own. And if you have read the "Extracts" I sent you from the *Theologia Germanica*, and believe that in this renunciation of self lies the highest earthly happiness, you will think that as long as we are wise enough to act on this principle and in this faith, we surely must be happy.

Very sincerely yours, A. C. L. BOTTA.

NEW ORLEANS, LA., April 27, 1855.

. . . Mr. and Mrs. B—— went with us to the slave-market, where we saw a mother and child sold for $325, and many others on the stand, of all sexes, ages, and conditions, to be sold. This was a most painful scene, to see human beings sold as cattle.

A. C. L. Botta.

New-York, December 23, 1855.

My dear Friend: I have just heard that my friend G—— has very suddenly lost his only son, who was a promising young man; and the blow falls very heavily upon his parents. In thinking of such events, how fleeting and transitory life and the world and our little desires and efforts all appear! How strange it seems that we do not live farther above them! Yet perhaps it is wisely ordered that we should lose sight of the vanity and uncertainty of all things earthly; for if we did but realize the truth, we should be so appalled and overwhelmed that we should sink down in the apathy of despair. It is well, then, that we do not feel all the truth; but it would be better, and we should be more serene and tranquil, if we thought more earnestly, or could bring the truth more vividly to our minds: that so far as this life is concerned we are but the beings of a day, and that the only reality of this phantasmagoria that we call life, is to be found in the exercise of our highest and best faculties,—in being and doing good, in loving God supremely, and our neighbor as ourself.

How simple and how beautiful is this sublime precept! It seems to me to contain the essence of Christianity, and if we could but live up to it, and act upon it, how soon the millennium would be here! . . .

I am most truly yours, A. C. L. Botta.

Anne C. L. Botta

PALENVILLE, CATSKILL CLOVE, July 18, 1858.

My dear Friend: We had a charming sail up the Hudson River. I went immediately to the pilot's room, and asked permission to sit there, which was accorded to us cheerfully. The view of the river was splendid, and when we landed, the drive here to this place was delightful, and the scenery really beautiful. The inn is just by the creek, which roars steadily all the time, producing a most somnolent effect. The mountains rise on both sides for several hundred feet, and are surmounted by bold rocks.

I should like to introduce you to the woods, hills, and waterfalls of this charming region. It is raining to-day, but yesterday was beautiful and the landscape magnificent. From our window we can see through the opening of the Clove the blue hills of Massachusetts, and the varying light and shadow upon them makes them an unfailing pleasure to look at. I have never seen them so beautiful as yesterday. The falls are very beautiful, and the view from the Mountain House is really grand. I enjoy it all very much, and shall try to do some painting while here.

. . . I am reading a charming book called "Celebrated Characters," by Lamartine. Those of the first volume are Nelson, Heloise, Columbus, Bernard de Palissy, and Cicero. Although the subjects were not new to me, it is extraordinary with what a new charm he invests them all. It is a book worth owning, and if you have any leisure for reading this summer you will be charmed with this.

. . . We have had a delightful drive home from the ferry; the air hazy, and the mountains more blue and beautiful than I had ever seen them before. I was very glad to have Botta back, you may be assured; for I was rather forlorn without him. I did not know or realize before how much I am indebted to his sweet and gentle influence for the degree of equanimity to which I have attained. He is my balance-wheel, I find, and his devoted and untiring affection a necessity that cannot be dispensed with. To live, even for a few days, among persons who are perfectly indifferent to me, I find is no more easy for me now than when I was younger. Affection is my atmosphere; I cannot live without it, although I sometimes have; but it was like a fish trying to sustain himself out of water. I must love those I am with; they must love me. I think, dear friend, you have something of the same weakness,—if it is weakness,—and this is one bond of sympathy between us, among many others, all of which, as far as I know, are harmonious, none discordant.

What a sweet and pleasant friendship ours has been!

. . . No sound breaks the Sabbath stillness but the murmur of the waterfalls and the hum of the insects. We have found our cathedral to-day in this magnificent temple of nature, where God himself speaks in tones more eloquent than human tongues can approach.

His almighty power, his infinite goodness, his

boundless love, we behold at every step: in the mountains heaved up from their rocky beds, in the fields waving with their wealth of grain, in the myriads of beings, all seeming happy (except only man), in the beauty, the lavish beauty, which clothes and mantles all.

How strange that in a world of such harmony, man alone should make the discordant note! that in this great symphony of creation we only should sing out of tune, and spread over this beautiful world the pall of our own unhappy individuality!

. . . I have been reading Homer, and cannot say that I am much edified by it. As you know, "The Iliad" is a collection of poems written by poets of different ages in the history of the civilization of Greece. These were collected by Homer, who gave them the unity of an epic poem. At least this is the opinion of Vico and other eminent critics. The artistic form is beautiful and sometimes sublime; but the poem describes periods of civilization that were entirely primitive and semi-barbarous. I feel sure that the world has advanced since that time, and that our own war for the abolition of slavery and the permanence of free institutions deserves an epic poem a thousand times greater than "The Iliad."

P. S.—These lines I copied from some late work of Bulwer:

The world's most royal heritage is his who most enjoys, most loves, and most forgives.

A. C. L. B.

NEW-YORK, January 2, 1859.

My dear Friend: What a life of possibilities this is, and realities too! It is good to have lived—and good to die, when the hour comes. I think most every one feels this when the moment arrives. So many aspirations are stifled, so many hopes crushed, so many disappointments and vexations, great and small; such losses, such changes, such trials, such dangers in this "fitful fever" we call life,—that there must come a certain calm and sense of repose when we can cast it all aside, and enter on a new and higher plane. Three of my friends have passed away in the last three months, and yet, as Thomas à Kempis says, "We think more of the length of life than of the certainty of death."

. . . Why, here is your birthday coming round again! They are not "merry-go-rounds" either, to any of us. But the days pass on swifter and swifter to the end. I sometimes wish we could have another chance in life; the privilege of returning and trying it over again. We make so many mistakes, and lose so much time in learning to live; and before we have learned, we are gone. How many of our friends are gone! How few of us are left! But if in departing from this earth we can but leave behind us "footprints on the sands of time," there is nothing to regret, except the separation for a time from those we love.

. . . Everything is ordered wisely and well, and whatever we cannot control must be for the best in the end. If we could only keep this in mind, we could float over the stormy waves of this life in peace. It is the want of faith and trust that causes all our perturbations and distresses; or, the most of them.

Sincerely yours,

A. C. L. B.

. . . I have been reading a letter of Franklin which is very cheerful in its views of death. Our ideas of death seem to me to be altogether too gloomy. If there is an eternal life awaiting us on the other side of that dark passage, where we shall meet those whom we have known and loved here, and be reunited to them forever, where there will be no more sin, nor sorrow, nor parting, why do we "linger shivering on the brink, and fear to launch away"? It is because we do not live up to our belief. Practically, we are unbelievers.

New-York, December 23, 1859.

My dear Friend: . . . We are so happy in our relations with each other, Botta and I. He is so affectionate and good, and my lonely, sad life is so brightened and blessed with his beautiful affection for me. My blessings are so great and so numerous that I say often with the Psalmist, "My cup runneth over." I, more than any one, ought to be happy, and I am. Only I have talked so long and so loud about doing something that it is difficult to relinquish the idea altogether, and I have not yet done so. You well know that I have always been opposed to settling down; and I have thought that those women did wrong who left the world and restricted their sympathies and their affections to their own narrow circle.

But I begin to feel creeping over me a very strong impulse to let the world go by, and drop behind into a quiet nook,—there to stay, with the two or three who love me, while the great "machine" rolls by with its noise and dust. This, I say, is my impulse; but I shall not yield to it, because I think it a selfish one, and because I think it better for Botta that I should not, as he is already too much disposed to retire within his shell. It is clearly my duty to be "a thorn in his side," and to prevent his becoming too much a recluse and too hard a student. But society, as it is constituted, is certainly a very poor affair, and pays a very small dividend on the investments in finery and carriage hire. Still, if I can do something to make it better in my own house and by my own example, do I not owe it to "posterity" to do it,—although, as some one said, "posterity has done nothing for us"? . . .

Ever truly yours, A. C. L. B.

My dear Friend: . . . I believe I have often quoted to you these favorite lines:

> Give me the spirit that on life's rough sea
> Would have its sails filled with a lusty wind:
> Even till the sail-yards tremble, the masts creak,
> And the vast ship runs on her side, so low
> That she drinks water, and her keel plows air.

My sails, however, hang flapping about the masts, and my ship lies rolling in the harbor. I am like the great "Pennsylvania," the war-ship that was built in Philadelphia so long ago, and which has never left the harbor.

. . . There is something in this New England air that is native to me. All my early life was passed here, and this I consider a great advantage. Certain modes of life and habits of thought peculiar to this section cling always after to those who have passed their youth in it.

. . . I have just come from the funeral of a friend. Only a week ago I met him and had a pleasant little talk. How small and insignificant our little cares and troubles seem in this great presence of death, so near to each one of us! Pray, think, at the longest how soon all will be over for every dweller on the earth at this hour!

A. C. L. B.

New-York, 16th November, 1863.

. . . Do not feel, my dear friend, that your beloved son is no more. He still lives, but in another and a higher sphere, far above the cares and sorrows of this poor life, in which we wander as in a troubled dream, and which is so incomplete and unsatisfying to those who live longest here. "Whom the gods love die young," was a saying of the ancient heathen poets. May it not be true in our higher and Christian view? Except for the few who love us, and whom we love, there is nothing here to live for but our duties, which we ought to be willing to lay aside when we are called to a higher destiny. But there is everything to die for — a more enlarged sphere of action and development, the company of the great and good, the "saints of all ages," the "noble army of martyrs," the more immediate presence of the Father of love and light, and his divine love.

Why, then, should we not feel that those who have preceded us on this heavenly journey are "not lost, but gone before"? Why should we not regard their departure with cheerful resignation, and, with our "lamps trimmed and burning," prepare to follow them?

Dreams cannot picture a world so fair;
Sorrow and death may not enter there.
Time doth not breathe on its fadeless bloom
Beyond the skies and beyond the tomb.
It is there.

New-York, February 14, 1868.

My dear Friend: . . . This is your birthday, and I wish we could do something to honor it more worthily than to send these few lines of congratulation,—if it is a matter of congratulation to get a year older.

. . . Here are some sentences from Alcott, who gave a series of conversations some time ago at Dr. Bellows': "Our despair is the measure of our aspirations." "We become drudges because we cease to be ideal." "Every act of our lives should be religious." In the conversation on Victories he said, "Health is victory—one of the greatest—Position, Blessedness, Forgiveness: but the highest of all is Friendship. Whoever has not won a friend, has not entered into the kingdom of heaven. What is all this planet and universe if we have not found a friend? This is the victory of victories." "In our daily life we do not economize our solaces. Life is too mighty a trust to be wasted as we waste ourselves." Emerson says: "The one event which never loses its romance is the alighting of a superior person at our gate."

A. C. L. B.

August 4, 1877.

My dear Friend: We were grieved to hear the sad account you gave of Mr. O——. As you had no hope, we are expecting to hear that all is over, and that that genial and kindly spirit, so full of energy and life, has passed away from us forever. Looking back over an acquaintance and friendship of so many years (for I knew him long before I knew you), and remembering what a power he has been and how much he has done, I find it difficult to realize that the world will soon know him no more. But religion tells us that with death the scene of our activity only changes, and science confirms this belief in the great doctrine of the "conservation of forces." What we shall do in this untried state; how much of our individuality we shall retain; whether we shall know and love those whom we have known and loved here,—these are great questions which are always asked and never answered, and never can be answered except by those who have passed to "the undiscovered country, from whose bourn no traveler returns," that country toward which we are all hastening so fast.

Sincerely yours, A. C. L. BOTTA.

TO MISS S. A.

NEWPORT, R. I., July, 1849.

My dear Friend: Feeling that you would be very much interested in the events of the past few days at this charming resort, and particularly in the reception which was given Mr. Clay, I do myself the pleasure of writing to you and giving you an account of it. When he arrived here, a dense multitude covered every inch of ground in sight; the flags were all flying, and as the cars approached, the bells began to ring most merrily. When the venerable head of Mr. Clay appeared towering above the crowd, handkerchiefs waved, cheers rent the air, and the coldest hearts were stirred with enthusiasm. Hero-worship, it appears to me, is one of the original and higher instincts of our nature, and one which is closely allied to the religious sentiment. We see what is great and good and superior to ourselves, and we seek to ally ourselves to it by our admiration and reverence; we touch the hem of the garment, and a virtue is given out from it.

The personal popularity of Mr. Clay, aside from his political standing, is no mystery to those who witness the extraordinary kindness of his manner toward all who approach him. Ill and wearied, as he must be to the last degree, he loses all thought of himself in his desire to give pleasure to others, and it is painful to see with how little consideration they avail themselves of this high-bred courtesy. Deputations of men, women, and children from the surrounding towns pour in upon him, and he is introduced to sixty or seventy people; he shakes hands, says something agreeable to each one, with the courage and fortitude of a hero and a martyr,—as he is,—and retires to his room to recruit for the next mission. It is of no use to refuse to see them; they will be admitted; and it was announced the other day, in the advertisement of an excursion that was to take place from New London to Newport, that persons would thus have an opportunity to see and converse with Mr. Clay. Whatever our national faults may be, a fastidious delicacy is not one of them. The presence of Mr. Clay and the members of his family which accompany him has made this a most attractive season at Newport. To have seen and spoken with one so beloved of our country, who belongs to her history,—a fixed star in her constellation of statesmen and patriots,—is an event to be remembered and spoken of with equal pride and pleasure.

You well know there has been much said and written on the subject of manners at watering-places; and some persons are disposed to take offense because a millionaire, or a clique, or a set, chance to be exclusive. From my point of view, I must say that in the absence of an hereditary and acknowledged aristocracy in our country, there is also—unfortunately too often—an absence of that personal dignity and self-respect which supplies an entire confidence in one's own position.

If as a people we were more eager for the respect of ourselves, I am sure we should find less difficulty in commanding that of others.

Now, my dear friend, write to me very soon, and believe me

Most affectionately yours,

ANNE C. LYNCH.

NEWPORT, R. I., September 3, 1849.

My dear Friend: I was very glad to hear from you, and will certainly try to keep you informed of any interesting event connected with life here in Newport. . . . Society people have been very busy preparing for the fancy ball, which has now passed, and with this the season of gaiety closes. It was a most gorgeous assemblage of people; and, you know, a fancy ball, like a republican government, allows each one the pleasure of displaying his peculiar attractions or gifts without restriction; and on this fair field the plainest person, with proper taste in the selection of costume, may often bear away the palm from acknowledged beauty.

Mr. Clay was present for a short time at the commencement of the ball, with his kind words and benignant smiles, delighting the gay groups that surrounded him. He leaves Newport this evening on his return to Kentucky. Notwithstanding the intense fatigue he daily experiences from calls and letters, which people continually pour in upon him about their own affairs, and to which he scrupulously replies, and various other annoyances sufficient to wear out an ordinary man in good health, he is, in spite of it all, essentially improved. An incident occurred yesterday morning at this house which occasioned some little sensation. It was ascertained that Levi, Mr. Clay's personal attendant, was not to be found. There was but one inference to be drawn from this fact, and that was that he had run away. Mr. Clay took no steps to regain him, for he had already freed his father and mother, and was about to do the same for Levi; but his great anxiety was in reference to the future fate of the absentee, who was not gifted with the Yankee faculty of getting along.

Mr. Clay admitted that Levi had done no more than he would do himself in the same circumstances, reconciled himself to the laugh his Abolition friends would enjoy at his expense, and supplied himself with another attendant. An hour after, to the surprise of all, Levi made his appearance and resumed his office of *valet de chambre*, to the great annoyance of the new incumbent. He stated that throughout the journey to the East he had been urged by Abolitionists, with every inducement that could be held out, to leave his master, and that at last they had offered him three hundred dollars. An old and freed servant of Mr. Clay advised him to go and accept the money and return to his master. Whether Levi had determined to act on this sage advice does not appear. At all events, the parties began mutually to distrust each other, and with an honesty worthy of imitation in higher places, Levi gave up the bribe and returned. The laugh has thus changed sides.

It is easily understood how an Abolitionist, or, indeed, any humane person, might secrete a runaway slave—a generous nature could not do otherwise; but to seduce by bribery or other means an attached servant, as in this case, is unworthy of the cause and its advocates. . . .

I am very sincerely yours, A. C. L.

TO MR. F. S.

NEWPORT, R. I., August 28, 1849.

My dear Friend: It is a long time since I have had a word from you; and thinking that the fault might be at my own door, I take my pen and proceed to communicate with you at once. I wish you would come here and spend a few days, for I am sure you would enjoy it. There are many nice people and much entertaining.

Among the most agreeable features of society here, Miss Jane Stuart has opened her cottage and studio for the weekly reception of visitors, and her rooms are always crowded with the fashion, beauty, genius, and distinction assembled here. Her extreme kindness in receiving, and her great talent in entertaining her guests, render the morning of this reunion the most delightful of the whole week.

Huntington, the artist who has taken a studio here for the season, also receives visitors one or two days in the week. He is just giving the last touches to one of his most beautiful compositions, "The Marys at the Sepulcher." The angel at the door, pointing upward, says, "He is not here; he is risen." The divine repose of this figure, the mingled sorrow and faith in the expression of the others, compare with nothing I have seen except the "Dead Christ" of Scheffer, which it far surpasses in beauty of coloring. This picture has been purchased by the Art Union, and will be one of the attractions of the gallery. Huntington is not content to reproduce flesh and blood in their ordinary forms: in his pictures he embodies the immaterial. He paints sentiments—soul; and this is certainly the highest province of the art.

I am sincerely yours, A. C. L.

TO MRS. M. L.

New-York, September 30, 1849.

My dear Friend: Here I am again in New-York, and to a genuine New-Yorker there is no season more delightful than this month of September. Then "the town" returns from its summer rambles and is again to be seen in Broadway, the front blinds above "Bleecker" are thrown hospitably open, the door-plates brightened, and friends and circles long parted meet in pleasant reunions, compare notes, and over all the retiring sun of the Indian summer sheds its golden rays and its genial warmth. This is really the beginning of the New-York year, which lasts only until the first of July or the first of August, when there is a universal suspension of hostilities,—the gay and business world treats itself to a vacation, which by this time becomes indispensable to its overwrought energies.

Life is measured by the number of thoughts, emotions, and sensations experienced, and hence there is an intensity of action in these mental processes that it is impossible to resist. Like atmospheric influences, or like that subtle and mysterious power that we call the "spirit of the age," it penetrates the closet of the scholar and the workshop of the artisan. Its outward manifestation is in the form of "hurry." People rush on to the ferry-boats before they touch the wharf, rush to the extreme end, and are prepared to rush off, at the imminent risk of drowning, as soon as the boat gets within jumping distance of the opposite dock. There is a universal want of time, though, as some one has very wisely said, "We have all the time there is." Why do we drive on so? . . .

Sincerely yours, A. C. L.

TO MISS EMILY O. BUTLER.

EVERGREEN FARM, N. Y., August 9, 1855.

Dear Emily: . . . The country about here is charming. We are about midway between the Sound

18

and the Hudson River, and, contrary to our expectations, we have found it very cool. I am becoming so much in love with it that I am almost willing to give up New-York for the country. These splendid skies and gorgeous sunsets, in contrast to the little patch of blue that we catch a glimpse of in Ninth street, these beautiful fields and waving trees, compared with our dusty streets and brick walls, all seem to tell me that life in the country is the truest life; and a better reason still is: "God made the country and man made the town."

However, when I am once more in the whirl of New-York life, I shall listen to arguments on the other side, doubtless, and be reminded that the city has attractions not less than the woods and the fields, although so different in kind.

I hoped to have accomplished some reading this summer, and to have again taken up my favorite pursuits of drawing and painting. The most I can say is, I have made a beginning. I have commenced reading some historical works, making notes as I go along. I am teaching my nephew, a boy of fourteen years, two or three hours of the day; and this, with a little walking, driving, and all the other details of life, makes up the day, and makes off with it, long before I am ready to part with it.

Let me tell you a secret, my dear, that may be of value to you, as you are young and just beginning in life. I have a secret sorrow, a feeling of remorse, that nothing in the present or the future can remove or alleviate; and this is a sense of time wasted, of faculties unemployed, and of both having been frittered away during the past years of my life. How much I might have done, and how little I have done, is the thought that always oppresses me. It is too late for me to remedy the evil, but not too late for you to prevent it; therefore I would wish you to take warning from me, and spare yourself these bitter reflections when you reach my age. A word more: make notes of what you read; in the "Queens of England," for instance. Each one had prominent events in her reign; note these down, and look them over until they are firmly fixed in your mind. This may seem laborious at first, but the advantage you will derive from it will more than compensate you for the effort. . . .

The cool mornings and evenings now begin to remind us that the summer is "bearing hence her roses," and that we must soon be preparing to return to the city. I have passed the last few weeks so pleasantly here that I am really unhappy at the thought of leaving this lovely spot.

Miss Bremer tells a story, in one of her books, of an Eastern prince who asked a sage for some maxim that should enable him to bear both prosperity and adversity. The sage gave him these words, "And this, too, will pass away."

Now, my dear young friend, good night. Let me hear from you soon, and believe me always affectionately yours,

A. C. L. B.

Anne C. L. Botta

TO DR. H. W. BELLOWS.[1]

NEW-YORK, December 6, 1858.

My dear Dr. Bellows: As I have not for some time had an opportunity to speak with you, I must take the opportunity to write. I confess that my instincts of humanity are outraged at the idea of exciting among the negroes of the South a servile insurrection, which it was the avowed intention of John Brown to do, and which Dr. Cheever and others seem to regard as the highest manifestation of nobleness, patriotism, and Christianity. On Sunday last, Dr. Cheever invoked God to preserve us from mob violence, in view of his own church being attacked, and is quite ready to fall back for protection upon the laws of the land in such an extremity, while he despises them so much in other cases. If the violence of a mob in a Christian community is to be deprecated, with how much more abhorrence should it be regarded among such an

1 This letter was written some three years before the South took up arms against the United States Government in defense of slavery. On her wedding-tour, in 1855, Mrs. Botta had visited some plantations owned by friends in the South, and had noticed the intense anxiety amounting almost to a panic which there prevailed, due to the fear of slave insurrection. This was prompted and encouraged by a small party of fanatics in the North, who thought the abolition of slavery could be obtained only through such an insurrection, which would have wiped out slavery by a general slaughter of the slaveholders. While Mrs. Botta openly condemned slavery, both in itself and in its results, she protested against, and could not but denounce, such a barbarous method of dealing with this problem. And she rejoiced when the subsequent war, which was brought about by the Southern people, supplied a radical solution of this problem through the regular action of the government.

ignorant, half-barbarous population as the slaves of the South, when the victims are to be the wives, sisters, and children of our friends and brothers!

To me the terror manifested through the South at the bare idea of such an uprising is not ridiculous, as it seems to be to most of our Northern journals and some of the people. I deeply sympathize with it, and unhesitatingly condemn John Brown for his reckless disregard for human life, and his one-sided philanthropy that would secure a real or imagined good to the slave, no matter at what cost to humanity or to civilization.

I admire courage; but without wisdom it is a dangerous gift. If John Brown has manifested the highest Christian principle, as his admirers claim, then for me the lessons of Christ must be learned anew; for I do not think his course sanctioned by our Saviour's example or precepts, any more than the burning of heretics by the Inquisition, or of Quakers by the Puritans, though both were done in his name.

John Brown was simply, in my view, a brave and worthy man who had dwelt on the subject until he became a monomaniac. It seems to me that many people of intellect and discretion in our community are losing their mental balance, and allowing their instincts and passions to guide them in this great crisis, rather than their higher judgment, which the state of things so imperiously demands the exercise of. We all know that slavery is a great evil, and the blot on our national escutcheon; and we have a right to say so, and to express our abhorrence of it. But that we have the right to murder the slaveholder in order to free the slave, or to incite the slave to do so, or even to glorify him who does, I do not believe, though he may do it in the name of God. Slavery is the inherited curse of the South. She came into the Union with this mark upon her, and was accepted with it by our fathers, whose patriotism and wisdom we never tire of praising. In the struggle that achieved our independence, the South bore her part bravely; and Virginia gave us Washington, through whom we established our nationality and formed a republic which is even now the forlorn hope of humanity throughout the world.

Suppose we dissolve the Union by withdrawing ourselves, or by driving the South out of it. Do we thereby extinguish the evil of slavery? I do not see that we do, but we certainly do extinguish the hopes that humanity has risked upon our experiment of self-government. Slavery is the growth of more than two centuries. It cannot be destroyed in a day, nor in a longer time, without producing a moral shock that would be, perhaps, a still greater evil. I would watch, and pray, and wait. This is not the doctrine of the fanatics on either side of Mason and Dixon's line, whose limited and distorted vision is confined to the narrow limit of the present, and whose mutual bitterness and hate are sowing a wind which, apparently, will rise a whirlwind upon us all. In this emergency it seems to me that all who have a calm word to utter should speak out, and at once.

I am most respectfully and sincerely yours,

A. C. L. Botta.

EXTRACTS FROM LETTERS TO MR. BOTTA.[1]

NEW-YORK, March, 1865.

My dear Botta: . . . I am reading Marcus Aurelius,— every day a few sentences, and they seem to give me wings. Here is one "wing": "On every occasion which leads thee to vexation, apply the principle that this is not a misfortune, but that to bear it nobly is good fortune." "Out of the universe, everything from the beginning which happens, has been apportioned and spun out to thee." "Everything harmonizes with me which is harmonious to thee, O Universe! Nothing for me is too early, nor too late, which is in due time for thee. Everything is fruit to me which thy seasons bring, O Nature! From thee are all things; in thee are all things; and to thee all things return." . . .

. . . I have all the time a great sense of wasted life, undeveloped powers, and unused faculties, which presses upon me with a dreadful weight. Still, I do not see how it is to be avoided; so I try to be cheerful under it. There are so many books I wish to read, so much I would know, so much I would do; and I live on learning and doing — nothing — except complaining.

[1] These extracts are from letters Mrs. Botta wrote to her husband while he was in Europe.

. . . I am sure it would not be well for us to have everything we want. Life would be too pleasant, and we should not be willing to leave it when our summons comes. We have just now been speculating as to when you will come, but are lost in conjecture.

. . . I know that danger and death are at our sides every moment of our lives, and you know my unwavering conviction, that an inscrutable series of cause and effect constitutes all the phenomena of the world; so that there can be no accident, no occurrence, in the universe, except such as was designed to take place from all eternity. All that remains for us to do, then, is to launch ourselves on this great sea of being—to strike out for the great landmarks we wish to reach, and in our feeble way struggle toward them, well knowing that the great currents will bear us along: perhaps to our proposed ends, perhaps to absorb us in its own essence.

. . . I look off on the ocean and think of it as the emblem of that great unknown and untraversed sea that we must all launch our boats on, sooner or later. But it would be a very pleasant thought if we knew that before doing this one might live out one's idea of life. Mine is, and always has been, so distinct and so unlike the actual life, and so different from that of most other persons. I have always felt like those eagles which have been hatched in Central Park. They hop from one perch to another in those little cages, their wings, that were made to sweep the empyrean, folded uselessly by their sides, and their eyes that could face the sun, bounded in their vision to the limits of a few hundred feet. Now I must say good-by for this time; so fly home, my eagle, and we will open our cage-doors and go forth together, you and your Anne.

. . . I am reading now De Tocqueville's life and letters; but am sorry to say I do not get much time for reading. How I would like to be able to study! There is so much that I would like to know in science, in art, in history, in biography; so many noble people that I might be acquainted with in books, where their lives and thoughts are chronicled, if they are not often met in real life. But after it all, some people say, it comes to the same thing in the last analysis: a little carbon and a pailful of water. But the sense of life, and of intellectual life, in me is very strong and vivid, and claims its proper food, before it comes to that point. This is the only complaint I have to make of life: that circumstances, and physical inability on my part, prevent my wings from doing much more than flapping idly by my sides.

. . . Take all the pleasure you can, my love, as you go along. The present we are sure of, and if we store up sweet memories, we are sure of the past, and of something pleasant in the future,—your *bête noire;* for you always see it through the present, or allow it to steal the present from your sight.

. . . It is not the swiftness of time that disturbs me, but only the thought that it is so poorly filled up. I want its sands to be " diamonds as they pass," and they prove to be only very coarse desert sands.

. . . The summer is passing away so rapidly, and our summers, mine at least, are getting so few; but I do not mind that; I only want to make the most of them, to employ and enjoy them to the best advantage. If I could only stop longing and aspiring for that which it is not in my power to attain, but is only just near enough to keep me always running after it, like the donkey that followed an ear of corn which was tied fast to a stick! But now I must stop short in my reflections. Perhaps, if you should be detained in Italy until the winter, I might join you there. How I would enjoy it! You Europeans can never know what a charm the Old World has for us, who have no antiquity, no romance, and so short a history (though in every other respect the greatest people the world ever saw); and for one like me, who loves history, poetry, and art so much more than anything besides, and who lives only in that atmosphere, and merely vegetates in all others, it is indescribably delightful.

I look forward with much pleasure to the sometime when I hope to enjoy it all with you.

. . . You know, my dear, that we can die only once; that death is only a swallowing up of our poor individuality in the great ocean of being ; and that life, while we have our small "pipes" in communication with this ocean, is full of variety, emotion, sensation, joy, pain, and pleasure. So let us dash on with it, enjoying what we can, bearing what is to be borne, and meeting the close of it all, which at the farthest cannot be far off, with heroism and calmness. Death may come to us any moment; or to those whom we love, which is worse. My desire is to live for your sake more than for my own. And while we both are as well as we are now, what is the use of looking forward and fearing something which may never happen?

My dearest one, I could go on preaching through another sheet; but, as you know, I have always to turn the crank to my own organ; so I will stop here. . . .

. . . The time is passing away very fast, even here; and between reading and modeling I am very busy. I have just finished reading the third volume of the "Dutch Republic," making in all about sixteen hundred pages in less than three weeks. It is extremely interesting and brilliant, and I have learned a great deal in reading it. I have now just begun one of Scott's novels. Now that I have a little real leisure, I am overwhelmed with the number of books I want to read.

. . . Mr. V—— came to see me yesterday. I met him at Goupil's, and had a very pleasant talk with him; he called to finish the conversation. You know he is an artist, and paints extremely well. I showed him my two busts, and he was delighted at the power he said they evinced. He praised them more than (with my modesty, which you know is so great) I dare to repeat; and exhorted me by all means to give up every other pursuit and devote myself to this art. He was sure that I could distinguish myself and do honor to the sex even now. I do not care so much for these last results; but if I could give expression to the love and idea of beauty that is in my soul, I should be happy.

. . . I have been reading in the "Journal of Speculative Philosophy" an article by Schopenhauer on Immortality. Did you read it? He says, "That which cries out, 'I, I myself wish to exist!' is not yourself alone, but all that has the least vestige of consciousness. Hence this desire of ours is just that which is not individual, but common to all without exception; it does not originate in individuality, but in the very nature of existence itself. It is essential to anybody who lives; nay, it is that through which all conscious individuality exists. It seems to belong only to the individual, because it can only become conscious in the individual. What cries so loud in us for existence, does so only through the mediation of the individual; immediately and essentially it is the will to exist, or to live, and this will is one and the same in all of us."

I cannot follow the argument. Our own essence

is this universal will to live. Individuality is a restriction to be got rid of. I always said so! But the day is cloudy, and so you will say is Schopenhauer, as manifested through this medium. . . .

I am always with you in spirit, and hope you will soon return to your own ANNE.

TO MISS N. W.

NEW-YORK, March 25, 1867.

My dear little Friend: . . . I am deeply interested in you because you are young, and youth has such splendid possibilities for the future. If you only knew it, you would avoid all our mistakes.

Some years ago, in order to remedy one of the mistakes or deficiencies in my own education, I compiled the volume which I send and beg you to accept, from about seventy of the best works I could find on the literatures of different countries. It was so useful to me that I published it for the benefit of other learners. You are yet too young, perhaps, to care much about the subjects of which it treats; but you will soon wish to know something of the works which make nations great, and of their great writers, and I am sure this book will assist you. If you will provide yourself with a blank book and each day select and transcribe a few lines from each author named, or from the most prominent ones, at the end of a year you will find yourself familiar with all the great writers of the world, or with their names and the character of their works. Translations from them all are easily accessible, and if at any time you need any assistance or suggestion, if you will write to me, I shall be most happy to aid you.

With my best wishes, I am sincerely your friend,

ANNE C. L. BOTTA.

TO THE HON. L. M., OF LONDON.

NEW-YORK, November 15, 1870.

My dear Sir: I wish to thank you, in my own name and in that of the friends who were with me last evening, for the noble thoughts you expressed, the wise and friendly counsels you gave us.

We need very much many things that you of the Old World can give us, and I am sure that if the English and American people could see more of each other, the effect on both would be most salutary. However we may fall short of our ideal, we have one; and I believe that nations and individuals who have an ideal can never become wholly degenerate.

The political corruption among our public men, odious and disheartening as it is, after all is confined to the few. The great masses of our people are not unprincipled and venal, however neglectful they apparently may be of the public good. And when our officials reach a certain lower depth, they will be overthrown, as you told us they had been in England.

The recuperative powers of humanity under the conditions that our country offers are wonderful. During the winter that followed the election of Lincoln, when the South was seceding from the Union, State after State, and there seemed to be no power to prevent the disintegration of the country, the feeling that our nationality was destroyed became universal. Politicians were aghast and powerless; patriots and wise men believed that the States would become independent, and New-York a free city. (By the way, I am sure it was the general tone of the people and the press that so misled England.) But when the flag was fired upon at Fort Sumter, the great heart of the nation was electrified into life, into a new life; the crumbling elements of nationality crystallized and took permanent form; and the abstract sentiment of patriotism became vital and active. Since then, like you, we do not despair of the Republic.

But while we admit that our institutions have much unsound fruit, our apple-trees have done better for us, and I hope you will not think it a liberty if I send you, as I do with this note, a box containing some Newtown pippins, which I am told bear exportation better than any other variety. And since you are interested in education, I send also a little book which I have compiled from various sources in order to give young persons a bird's-eye view of the great field of literature, and a hint of the treasures it contains.

We shall be delighted to see you here again, and

let me hope that you will bring some of the ladies of your family with you.

Wishing you a pleasant voyage on the part of Mr. Botta as well as myself, I am, dear sir, very truly yours,

ANNE C. L. BOTTA.

TO MR. ANDREW D. WHITE.

NEW-YORK, November 4, 1864.

My dear Sir: A friend in Boston has sent me a copy of your "Outlines of a Course of Lectures on History," the reading of which has afforded me a degree of pleasure that must be my excuse for the liberty I take in writing to you, and for expressing the hope that the lectures themselves will not long remain hidden in manuscript.

We have valuable special histories, but no general history that I know of, of such vast scope and able generalization as that of which your comprehensive analysis must form the basis. Such a work—which in its complete form would include the Oriental, Egyptian, and Grecian civilizations, as well as the best, and in my opinion the grandest, development of humanity in our own country,—would be a literary monument worthy of the nineteenth century. And to produce such a work especially at this time would be one of the highest efforts of patriotism. Our people have "builded better than they knew," and they have accepted our free institutions as they accept the sunshine and the air, without knowing what it has cost the race to attain such a condition of freedom. In general, they are not only ignorant of the great facts and significance of history, but they are unacquainted with the method of studying them. Special histories, however elaborate and complete in themselves, must from this nature be fragments of the great whole. An artist can never comprehend the grandeur of a vast cathedral by the minute study of its detached arches and columns. The structure must be first seen as a whole; and so, it seems to me, we should contemplate history,—first, in its unity; then, in its details.

To lift the veil from the past, and rehearse to the American people the grand drama of the ages, to interpret to them the significance, the importance, and the dignity of the *rôle* they are to perform in it,—that they may not play their parts as the daughters of Milton read the Greek poets, without any intelligence of their meaning,—would be a great and noble work. And without pretending to be a sibyl or even a medium, I feel inspired to predict that you are to be the author of such a work, and that a brilliant future lies before you. I am glad to hear that you are still young. Our young country requires for its highest expression the ardor and enthusiasm which rarely survives the meridian of life.

It was my wish to have spoken of some plans of my own relative to a school history, and to have asked your suggestions and counsel. But my letter is already too long. I will only ask your acceptance of a copy of a "Handbook of Universal Literature," which I have prepared for popular reading, and in which I have aimed to give to the history of literature in an elementary form, that unity which seems to me so desirable in all history.

Very respectfully yours,

ANNE C. L. BOTTA.

NEW-YORK, November 5, 1884.

. . . I have just laid down your speech before the German Society, after reading it with very great pleasure and at a most opportune moment,—when assurances that all is not scum in the cauldron, but that below there is noble endeavor and earnest purpose, are so much needed. Of late we must admit that the scum has fearfully predominated.

I have not yet really begun the "History," for I find it difficult to get the books I need. When they are owned by the libraries, they are always out. I am, however, looking over what I can find of the "Philosophy of history," and would like you to suggest any work that you think would be of use. Just now I am reading "An Inquiry into the Theories of History," by Adams, which I find interesting, but too argumentative. I would like to set forth in a few pages the most conclusive or probable theory or theories on the scope or meaning of this great drama that the human race has been performing for thousands of years, and what the probable tendency is; or showing that it is toward a higher development.

I think that the grouping together of the great events in the history of each nation in chronological order, preceded by a summary of the significance of it all, would be interesting and popular.

So few, except scholars like yourself, have time to gather all these materials together. If you could spare me one of those small condensed works of which you spoke to me, I would return it in a very few days.

A. C. L. B.

PARIS, October 21, 1887.

. . . Although we are leaving Paris to-morrow morning and I am very busy, I feel impelled to write you just a few lines on this sad anniversary.

You have now sounded the depths of your sorrow and despair; but in these depths you must not linger. "Stand where you are" was Goethe's translation of Archimedes' fulcrum for lifting up the earth. See what you can do in the blank future before you. There are two great principles that we must adopt and live up to as far as possible if we would have life endurable,— one, that all is wisely and well ordered; and the other, that we accept it. When Carlyle shouted in derision at Margaret Fuller when she said that she accepted the universe, he expressed the sum and substance of Froude's biography of him. He accepted nothing, but was at war with himself and with everything around him. "Learn to bear the cross," says Thomas à Kempis, "and it will soon bear thee; but if thou resist it, it becomes an intolerable burden."

Death and old age await us all, and this world is not such a beautiful place that we should wish always to stay here, if we could. Happiness is certainly not the end of existence; but struggle, evolution, disappointment seem to be. But of happiness have you not had a larger share than most men? Thirty years of wedded life with one of the purest, most beautiful and lovely of women is an experience that falls to the lot of few. That she left you without a moment's warning seems to me to be the most desirable end: no lingering disease, no agonizing pain; but passing away like a dream, in the fullness of life and beauty, without even on her part the agony of separation. I can only say, may my end be like hers.

Think of Longfellow, who saw his wife burning to death before him; of Mrs. P—— suffering for nearly three years pain like a dagger in her heart. You are bereft, indeed; but you have yet something left. You have children who love you; you have not to toil for your daily bread; you have a knowledge of the past,—that, as Sir Thomas Browne says, "makes you as old as the world." Yet you are in the prime of manhood, with fair health, and there is much for you to do. Do not, I beg of you, let the past be a tomb in which you bury yourself; she would not wish it, I know, if she could speak,—she would rather be a beautiful memory that will be always with you, that "age cannot wither." Rejoice in the past, and courageously face the drear future. I spare you any further words, but I felt that I must say as much as I have: because having, as I said, reached the depth of your despair, you must turn away from it as far as possible, and give yourself to regarding it in other aspects.

With deep sympathy from us both, and hoping soon to see you, I am always sincerely yours,

A. C. L. B.

November 24, 1888.

. . . Let me ask you, my dear friend, why you continue to give yourself up to the keeping of all these sad anniversaries? You have descended to the very depths of your sorrow; why indulge yourself in brooding over it, in cherishing it, and in holding yourself always there? Without any disloyalty to the dear one, you owe it to yourself and to her memory to be "up and doing," and, above all, to accept the burden that has been laid on you, and to bear it with heroism and with resignation.

You see I cannot help preaching, do what I will; but even that you by this time have learned to bear.

A. C. L. B.

December 26, 1888.

. . . Do not think that I really meant to find fault with you in my last letter, or to reproach you in any way. I know that you are making a desperate struggle to keep up, and doing all that man can do under the circumstances. While I preach courage, occupation, and all that, perhaps you will scarcely believe that I have, ever since I grew up, been subject to attacks of depression that, while they lasted, made life almost unendurable. A sudden realization of the emptiness, shortness, nothingness of life comes over me; such, as I am persuaded, it is not in the plan of creation that human beings should have. And then I need preaching to, and praying for, badly. As people are said to whistle sometimes to keep their courage up, so, perhaps, they sometimes preach.

A. C. L. B.

December 31, 1888.

. . . While in Rome we were taken to the studio of Monteverde, where we saw a most beautiful monument: a recumbent figure with an angel bending over it. I have never seen anything of the kind to compare with it. I would have liked very much to have a photograph of it; but I learned that some American, who liked the work very much and pretended that he would order a copy of it, obtained a photograph from the artist, sent it to Carrara and had it copied; so I did not like to ask for one, lest I should be ranked with my thrifty countryman. What sad news about the Crown Prince! You who know him so well must feel it deeply, when even strangers who never saw him find the case so pathetic.

A. C. L. B.

TO MR. J. M.

July 31, 1875.

My dear Friend: Referring to our conversation of a few days since, I send you the copy of a letter written one hundred years ago by Mrs. Samuel Gray, of Windham, Conn., to her son, Lieutenant-Colonel Ebenezer Gray, who was my grandfather. At that time he was serving in the Revolutionary Army near Boston, Mass., and this letter shows the patriotism, heroic courage, and religious faith of the women at that period. It also shows that I come directly from a race which filled a prominent place in the establishment of our national independence. Of this, indeed, I am very proud.

A. C. L. B.

WINDHAM, CONN., July 31, A. D. 1775.

Dear Child: I this morning heard that Mr. Trumbull, who passed through town in haste last evening, said that you are preparing to meet the enemy, or to drive them from their new-begun intrenchments. I could not hear it without some emotion of soul, although I firmly believe that God is able to deliver, and will deliver, us out of the hands of these unnatural enemies in his own time. Our cause is just, I don't doubt; and God in his holy and righteous providence has called you there to defend our just rights and privileges. I would commit you into the hands of a just and merciful God, who alone is able to defend you. Confessing my utter unworthiness of the least mercy, I would trust in unmerited mercy through Jesus Christ, for all that strength, courage, and fortitude that you stand in need of in the business he is calling you to. Trust in the Lord and be of good courage; the eye of the Lord is upon them that fear him, upon them that hope in his mercy. Confess your sins daily before the Lord and forsake every evil way; walk in all the Commandments of the Lord. Be careful to set a good example before those that are under you, especially in observing the Sabbath. The surest way of conquering our enemies is to turn from every evil way and seek the Lord with all our hearts with confession of our sins. I am more afeared of our sins than all the forces of our enemy. As to profane swearing, which is very common in camps, I always thought you were not inclined to, and I trust you will take all possible care to prevent it in those that fall under your care.

I think we have abundant reason to praise the name of the Lord for his wonderful assistance and deliverances our people have experienced at one time and another, especially at Bunker's Hill. Well may we say, had it not been the Lord who was on our side, when such a number of troops rose up and surrounded our people, then they had swallowed us up quick when their wrath was kindled against us. These merciful assurances of God for us ought to encourage us to call upon God, and strengthen our faith in him. That you may put your trust in God, and go on with courage and fortitude to whatever work or business you may be called to, is the sincere prayer of your loving mother,

LYDIA GRAY.

TO MR. EMERSON.

NEW-YORK, April 13, 1868.

Dear Mr. Emerson: I have delayed acknowledging your letter of February 24th and the very excellent photograph which accompanied it, hoping that I might see Edward on his return; I was so unfortunate as to miss him when he passed through here.

I thank you very much for the picture; it seems to me to convey a better idea of the "real presence" than any I have seen of you. The other which you promise I shall hope you will bring when you make to me the long-expected visit. Now, I am afraid if I say anything about this visit you will think me importunate, and perhaps I am. But life seems to me so short, the terminus so near at hand, great and noble souls so rare, that I would crowd into this remnant of existence that is left, all the beautiful experiences that I can lay hold of. I have heard the admonition of the poet :

> To take in sail,—
> Contract thy firmament
> To compass of a tent ;
> Economize the failing river ;
> Leave the many, and hold the few ;
> Soften the fall with wary foot,

and I am seeking only to carry out his thoughts. Let me say, then, once for all, that whenever the curtain of my "tent" is lifted for you to enter, there comes and always will come with you the most serene and beautiful influences. And so you will not wonder that I always wish you to come.

I know well how little there is in this great city with its too material life to attract you from your home and your study, and how little I have to offer you: only the consciousness that I have aspired without attaining. But if, as some one says, "our despair is the measure of our aspirations," mine have been great indeed.

A. C. L. B.

Anne C. L. Botta

TO MR. JAMES A. FROUDE, LONDON.

NEW-YORK, October 16, 1873.

My dear Mr. Froude: It is just one year ago to-day that I first met you here, and I celebrate the anniversary by indulging myself in the pleasure of writing to you, a pleasure I have postponed from day to day for a long time, partly from the many distractions I am always subjected to, partly too, perhaps, from the desire to have something so pleasant in anticipation; for as soon as my letter is mailed, it will be such a long time before the reply will come to give me the opportunity of writing again. To me there is a great charm in having friends on the other side of the Atlantic; the enchantment of distance gives such scope to the imagination; and then getting letters is like receiving "communications" from the other world. I have observed that all believers in spiritualism are the happiest of people, and I suppose it is that their relations with the invisible world lift them out of the press and weariness of every-day life. . . .

We are delighted to hear that you so far favor pilgrimages that in another year you will make one to the shrine of St. Jonathan: he goes on working miracles, sometimes in the name of the powers of light and sometimes in that of the powers of darkness,—but so that it is no wonder that you in the Old World cannot tell which. As I think that everything works together for good, I do not fear the result. Besides the pilgrimage, I see that some of your clergy are advocating a return to the confessional. Sometimes I think that this institution is founded on some great necessity of the human soul for the expression of what is deepest in it, to some higher intelligence capable of understanding its needs, aspirations, and doubts. If the priest was always the really superior being he claims to be, living in an atmosphere so far removed from earth as to be above the line of perpetual congelation, I should for myself think it a privilege to confess; but, as it is, we must wait for a new order of beings. One of our poets says we carry about within us unwritten and unspoken tragedies:

> We are spirits clad in veils;
> Heart by heart was never seen;
> All our deep communion fails
> To remove the shadowy screen;

and this isolation alone would make religions a necessity, especially for women. Men, being made of sterner stuff, may perhaps do without it; but we never can.

Since our return to the city there has been a great deal going on in New-York. We have had two great opera companies, with Lucca, Nilsson, and hosts of other celebrities; Salvini, the Italian actor, perhaps the greatest living performer; the Evangelical Alliance, in session for ten days with delegates from every part of the world; followed by the Free Religious Convention, the Woman's Suffrage Association, with lectures of more or less note, and others that fill up the interstices; and, above all this, a great financial crisis which has shaken Wall street to its foundations, ruined very many people, though no one among my immediate acquaintances. In all the rushing and surging of the elements that go to make up the young and vigorous life of this country, I often long for the repose of an older civilization. I am sure I should enjoy nothing so much as to spend a year or two abroad,—provided you were not to get up a revolution in England, and provided France, Italy, and Germany were bound to keep the peace. . . .

Believe me, very sincerely yours,

A. C. L. BOTTA.

February 18, 1874.

My dear Mr. Froude: The telegraph of Sunday brought to us the news of your great loss, and I am unwilling to let a steamer cross the Atlantic without carrying to you some expression of our sympathy. Death has come so near to me within the last few weeks that I have a keener sense of your bereavement than I could otherwise have had. My mother, it is true, had outlived her family and friends and her interest in everything except her affection for me; and I could not have desired to prolong her life, if it had been in my power to do so. But in parting with her, it seems that a portion of my life has been sent away, and an overwhelming sense of loss all the while oppresses me. I can well understand, then, what you suffer in the losing of your companion, friend, and wife, in the prime of womanhood and without warning; for doubtless the event must have been very sudden. If I have read you aright, you, like all men of the finest type, have especial need of all the care and devotion that you have enjoyed. Women have so much to suffer in this world, and have so much more endurance than men, that, weak as they may be in some respects, they are yet strong enough to support and sustain them. But, bereft as you are now of your sweet consoler, do not, I pray you, curse God and die. "Despair is equally opposed to religion and to science," as Thomas à Kempis says. "The cross is always ready for thee, and everywhere waits for thee; thou canst not escape it; but if thou bear it cheerfully, it will bear thee, and lead thee to thy desired end. If thou bear it unwillingly, thou makest for thyself a new burden and increaseth thy load; and yet, notwithstanding, thou must bear it." This is all true in a philosophical as in a religious sense. . . .

I am, very sincerely yours, A. C. L. B.

March 28, 1874.

My dear Mr. Froude: On coming home from my walk, a day or two since, under a sky that had in it more of the last of November than of the first of April, I experienced the effect of a genial burst of sunshine in the shape of your letter of the sixth.

I can never quite get over a certain surprise when, after dropping my missive in the ugly iron box at the street corner, in a few days the reply comes back to me, across ocean and continent; or without feeling that the civilization that has given us the postal service ought not to be despised. But the telegraph is the miracle of the age. That you can sit in your study in London, and I here in mine, and carry on a conversation limited only by our pounds, shillings, and pence to pay for the privilege; that the message which goes down to the depths of the Atlantic's unexplored water, reaches you almost as soon as if spoken across the table,—this puts necromancy in the shade. Since you were here we have the district telegraph, which signals for a messenger, a policeman, or a fire-extinguisher. We have had it brought into our house. On a bracket at the head of my bed stands a little instrument like a very small clock, connected with a wire which enters the upper story from the neighboring station. The other day, wishing a messenger, I touched the spring, and by the time I reached the bottom of the stairs two men, out of breath, were at the door to see what was the matter; it being my first experience, I had made a mistake and telegraphed for the police. I think that progress in the useful arts will be wonderful even in the immediate future, and I almost wish that I or my ghost could be here to see.

Carlyle wrote to Mr. B. some time since, and spoke of you, and of meeting you three or four days in the week to take a long walk together. When I read it, I was very envious of you, and of Carlyle too. I hope that when you reach your study you at once transcribe the conversation. If you have not done so, pray begin at once, and send the notes to me in your next letter. It is too bad that all light elicited by the contact of two such minds should die out on the spot.

I have no great faith in our good B—— in his *rôle* of prophet, and yet I do believe that the world is tending toward democratic institutions, and that the war of classes that you in England are drifting into, is one proof of the approaching struggle. If England is upset by it, she will doubtless rise again, reconstructed and filled with new life, perhaps, as we have been since our war.

We all help the Great Master to carry out his purposes, whether we will or not. But the creature man is possessed of such unlimited conceit that he cannot believe that he is doing otherwise than carrying out his own. If he would remember that his birth, his death, his nationality, his moral and religious nature, and every event of his life that determines his destiny, is entirely out of his power, even in his own body—his assimilation, circulation, respiration, he has nothing whatever to do with—he would find the limit of free will narrowed down. But it is not in the plan of creation thus far developed that we should know ourselves just as we are, and this being the case, of course it is best that it should be so.

I am very truly yours, A. C. L. B.

New-York, October 28, 1875.

My dear Mr. Froude: Our beautiful Indian summer has come again with its hazy skies, its warm winds, and its many-colored woods, bringing with it pleasant memories of you, as it always has done ever since that bright October morning when you came to breakfast with us, and we saw you for the first time. And yet these thoughts are not altogether pleasant when I remember how long it is since we have heard a word from you. To this complaint you will perhaps answer that a chance acquaintance that has survived the interchange of half-a-dozen letters has lived out its appointed time, and come naturally to an end. Then I shall say that since life is so short and so poor and arid, the persons I admire and like so few and so rarely met with, that when I do find them I am not going to give them up without a struggle; hence this letter and "then tears."

If I live to be as old as the patriarchs, I shall never outgrow this necessity for friendship, than which, says Cicero, "there is nothing in the world more excellent." You remember Emerson's charming essay on the same subject; since, then, I have Emerson and Cicero on my side, do not set me down as a sentimentalist, but, instead of that, take your pen and paper at once and write me a long, charming letter, as you know so well how to do: all about every thing in public affairs, in science, and in religion. The great undercurrent of thought rolls along, and it is extraordinary to see what silent evolutions follow the allusions of poetry to the phenomena of nature. "So science applies the scalpel even to poetry," as Emerson says in a letter to me.

I have just been reading with great interest your

essay on Spinoza. His doctrines have a great fascination for me; for I owe to them, and other similar works, whatever of peace and repose I may enjoy. "We cannot fear when nothing can befall us except what God wishes, and we shall not violently hope when the future, whatever it be, will be the best which is possible." . . .

Believe me, sincerely yours, A. C. L. B.

NEW-YORK, ——, 1878.

My dear Mr. Froude: I do not share your fear of the spread of Catholicism in the country. Perhaps because I do not fear anything. As for going over to the Catholic Church, I am in one sense already over, since I was baptized in it as an infant, to gratify some friends of my father. When I reach my second childhood, I cannot now say what I shall do; but in the present condition of my mental faculties, while I can study nature, which Goethe calls "The freshly uttered word of God," and while I can observe, even as imperfectly as I do, the wonderful developments of modern science, there is little danger of my turning back to the cloisters of the middle ages, or to the childish superstitions that have come down from them. You, surely, are the priest of a new religion, though you may not know it. I think with you that we should not grudge to our fellow-creatures any belief in which they find consolation and hope. We all have our illusions of one kind or another; life would be impossible without them, though they may not relate to the Virgin Mary, or to the views of Moody and Sankey, or to so-called religious people who, feeling sure of an eternity beyond this life, and of preserving their very insignificant personal ties all through it, can afford to do many things that those who have their doubts about it cannot — as possessors of fortunes may squander their great wealth in a way that would be ruin to those of more limited means. I am thinking more particularly of our friends and our domestic and social relations. You have said the same thing, I am sure. I need not tell you that I am acting up to my creed; that, being absolutely certain of the present only, I am making the most of my friends here, without waiting for that future life which, if it comes at all, will doubtless bring with it new thoughts, emotions, and affections.

To prove that I am in earnest in your case at least, I forbear to spin my letter out to another page.

Always sincerely yours, A. C. L. B.

EXTRACT FROM A LETTER TO MISS A.

NEW-YORK, October 4, 1889.

. . . Whenever you have any occupation or pursuit which you dream of at night, it is an evidence that you are overdoing. The fact that you see skeletons and dead-heads in your sleep is a warning that Nature kindly gives you to let them alone for a while. Do not be so foolish as to slight it. The penalties she exacts for disobedience of her laws are fearful — far more so than the penalties attached to the violation of human laws. Do not be so unwise as to defy them :

> She knows not wrath nor pardon;
> Utter true her measures mete,
> Her faultless balance weighs,—
> Times are as nought, to-morrow she will judge
> Or after many days. . . .

A. C. L. B.

TO MRS. B. C.

NEW-YORK, June 6, 1889.

My dear Friend: I am slowly preparing for our departure. It is extraordinary how many details go to make up life, and how complicated it has become. I look back to our ancestors who lived in trees, according to the new dispensation, and wore their furs all the year round, with positive envy. No house-cleaning or cooking, no summer outfit, no misfit, no misfortune. . . .

Always most affectionately yours,

A. C. L. B.

TO MLLE. BADÈR, PARIS, FRANCE.

NEW-YORK, April 27, 1883.

. . . We who live in this Babel of New-York need the rest of a sea-voyage and the repose of the Old World for a season every year. You can have no idea of the pressure under which we all live here. An Englishman has lately said of us that "we all seemed to have been born an hour too late, and were each trying to overtake that hour or to make up for it." I enjoy the practice of this art of sculpture more than any other occupation; and if I could live in a studio for the rest of my days, engaged in it, I should be content. But I take my rest on modeling.

A. C. L. Botta.

Paris, October 20, 1887.

My dear Friend: Passing the flower market this morning, I selected two or three plants which I shall like to think of as adorning your studio: one to stand in your window, another to bloom on your table, and a palm for victory, though I believe it is also the emblem of martyrdom. But, whatever may be its significance, it is ever green and has a root; and may I not hope that it will be, in this regard, emblematic of a lasting friendship between us, which has thus so happily begun?

A. C. L. B.

TO MRS. STEBBINS-THOMPSON.

New-York, December, 1888.

Dear Mrs. Thompson: Few of us in New-York can deny that we live in a high state of nervous tension, fulfilling literally the injunction to do with all our might what our hands find to do, and always finding far more to do than we can possibly accomplish. This chronic constriction of the nerves, never relaxed, involves such an expenditure of vital force as often precludes the possibility of rest, which is found only by going to Florida or to Europe, to Lakewood or to Weir Mitchell. For this condition the system of Delsarte offers a remedy, as you have shown, by teaching *how to rest*, how to train the nerves not less than the muscles as a necessary part of physical culture, how to move and act with the greatest economy of force, without wasting the vital powers in superfluous action as we all do: teaching, in short, both repose and action, relaxation and concentration, and that command of reserved force so essential in character as well as in all the arts. In these particulars the splendid system formulated by Delsarte can be studied by every one, old or young. In its wider and more general application to the young, the education of two or three generations in these great principles would do away entirely with round shoulders, hollow chests, and spinal curvatures, now so common, and, I fully believe, would produce a race which in beauty of form and expression would compare favorably with those antique statues whose forms and attitudes you can so beautifully represent. I am happy to tell you that I have formed a class to meet here twice a week, on such days as will be convenient for you to give the lessons.

Sincerely yours, ANNE C. L. BOTTA.

Anne C. L. Botta

A LETTER TO MR. JOHN BIGELOW.

NEW-YORK, January 8, 1877.

My dear Mr. Bigelow: Inclosed you will find a copy of my sonnet "Accordance," on which I should like your criticism. While I may be somewhat doubtful of the poetry of the sonnet, I am perfectly sure as to the doctrine, which is to me a source of great serenity of mind. Every day's experience proves to me that we have only to do "the duty that lies nearest to us" and the result must be good, though we may not see it at once, or may never see it; and this conviction takes the edge, however keen it may be, from all disappointments and annoyances.

The idea I strived to express is as follows: As he who plays the cathedral organ hears only a roar, yet, secure in the motive of the composer and in the laws of harmony, knows that the psalm or hymn is heard throughout the building, so he who on the chords of life plays the score of duty and love knows that far beyond the present noise and strife these notes must accord, though he may not hear; or, in other words, the performer on the organ does not hear his own music though he knows that he makes the music; and the man who does his duty does see the good results or may not see them, though he knows that in accordance with moral laws they must inevitably be produced—this is the meaning. Let me know if you think I have expressed it with proper clearness and force.

I am far from believing that obscurity is one of the beauties of style, either in poetry or prose. I do not enjoy the poetry that requires the same study as a mathematical problem. I have been reading the new poem of Matthew Arnold, "The New Sirens," and I confess that I can make nothing out of it but nonsensical versification. I have read it only once, however; perhaps by study I could better understand it. But as I do not propose to give any more time to it, I send it to you. You may, perhaps, see the drift of it. If you guess it, do let me know.

Very truly yours, ANNE C. L. BOTTA.

EXTRACTS FROM LETTERS TO MRS. A. H. LEONOWENS.

NEW-YORK.

. . . H. H.—who is visiting us—is very enthusiastic on the subject of the Indians and their wrongs, and has published several articles in the papers, which have made quite a stir and called out explanations from the Secretary of the Interior. There is a Ponca chief here, with "Bright Eyes," his interpreter, and some others, in whom she has been deeply interested. I invited them last Monday to our house, and "Standing Bear," the chief, made a short speech. He wore a scarlet blanket and a dark-blue coat worked with beads, a very handsome eagle's feather in his hair, and a necklace of grizzly bears' claws about his neck. He is a sad, dignified old man, and everybody was interested in the story of his wrongs. We had about seventy people present, and the evening went off very pleasantly. . . .

My dear Friend: . . . The painful part of your letter is that in which you tell me that you will not come here to embark. There were so many things I had to say to you that I put off for this last or later meeting that must now remain unsaid, and I am sadly disappointed. You are the one of all others that I have the deepest sympathy with, and now we are to be yet farther separated. As you say, we are united in the eternal. If we would only keep that in mind, and ourselves "on the heights," life would become ideal. But strive and struggle as I will, I go stumbling along, the light within often burning dimly or becoming quite extinguished. I seem to myself like some land animal dropped into the sea, struggling to keep its head above water, now and then finding dry land ; but a tidal wave breaks over it soon and swamps it back, drowning the floundering and striving creature. The mystery of life grows deeper and darker to me every day, and yet I know that it cannot be solved, and that it is the only wisdom to accept and not to question.

. . . What a delight it would be if we could live near each other ! I am sure that there are very few who are intellectually and morally as near as we are, and yet "so near and yet so far" personally. As you say, we have been in close communion in some former existence, and let us hope that we may continue it in the next. There is a verse in the "Kindred Hearts" of Mrs. Hemans that is often in my mind:

> Oh! ask not, hope not thou too much
>   Sympathy below:
> Few are the hearts whence one same touch
>   Bids the sweet fountain flow,
> Few—and by still conflicting powers
>   Forbidden here to meet—
> Such ties would make this life of ours
>   Too fair for aught so fleet.

While we have not been forbidden here to meet, we may not abide together; and we will be grateful that we may still communicate even from a distance. Accustomed as we are to all that civilization does for us, it is a strange experience to be suddenly deprived of much that it gives us. . . .

. . . Yesterday I read a review of Mallock's new book, "Is Life Worth Living?" It seems to be a perfect jeremiad over the loss of faith, the growth of scientific materialism, etc.,—the remedy for which evils he finds in a return to the bosom of the Catholic Church. Is it not strange and painful that in this age of progress there can be found no better solution of the great problems of life than this—to shut our eyes and go to sleep in the bosom of an ecclesiastical organization made of men like ourselves, subject to all errors like ourselves, notwithstanding their claims to a supernatural power, wisdom, and infallibility!

Anne C. L. Botta

. . . I send you an interesting review of "Esoteric Buddhism," by Sinnott. It is an interesting book: its fundamental idea is the progress of the human race. That man will advance as far beyond his present development as this is beyond his "Scimian progenitors," is what I have long believed; and this faith gives me consequent hope. If this were the best of us, I should be miserable indeed.

A. C. L. Botta.

Selections from Letters to Her.

Selections from Letters to Her.

A LETTER OF MRS. L. H. SIGOURNEY.

HARTFORD, CONN., December 27, 1836.

My dear Miss Lynch: I have heard nothing from you since your departure from Hartford, but cherish the hope that your situation is agreeable, and that the excellent motives which induced you to undertake the education of the young are rewarded by the exquisite pleasure of witnessing their improvement. I write now to say that I have consented to interest myself in a "Religious Souvenir," which was originally commenced by the late Dr. Bedell, and that I should be happy to number a poem from your pen among its articles. I am pleased thus to convey to you my high opinion of the character of your writings, and also to point out an appropriate channel for their circulation, as the list of contributors to this Annual comprises some of our most gifted writers. I scarcely know whether you are fond of writing prose, but if you should find in the scenery of that beautiful island, or in the legendary lore of the ancient family who inhabit it, or if in your own imagination there are materials for a religious tale of some ten pages, I think I can make room for it, and shall gladly insert it. Whatever is intended for the Souvenir must be sent by mail to the care of the publishers, who allow the remuneration of $2.00 a page. Trusting that you will favor us with the contribution as desired, believe me yours, with sincere regard,

L. H. SIGOURNEY.

Anne C. L. Botta

A LETTER OF MRS. LYDIA MARIA CHILD.

PROVIDENCE, R. I., 1839.

Dear Miss Lynch: I thank you for your kind invitation to visit you, with Mr. Furness. If I ever went anywhere, I certainly should have come. But for ten years past I have made no visits and formed no new acquaintance. I am considered a very odd woman; but my only oddity consists in an unaffected love of seclusion. I have not the smallest particle of social ambition. I would not take the trouble to go to two parties for the sake of obtaining the most flattering honors society could confer. It would, in fact, be taking what I do not want; for I have the most sincere aversion to being conspicuous in any way. To this natural love of keeping out of sight, is added weariness of spirit. Life has been to me a hard battle, and I would fain rest by the wayside. I am careful to do injury to no one, by act or word; and I strive to do, in a noiseless way, as much good as my limited means will allow. From what I am told of your independent character, I think you will admit that I have an undoubted right to live in retirement, since the choice springs from no imagined superiority and no deficiency of kindly social feelings.

The world has tried hard to fasten its fetters somehow upon me, but it is quite as much to the purpose to pour water on a duck's back. I wish well to everybody; I delight in beauty wherever I meet it; I am thankful I am poor; and I do not want a single thing that the world can either give or take away. With the most cordial wishes for your happiness, I am truly your friend, LYDIA MARIA CHILD.

LETTERS OF MRS. BUTLER (FANNY KEMBLE).

PHILADELPHIA, PENN., 1845.

My dear Madame: I was at Mrs. Morrison's this morning, where I had the pleasure of reading some poetry of yours, for which I am much obliged, as all who read it worthily will be. It naturally suggested to me immediately the idea of how desirable the society of the writer must be, if one could but obtain it; and with this, I confess, rather selfish motive, I venture, my dear madame, to ask you if you will not occasionally give me the favor of your company. I am at home almost every afternoon and evening, and if at any time your leisure and inclination stand so far, my friend, as to induce you to visit me, I shall consider myself fortunate in the opportunity of becoming better acquainted with you.

I hope this will not appear to you a liberty, or that if it does you will excuse it in favor of the sincere interest and admiration with which I am, my dear madame, yours truly,

FANNY BUTLER.

Many thanks, dear Anne, for your book, over which I have been crying, sighing, and thinking—and every leaf of which, as I turned it, brought to my mind and lips these words, "God bless you." These gifts always seem to me to demand his most especial providence for those who own them. . . .

Affectionately yours, FANNY BUTLER.

My dear Anne: Thank you very much for the sonnet you have sent me; its poetical merit is great, its moral value even greater; and it is very comfortable to me, dear Anne, who am walking along a rough and thorny path and carrying at my heart the burden of an irreparable loss, which, however, I take it, is lighter than an evil deed.

I am just now acting an engagement in London with Macready, I think very probably the last I shall perform in England; for I shall sail for the United States in the middle of July at the latest, and am much solicited to give readings from Shakespeare. I have even been urged to lecture upon his works, but am not bold enough for such an undertaking. Some years hence, perhaps, when I have thought and studied as carefully as I have now felt deeply over those wonderful productions, I may venture to bring my farthing rushlight to help the light of the sun.

The two years of labor I have chalked out for myself rather weigh upon my spirits. My Paradise by the Lake Fucino in the Abruzzi will have been fairly earned, if I dare say so, by all that I have gone through of misery, of bitterness, of disquiet, of irksome labor and most unrecognized effort, before reaching that haven of my rest,—to which I look, however, with constant hope, and a flattering thought that perhaps with peace and leisure I may yet achieve something worthy in those higher regions of intellect from which my theatrical career has perpetually drawn me—exhausting and inspiring in some degree to those mental faculties, to which, nevertheless, it cannot give adequate scope or employment. God bless you, dear Anne, and if you can make use of me in any way, remember that you do me a service in asking one of me.

I am ever yours very affectionately, FANNY.

LETTERS OF N. P. WILLIS.

NEW-YORK, 1845.

Dear Miss Lynch: . . . Poetry is a shadow over the heart that enables us to see to the bottom-like clouds cutting off the sunshine from a well. I now see the truth in the well of your heart, but I do not know as I dare tell you what it is like. You would be bound to deny a part of it, true or not, and (to tell a truth that is all my own) I do not yet feel sufficiently taken into your confidence to venture on translating your pulses to yourself—no ; I will not venture !

This much I may say, as a literary godfather, and with a freedom given me by never having seen beyond the edge of your bonnet till a month ago, that the intense passionateness of your nature is all ready for utterance in undying language ; and that if you do not breathe your heart soon upon an absorbent object, you will either be corroded by the stifled intensity of undeveloped feeling, or you will overflow with poetry and (like other volcanoes that find a vent) blacken the verdure around you with the cinders of exposed agonies. In short, you must *love* or *be famous!*

Wretched dilemma! I have studied people of genius more than you were prepared to guard against; and I read in the poems you send me exactly what your looks and conversation betrayed—boundless capability of love, and no present flow from the fountain. I cannot enlarge upon this without the hazard of running against some "Ideal Found," and I leave it till you make me your confessor—not to say, your "pilgrim prophet."

By the way, I do not see a fault in your style or versification. You have only to trust your pen.

Yours, with strong interest in your unturned leaves of life,

N. P. Willis.

Leipsic, September 27, 1845.

My dearest Friend: Your sweet letter and beautiful sonnet reached me at Wiesbaden a few days ago, and since that time I have been on the wing, getting northward to see my brother who is studying at this place. I write now merely to "make affidavit" that I wish my place kept in your friendship, and to assure you that there is no one in America whom I wish to see more. A glorious nature, prodigal of sweetness and genius as yours is, becomes a sort of "Isola Bella"—a sighed-for island in the great ocean of memory. I must explain the poetry of this by telling you that of all my years of travel, the day I spent at this lovely island in the Lago Maggiore is the most treasured and freshest in my remembrance. So, hereafter, please answer to the name of "Isola." . . . N. P. W.

Ramble-Brook, N. Y., February 12, 1853.

Nellie sends up to inquire whether I have "anything to say to Lynchie." Why, of course, I have! Well, how are you, dear equally-beloved-of-man-and-woman? Does our often talking and always thinking of you have any perceptible effect on your general health? Are you sweetened at all for those who see you by the blessings sent to you in great lumps by those who don't see you? It is otherwise a world of mournful shortcomings. . . .

Write us the news, dear Lynchie. Tell us if you are loving

anybody more than his fellow-man. God bless you,— but of course he will,— and may you be happy in what ought to make anybody happy, the sweet and blissful privilege of occupying your own charming existence.

Yours ever, sincerely and affectionately, N. P. Willis.

Idlewild, N. Y., December 3, 1853.

Beloved and adorable Lynchie: Is it possible that it is true, and you are back again? Gracious, how we want to see you! Nellie would give everything but her new baby (Miss Honora Willis) to get her arms round your neck. When can you and your mother come up and spend a week at Idlewild? Write and tell us. God bless you, and welcome home.

Ever yours, Willis.

March 24, 1855.

My dear Lynchie: The positive news of your coming marriage affected us very strongly, of course. Nellie and I love you so well that we tremble while we rejoice in new wings so venturesome, though so expanding of scope and lift. I believe, however, that you are one of those who carry your own "happy star," and, as to happiness, can *planet* for yourself. You are above destiny — subject naturally to nothing. If you promise to love, honor, and *obey*, it is as a volunteer altogether; please say to Mr. Botta, with my best respects, may God bless you, husbanded or wasted! Nellie is my "business man," and has doubtless told you what we expect in the way of a visit from your better half and you. Our glen is a place for the happy — geologically viewed, I believe — only "more so." But there will be time to spare, besides, for letting us see and know Mr. Botta. We trust you will both feel more at home at Idlewild than anywhere else.

Well, dear Lynchie, no woman ever deserved more love, and few mortals ever were better constituted to have all that belonged to them. *He* will love you all he can, till death — and that, for such a universal idol as you are, will be the "last drop" which you alone require. And so, with all the blessings, ever yours most truly, N. P. Willis.

Selections from Letters to Her

April 26, 1857.

My dear Friend: Please draw on me "at sight" for any amount of thanks, for your long and kind letter of information. I was exceedingly interested in it, and we will consult as to what is to be done about it. How is it possible that a man can be so victimized in a civilized country? But we will talk of it—easier than this weary inking over our ideas. Nellie was much interested in your letter, and wants to see you—as who does not? We both send love, and are ever faithfully yours.

N. P. W.

NEW-YORK.

Here you are, dear Lynchie, portrayed as the angels take portraits,—a good likeness of you,—probably as you will figure in heaven; may I be there to see! Meantime you must eat terrestrial dinners, so can't you navigate this way in unangelic overshoes at four mortal P. M.?

Yours always, N. P. W.

LETTERS OF FREDERIKA BREMER.

STOCKHOLM, 1845.

To Anne C. Lynch: Whoever you may be, sweet lady, whose harmonious voice has passed the great waters to reach my distant and lonely shore, let it be a satisfaction to your noble heart to know the effect your lines have produced in the home of her to whom you have directed them. I read them aloud to my mother, my sister, and my cousin, Sir Fabian Wride (who after the death of my brothers is my only brother); but often I must stop, so deeply touched was I with the beauty of the poesy and affected with the meaning it conveyed, so gratifying to my fondest wishes—yea, to my *only* wish in life, in respect to men, or mankind; and the glistening tear in my eye was reflected in those of my relations. So do not fear, dear lady, that the ambrosia of *such* praise can do anything but good—purifying and vivifying the soul of the mortal who receives it, spurring it the more to try to merit what is offered by the hand of grace.

So blessings on you, sweet and noble muse of America, and thanks forever from the family and the heart of your Swedish friend and sister-mind, FREDERIKA BREMER.

STOCKHOLM, 6 April, 1840.

Dear Anne Lynch: I have to thank you, dear Anne, for a sweet letter, and, moreover, for a welcome promise to write to me "something" about yourself, your society and life in America. Do, my dear young friend! It will greatly interest me to see a truthful and unbiased picture of private life in that part of America where you reside, its influence on the morals and happiness of individual man and particularly of woman. It will be to me a precious introduction to the chapter I myself wish to study, if I once can come to your shores.

In my next book you will find some characteristics of our inner and better life, of what there is going forward under the eyes of the Scandinavian genius. Danes, Norwegians, Swedes, though brethren in history, literature, and social life, are still very different in spirit. I cannot but acknowledge that I am very partial to that of my own people.

But we should be so, my dear young friend; every one should be partial to his own land and view its life through the eye of love,—the only truly sharp one,—and every one endowed with genius should employ it in bringing out the characteristic genius of one's people, and let it light on its own soul as on those of other nations.

I long for your poems; I know I shall love them. Your mission as a poet is one of the noblest. May it prosper, dear Anne, and the happiness of a great and good heart be your lot.

Most affectionately yours, FREDERIKA BREMER.

STOCKHOLM, December 1, 1847.

Dear Anne Lynch: . . . I have not yet discarded the hope of seeing the shores of the New World and its noble-minded, benevolent people, its beautiful and refined women. I hope yet once to visit the Penates of America and to compare them with those of my Scandinavian home.

You, dear Anne Lynch, I then hope to see and converse with. Your beautiful talent is of a cast which must be conducive to happiness for you as well as delight for your fellow-men. The deep melancholy which at times has cast its shadow over you is but the dregs in the inkstand of existence, which every deep soul takes ere it can pen the strong inspirations of life, the depths of sorrow or joy, or mysterious nature and heavenly grace. So I do not fear the plunge, my dear young friend. Believe me, you will rise from it rich of the treasures of the depths. And with wings such as God has given to you, you must soar over all the sorrows of earth in the sunshine of everlasting light. No fear! I should like to speak specially with you on this theme, but time is at this moment denied me. God bless you, dearest Anne, and make you so happy as wishes your obliged friend,

FREDERIKA BREMER.

CAMBRIDGE, MASS., December 20, 1849.

Dearest, sweetest Anne: There, now, you come to heap glowing coals on my guilty head, making me, through your sweet lines, feel still more bad not to have written to you long before! But I must tell you, dear Anne, that I have been constantly writing to you for weeks in mind, only that I could not come to pen it upon paper; and then you know how it is with me, and what a poor letter-writer I am. I know you will excuse me. But now, indeed, I must at least say, thank you, my dear Anne, for the past and the present kindness; I feel it more than I can tell, and long to make you feel it some time or other. The memories of your kindnesses are always with me, cheering and comforting me. . . . Dearest Anne, I must leave you now, but hope to see you and your dear mother, and your young ladies, in the course of February, if not earlier. Give my love to your mother, and best regards to your friends. Believe me, my dear Anne, yours affectionately,

FREDERIKA BREMER.

Anne C. L. Botta

GENEVA, SWITZERLAND, August, 1857.

Dearest Anne: Months have gone by since I received your dear letter, which found me in one of the remote valleys of Switzerland, where I was restoring myself after great fatigues and later illness. In your letter I saw you, all yourself, my own dear amiable Anne, sweet and serious and kind, and I blessed you in my heart for it. I like to think you are married with an Italian. The Italian character has a peculiar charm to me; there is in it a simplicity and a grace with a chivalrous feeling for women which delights me. I think an Italian must love you dearly, and in a peculiar way as a woman and a poetic soul, as you are; and it is sweet to be loved well.

Now, you will want to know something of the friend to whom you once were a kind hostess and friend. Dear Anne, she is well, and thanks God for her existence. She has had severe trials, dreary times to pass; but they are passed, and the fountains of hope and love spring still,—perhaps are more strong than ever. Love! did I say? yea, but not more of earthly friends. All those I have dearly loved are gone,—gone to the unknown land. My love on earth has become more like adoration, and I need not tell you for whom. I like to read *his* name, to study *his* meaning wherever I go; and in every page of nature and history of present life that I do study, I hope to see his light, and love more and more clearly, and to make others see it. This makes life dear to me. If I can carry out what I have planned for this purpose, many souls will be befriended and strengthened; and, my love, my constant, only true love will make my faults and errors pardoned by God and those who have any right to pardon me.

O Anne! This is my prayer and my hope! And this is a confession to you whose pure mind I know. As to my earthly plans and movements, they are now to go to Italy. The coming winter I intend to pass in Rome. Perhaps I may go to Greece and to Jerusalem. But this will depend on several circumstances. In two years after this present one I wish to be back in my own land, which I shall probably no more leave until my very last voyage on earth. God permitting, I will have plenty to do until that moment. May I not hope that when I am once more in my own land, you, my dear Anne, with your husband, will pay me a visit? I do hope it, and beg you to remember in kindness, your Swedish friend and sister,

FREDERIKA BREMER.

STOCKHOLM, February 16, 1864.

Dearest Anne: Your good and interesting letter from New-York has been to me a true treat: first, by its being from you and bringing good news from you; second, for the many interesting things of general import contained in it. Cheering and refreshing one, many things you tell about the regeneration of your people,—about its rising to manhood! Alas! that so bloody a baptism was needed, and still seems needed for it! I need not tell you with what intense interest I have followed, and do follow, all phases of this American war, which certainly is one of the most remarkable in modern, and perhaps also in ancient, history: next to the religious war of "thirty years," which closed the middle age and founded a new order of things in Church, State, and Society. I know of no war except the present one in America where so great and so life-teeming principles are working for the future of still unborn generations. And to have lived to see its probable issue, its certain fruits, is a great privilege. Oh, how I should wish to respond to your most kind invitation, your sweet words, by coming once more to that great country of my hopes and fond aspirations for human felicity; to sit down there with you and yours, looking out over a pacified realm rising new-born and purified out of the bloody strife, and observing with you the signs of the coming day; but that will hardly be! I feel old and weary, and do not believe I have many years left to live, and those I must devote to my country and to the work given me there in more than one way. But my heart and mind will never be absent from America. One of my last looks of love and blessing will be for that country where I have lived so much, enjoyed, loved, and learned so much; and on which still my fondest hopes for a better and more happy humanity do repose. I am delighted to hear you say that you "begin to find that life can be too short," and that happy love has made you feel so. If you once will have leisure and tell me more about your husband, your home, your pursuits, every-day life, and plans for future life, you would give me great pleasure. . . . Alas! when will this war cease? Though every pulse of my being beats for the success of Northern arms and ideas, I do suffer with the South, with its brave men and its much-suffering, self-sacrificing women, with its *good* slave-owners and *happy* slaves,—for such there are, though now they are confounded with the cruel and the unhappy.

In my new edition of letters from America I shall give a summary of recent political events and present state of things in your great land. Your last good letter is a help to me in this task; and I shall be thankful for any new hint or observation that you would give me. I must break off. Farewell, dearest. Best regards to your mother and husband, from your affectionate old friend,

FREDERIKA BREMER.

My dearest Anne Lynch: . . . I send you some pictures; the names on the several scraps of paper will not be strangers to *you*—wonderful little encyclopedian, universalistic literary lady, as you are! Yes, dear, I have got your "Handbook of Literature," a truly wonderful product of the genius of the New World. No woman but an American would, I think, effect gracefully and cleverly such a mammoth work. Many, many thanks for this book, as useful as interesting. . . .

Your obliged friend, FREDERIKA BREMER.

LETTERS OF HENRY GILES.

NEWPORT, June 23, 1847.

My dear Friend: . . . I will first refer to a question on which we have talked; and that is the relation of poetry to moral purpose. Extend the form of expression and say—the relation of art to moral purpose, and we shall cover nearly the whole ground of criticism—within which, of course, poetry is included. I maintained, if I remember correctly, that a moral purpose was not the proper end of art; therefore, not of poetry. I felt that I was right. What is it that one seeks first of all, above all, in art? Enjoyment. This, then, is the first and great end of art. Not merely through the senses, for art can never wholly belong to the senses,—nor yet purely through the reason, for art can never wholly belong to the reason. To specify all the elements which combine in the perfection of art would be to go through the whole philosophy of criticism. One thing is certain, that these cannot be confined by the limitations of ethical requirements, nor to the purpose of ethical results; if they could, all art would be but a mirror of morality. Art, however, has concern mainly with imagination, and not with conscience; and though it may satisfy the conscience, if it fails in the imaginary element its failure is complete. . . .

Yours truly, H. GILES.

QUINCY, MASS., October 29, 1860.

My dear Friend: It gave me no common pleasure to receive a note from you. You may be quite sure that long silence and distance have not caused me to forget you, nor in the least weakened my regard and friendship for you.

Your book I was glad to have; but have only had time to look at certain portions, which I found admirably well done. Considering how brief it is, and yet so clear and comprehensive, it combines also with its brevity a good deal of modern research. In the Italian section, I see fully appreciated the name of "Vico," the real founder of the "Philosophy of History," which late speculators have plundered without acknowledgment, gratitude, or conscience. . . .

Yours truly, H. GILES.

CHICAGO, March 23, 1861.

My dear Friend: . . . You know better than I can tell you how shallow the strata of our educational systems are. They were thin in the beginning, and so far as I can see now, they grow thinner year after year. The present is all in all. The past wears out of memory here; yet if men would only see it, a living knowledge of the past is only that which gives a deep and real knowledge of the present. This, however, is a lesson to which our people have never yet given themselves; socially and politically they are now reaping bad fruits from this historic ignorance, and by and by may reap yet worse. We have intellectual and moral *activity,* as a mass, and we want intellectual and moral *culture*. Culture is the growth of patient thought and study. We are not patient, thoughtful, or studious. . . .

Yours sincerely, H. GILES.

ST. LOUIS, November 23, 1863.

My dear Friend: I forward to you for examination a syllabus of the proposed course of six lectures on "Life in Shakespeare"; please to examine it, and I shall be greatly obliged if you will favor me with your criticism.

I. *Woman in Shakespeare.*

Ideal women — Romantic women — Impassioned women — Vice in womanhood — Tragic women — Untragic women — The heroic element in womanhood — Love in womanhood — The unity of womanhood.

II. *Man in Shakespeare.*

The unity and duality of human life — Man in his diversity — Man according to his era or nation — Man individualized — Intellectual men — Impassioned men — Sensuous men — Comic men.

III. *Shakespeare's Comic Power.*

The humanity of humor — Characters we laugh *at* — Fools and their varieties — Characters we laugh *with* — Wits, satirists, rogues — Characters that we both laugh *at* and *with* — Falstaff — The philosophy, imagination, and pathos which underlie Shakespeare's humor.

IV. *Shakespeare's Tragic Power.*

Pathos — The forces of passion, intellect, and thought as elements of the tragic.

V. *The Study of Life in the Study of Shakespeare.*
We study life as a whole in Shakespeare — We study it distributively, impartially, sympathetically — The value of this study is artistic, philosophic, and practical.

VI. *Shakespeare's Personality.*
Biographical sketch — Shakespeare in relation to his country — Society — Mankind — His associates and friends, and their relation to himself — The order and progress of his genius.

H. Giles.

A LETTER FROM MR. CLAY.

Ashland, Ky., September 30, 1849.

My dear Miss Lynch: Notwithstanding my great repugnance to letters for my poor autograph, and to idle letters from total strangers, there are other letters, my dear Miss Lynch, which I receive with pleasure, as I have yours with more than an ordinary degree of it. It assured me on your part, as I now do on mine, of the continuance of that friendship which we recently formed at Newport. And I have to thank you for the scraps (not of bread, but of praise) inclosed in your letter, in which you speak in such terms of kindness of me.

Jeremy Taylor has not described ill the sentiment of friendship in the passage which you have quoted, but its emotions are rather a proper subject of feeling than of description. If women were really without heads, as you unjustly estimate, you would coincide in that opinion. Their excellence, I think, consists in their blending together better than our sex does the impulses of the heart with the dictates of the head; or, if you please, tempering the severity of the sovereign head by the affections of the merciful heart.

I returned home about a fortnight ago, after passing through scenes of excitement, arising from the vast multitudes through which I passed, that I dare not attempt to describe. I wonder that I escaped from them with my life unhurt. At Syracuse, on the morning of my departure, I was locked up with a lady three quarters of an hour, as an asylum from the pressure of the crowd! I should have been happy if, to escape from them, I could have been oftener placed in a similar situation. As my secretary, you could in that time have written a dozen of letters for me.

I found my family in good health on my return. But you will be surprised when I tell you that Levi, my valet, was again seduced to leave me at Buffalo; and still more, that he has again returned, not, however, yet to me, but to Louisville, where he has reported himself to a friend of mine, quite penitent and sorrowful. I shall forgive him, but I shall not retain him as a valet.

I request you to present my warm regards to your good mother, and, feeling a deep and lively interest in the welfare of both of you, I shall be most happy to hear sometimes from you. You must not estimate the extent of my friendship by the brevity of my letters. As you anticipated, I feel myself encompassed by a vast number of them, to some of which I am forced to reply; but to none of those replies shall I subscribe myself with so much pleasure as I now do, that I am faithfully your friend and obedient servant,

H. Clay.

Having sent a copy of her volume of poems to Mr. Clay, she received the following note:

Newport, R. I., Atlantic House, August, 1849.

I beg you to allow me to tender to you, my dear Miss Lynch, my cordial and grateful thanks for your acceptable present of the volume of your poems. I had before enjoyed the gratification of perusing some of the productions of your pen, but in this collective form I shall consider myself as possessed of a precious treasure, which I shall value more highly from having made the acquaintance of the fair authoress. And notwithstanding my aversion to the collection of autographs, I shall ever cherish that of Miss Lynch, which she has placed under the lines which she has done me the honor to inscribe to me in the commencement of the volume, with great satisfaction and most agreeable recollections.

I request to be allowed to subscribe myself, most faithfully your friend and obedient servant, H. CLAY.

LETTERS RELATING TO THE CLAY MEDAL.

On Miss Lynch's return to New-York from Washington early in 1852, Mr. Clay intrusted her with a gold medal of himself, which had been presented to him by the Clay Association of New-York city. The committee had requested Mr. Clay to return this medal for some slight improvement which they desired to make on it. Miss Lynch willingly accepted the charge; she placed the medal in her satchel, and for greater security carried this in her hands throughout the journey. When she and the friends who accompanied her arrived in New-York, they took a carriage, and in the confusion this satchel was taken from her by some of the party and put up on the box with the coachman. On reaching home, she found it had disappeared and could not be found. She was deeply grieved over this, and wrote immediately to a friend in Washington requesting him to inform Mr. Clay of the unfortunate occurrence. Under the date of March 17, 1852, this friend wrote her as follows:

I called on Mr. Clay and mentioned the loss of the medal. I found him not at all affected by it; his spirits were as good and he as cheerful as I have seen him since his illness. He, I assure you, has suffered not the slightest depression on this account. That he appreciates this token of the respect and affection of his friends of New-York is doubtless true; but the token had performed its office. The motive and intention of the presentation gave it its value: that could not be lost; for things of the heart can never be lost.

He regrets that it should give you any pain, and I beg you will give yourself no further uneasiness on this subject. Mr. Clay suffers nothing from it, attaches no blame to any one; therefore I pray you to be happy,—for you deserve to be so,—and come to Washington, where you can minister so largely to the happiness of others.

Miss Lynch placed the case in the hands of the police; and a friend of hers advertised, offering a reward of five hundred dollars, which was the value of the medal, for its recovery. A few days after, the satchel was found in a back street of the city; it had been cut open and the contents taken. Thus all trace of the medal was lost.

Mr. Clay wrote to Miss Lynch requesting her not to give herself any more uneasiness about it; and as the committee proposed to have another medal struck, he said: "If my wishes could prevail, I would prevent the trouble and expense of the renewal of the medal. The fact of its presentation to me is gone to the record, and may be embodied in history. Of the honor of that fact, no thief can rob me, whatever he may have done with the medal."

The chairman of the committee, Mr. Daniel Ullmann, wrote also to her, saying: "I pray you, Miss Lynch, to give yourself no further concern on account of the loss of the medal. The accident is one that might easily have happened to any one. The subscribers regret only the uneasiness which the occurrence has caused to you. Such are their feelings toward Mr. Clay that they are rather gratified than otherwise to have another opportunity of manifesting them."

The mystery of the lost medal remained unsolved for many years. But finally it was solved by the statements received with the following letter:

TO MRS. V. BOTTA.

BANGOR, MAINE, March 10, 1867.

Madame: By the request of Professor Horsford, I will make known to you what I know of the fate of the Henry Clay medal.

In 1853 I passed the summer in Switzerland. I went one day to visit a friend at Lausanne on the Lake of Geneva. He invited me to pass the evening with his cousin, who boarded with Madame Noir. While there, Madame told us that her neighbor and tenant had a beautiful medal of one of our statesmen, and perhaps she would show it to us.

We called on her, and she reluctantly showed us the Clay gold medal, which I recognized at once as the one that had been stolen in America. I said nothing until we had returned to the hotel, when I reminded my friend of the facts connected with its loss, and said I thought it must be the same; he agreed with me on that point. Then I quietly asked Madame Noir where the lady obtained the medal. She replied that the lady's husband was a sea-captain, and bought the medal in Philadelphia for a small sum. She also told me that the medal was rarely shown; and that it was quite an honor for us to have seen it. The name of this lady I have forgotten. In Paris I described the medal to the artist who had made the design; and he was sure it must be the original, and I have never had any doubt as to its identity.

The history of the medal might be traced out by our consul at Geneva; and perhaps it might be obtained on his demand.

Very respectfully, AUG. C. HAMLIN.

Anne C. L. Botta

LETTERS FROM DANIEL WEBSTER.

WASHINGTON, October 31, 1851.

My dear Miss Lynch: On reading your note and the exquisite verses which accompanied it, I experienced feelings certainly such as no ordinary compliment or commendation could excite. Indeed, I was touched and moved by the vigor of the lines and the warmth of their sentiments. I know that poetry has its licenses, of which exaggeration is one; but allowing for this, and also for any degree of personal regard which you might entertain toward me, I could not but feel elated.

My dear lady, French scholars have a canon of criticism against which, I fear, you have greatly offended, so far as my name is concerned, in your stanzas. It is that "nothing is beautiful which is not true." Nevertheless, the beauty and the grace with which you write of the immortal lands of Greece and imperial Rome, of Plato, Demosthenes, and Tully, redeem you from the fault, since you say nothing which surpasses what history records of those sons of genius and renown.

I thank you, dear Miss Lynch, for putting my name on the same paper in which you mentioned theirs; and believe me when I say that the pleasure of the association is heightened by the hand which in so friendly a manner brings the names together.

With cordial regards and all good wishes, I am, dear lady, truly yours,

DANIEL WEBSTER.

Mr. Webster acknowledges with many sincere thanks the beautiful bouquet sent to him by Miss Lynch. He deems it a great honor to be thus remembered by so distinguished a person. At an earlier period of life, the gift by a lady of so many flowers from the garden might have excited Mr. Webster's ambition to attempt a return, either in flowers of *poetry* or at least in those of *rhetoric;* as things are, he can only ask of Miss Lynch to accept in acknowledgment of her present, a *cluster* of warm, rose-colored, various, and *unfading* good wishes and regards.

DANIEL WEBSTER.

Nov. 30, 1851.

Selections from Letters to Her

EXTRACTS FROM LETTERS OF GEORGE D. PRENTICE.

LOUISVILLE, KY., November 4, 1850.

My dear Miss Lynch: . . . I thank you heartily for your kind letter, and have intended to write you for some time and tell you how much I have enjoyed your volume of poems. There are three or four pieces in it that I long have been able to repeat, but there are others that I never saw before. I have read the whole book twice through, with constantly increasing admiration for the freshness, purity, and goodness of your heart, the strength and healthfulness of your intellect, and the sweetness, fervor, beauty, and affluence of your fancy. There are many of your sweet and beautiful images which, in the midst of the political strifes in which I am engaged, float upon the troubled current of my thoughts like lively water-lilies upon the bosom of a turbid stream. . . .

. . . I used to visit in Windham frequently years ago, when you were a little child; but I did not dream that the name of the sweet little child I sometimes gazed at was destined to become a familiar word throughout the nation. I respect you infinitely too much to flatter you; and it is no flattery to say that yours is one of the sweetest, purest, gentlest, truest, loveliest, holiest, and most beautiful spirits I have found upon the earth. The tendency of your poetry is to refine, to console, to purify, to strengthen, to ennoble, and to exalt; and I am sure that the world will be better for the sinking of such thoughts as yours into its heart.

You say that you live very little in the past, the present, or the future. I am sure, Miss Lynch, that you are mistaken. There are few, very few, who live as much as you do. You certainly feel more, think more, accomplish more, and *live* more in a single month than most men and women do in their threescore years and ten. I do not suppose that any strong and overmastering passion has ever passed over your soul; but I know that you have suffered, for the traces of suffering, subdued and chastened by a strong intellect and a high and holy will, are visible in your poetry; and you know that suffering "curdles days into years." Mrs. Prentice sends her best regards to you, and always believe me sincerely yours, GEO. D. PRENTICE.

LETTERS OF GEORGE WOOD ("PETER SCHMID").

WASHINGTON, December 19, 1851.

My dear Lady Anne: . . . I was every way pleased with your article on the city of Washington. It is written with all your admirable tact, and the illustrations are extremely well done. The few remarks on the social life of Washington are highly commended. I wish there had been more, but I suppose you could not make the article longer; perhaps you have a series of articles to be entitled "The Salons of the President's House, in the administrations of Washington, Adams, Jefferson, Madison, and Monroe." If you could get up such a series of articles, giving the personages who made up society in Washington in those days, they could not fail to be of great interest.

How are you? Pray drop me a line of your sayings and doings. With kind remembrances, I remain,

Very truly yours, "PETER SCHMID."

WASHINGTON, April 18, 1852.

My dear Lady Anne: . . . I thank you for your kind favor of yesterday, and assure you that I am desirous you should be about something which, while it will promote your happiness, will enhance your reputation as a writer. I am sure your taste, genius, and talents have only to be put forth in some labor of love to be successful. I am glad you are reading "Thomas à Kempis." There are the confessions of St. Augustine, as edited by Elizabeth Peabody, published some twenty years since, which, if you can get, you would find worth reading.

I beg you will present my affectionate compliments to your excellent friends, Mr. and Mrs. B——. I am glad you find it in your heart to value such friendship. It is a good sign; for I don't think there can be a sincere sympathy felt without oneness of affection for that great bond of sympathy—the supreme life of Christ, "our great God and Saviour."

With my great regard, I remain your friend,

George Wood.

EXTRACTS FROM LETTERS OF HON. JOHN M. BERRIEN.

Savannah, Ga., March 29, 1853.

My dear Miss Lynch: . . . I read with pleasure your account of the manner in which you have spent your winter. The true source of happiness and of a mind at peace with itself is such useful and especially such benevolent employment as that in which you have been engaged. In a populous city like yours there must be ample scope for the exercise of the feeling which animates you, and I bid you God-speed with all my heart—assuring you that the homage which I have cheerfully rendered to your native and cultivated intellect will be offered even in fuller measure to the benevolence which prompts the enterprise in which you are engaged. Speaking frankly to you, however, as I am accustomed to do, I am sorry to learn that you do not find the time you need for reading certain books which you would enjoy. "*Vis inertiæ*" is not a characteristic of the human mind. It must advance or retrograde, and such a one as has been allotted to you deserves better treatment at your hands. But I forbear, lest you should think I am going to assume an office to which I have no claim.

Let me hear more of the school. I shall be much interested in the issue of your winter's labors; and do tell me if you have found in those poor children the pure and lively pleasure which I anticipated for you. With cordial good wishes,

Very truly yours, John MacPherson Berrien.

Savannah, Ga., July 4, 1853.

My dear Miss Lynch: . . . That "splendid plan of intellectual culture" which has so long dazzled your imagination, and which, in the language of this age of dollars and cents, would "pay better" in every way than anything else, is, I am sorry to see, still postponed to "a more convenient season." Do not consider me intrusive in again reverting to this. The depository of a *single* talent was held criminal for burying it in the ground. How much more should be the one to whom *ten* talents were intrusted? But I fear I have exceeded my monitory privilege, and will forbear, only commending you to keep in mind the injunction, "*Carpe diem!*"

In some of your future wanderings, do, please, step on board one of those floating palaces which are continually moving between your city and ours. Besides the personal welcome you would receive, we will give you some new ideas of Southern society, and of the activity and energy of its members. Farewell! Your letters always give me so much pleasure, which I am sorry I cannot repay; but I am always very truly yours,

John MacPherson Berrien.

A LETTER OF GOV. T. H. SEYMOUR.

Hartford, Conn., January 11, 1851.

Dear Miss Anne: . . . Your esteemed favor of the 5th gave me great pleasure. I do almost envy you the friendship and society of Mr. Clay, Judge Berrien, and many others that are now in Washington. When I have opposed Mr. Clay, as I have sometimes politically, I have felt what Prentice in his life of Mr. Clay has expressed in a line of poetry—a sort of "remorse of love." The great statesman is associated in my mind with my earliest recollections of American eloquence and exalted patriotism. His present position is far above the reach of party strife and party attacks, and I pray that the remainder of his days may be as tranquil and happy as his life has been useful and honorable to his country and mankind.

. . . I did think of spending some weeks in Washington this winter, but it will be impossible; although the inducement you offer is certainly worthy of consideration. But I never got along very well with your amiable sex, and I fear it is too late for me to learn "new tricks." I am living more in "the ideal"!

> Thro' long, long years to seek, to strive, to yearn,
> For woman's love, and never quench that thirst—

No more! Will it be asking too much of you to request the pleasure of another letter? Renewing my best wishes for your pleasure and happiness, I remain, truly your friend and obedient servant,

THOS. H. SEYMOUR.

EXTRACTS FROM R. W. EMERSON'S LETTERS.[1]

CONCORD, MASS., May 28, 1866.

Dear Mrs. Botta: . . . I hope that having found so frank and intelligent good-will in your house, I may not lose it. I even persuade myself that my next visit will be better than the last, since we shall begin at some advance; and who knows but we shall arrive at our best experiences! For I think in the short winter days—and in New-York they are shortest—we left many good topics untouched, and hardly came into the precincts of those which interest each of us most. . . .

March 16, 1869.

I am glad you find Huxley interesting. He is an acknowledged master in England. As long ago as the Prince of Wales was here in Boston, Dr. Acland interested us much in him. But I have read him less than his compeers—Owen, Tyndall, and Darwin. Natural science is the point of interest now, and I think it is dimming and extinguishing a good deal that was called poetry. These sublime and all-reconciling revelations of nature will exact of poetry a correspondent height and scope, or put an end to it.

[1] For other letters of Mr. Emerson see pages 177, 178.

December 8, 1870.

. . . I read last night in Mrs. Hunt's little book her lines to yourself with real pleasure, and found them all true. Then I ran along through much more, and with great pleasure in the truth and the originality of the writing. It has what I think a high merit—the necessity of insight in the reader. Each poem is a riddle which only thoughtful people can solve. But of this and much more I shall hope to talk with you soon.

Yours faithfully, R. W. EMERSON.

LETTERS OF H. W. BELLOWS.

NEW-YORK, December 3, 1859.

My dear Mrs. Botta: I am overwhelmingly engaged nowadays, and don't do anything I wish, but only what I must. I thank you for remembering the existence of such an unsocial animal as I am; but I have found out that your charity is large and your long-suffering extreme. "These perilous times," abroad and at home, my heart is not big enough to feel *all* their significance; but it throbs with steady anxiety and sympathy for those who struggle for liberty on either side the ocean. Yesterday was a day to be remembered: whether Irving's death or John Brown's were the more perfect euthanasia, posterity will decide. But I should not wonder if the hero-martyr's were longer remembered than the well-beloved fountain of our American literature. What a terrible thing to have our sense of constitutional obligation of good citizenship and country at war with our instincts of humanity, our reverence for sanctity and honor, and disinterested nobility of soul! Was there ever such a terrible conflict in our country's history as that now silently raging—not in the newspapers or among the noisy partizans, but in the deep hearts of men who love their country, venerate law, and feel a profound responsibility for their words and their counsels at this juncture? God guide us aright! With love to Mr. Botta,

Ever cordially yours, H. W. BELLOWS.

Selections from Letters to Her

NEW-YORK, January 1, 1872.

Dear Mrs. Botta: I wish you and the Professor a Happy New Year!—and none the less seriously because of the strain of sadness that is scattered through your note. It won't do for such brave hearts as yours to talk about "our barren and prosaic lives." Who has covered life with more flowers (I dare say, watered with some tears) than your kind and ever-active ladyship?—or done more to throw the poetry of sentiment and friendship over its prose? Barren! Yes; so are the rocks that finally break into vines full of wine. Prosaic!—so are the facts that at last cumulate into principles, and then ripen into romances and poems. I won't have you saying things that minister so to my own sadness! The muffled drum in my heart wants no echo except from the tambour and pipe, that shall shame its melancholy away. Don't you dare to keep any time with it!

Dear Tuckerman! how refreshing it is to see the general recognition of his quiet merit and essential simplicity, and ever childlikeness of heart and smile!

We will hope that no such noble and beautiful throng of people will gather for a half-century to hear somebody younger by a score or two than I tell how good and amiable and gentle and faithful a soul had passed on! Dear old Sam Ruggles said to me a few days after T.'s funeral: "I was wondering whether your inventive mind could n't find something *kind* to say even of me in my coffin." And the old fellow's eyes filled with moisture that seemed like the approaching death-signal.

I will venture to say that I know nobody who has a kind of parallel position, a woman's place, in the hearts of scholars, artists, and belles-lettres society, in this New-York of ours, so firmly matched with Tuckerman's as a certain half-despondent friend of mine who lives near 25 West 37th street. May it be very long before my words are tested (to be wholly verified) by that Refiner who brings the silver out so clearly from what the Receiver of life and silence makes look often only like lead! . . .

Yours cordially, H. W. BELLOWS.

A LETTER FROM AMOS DEAN.

ALBANY, N. Y., March 28, 1855.

My dear Friend: I received this morning a letter directed in your own handwriting, which, whatever else I forget, I shall probably never entirely have erased from my memory. That same handwriting of yours on the back of letters has, in bygone years, raised such commotions among the depths profound of human feelings that I can never learn to see its tracings with indifference. I opened it with eagerness, as I always do anything from you; and although somewhat troubled at the outset in forming the word "Friend" out of ——, I halted not long there, but pushed through it, and upon sober second thought came to the conclusion that the envelope—at least the crust—was intended for me, and the contents—the kernel—for another; and I accordingly retain the one and return the other to you.

But you will not, I trust, do me the injustice to suppose I can remain indifferent to the fact the knowledge of which I have thus singularly acquired. You have occupied entirely too large a space in my own heart and affections for me ever to become indifferent to any important event that awaits you in life. It is true that for many past years I have seen and heard but little of you, but I have nevertheless thought a good deal. And you must know well that scarce any living soul, and perhaps not any, has a more perfect knowledge of the trials and hardships you have traveled through thus far than I have. I have got—and what I prize most highly, too—a record of them as they occurred, and of the effect they had upon your spirits.

And now it is to me matter of the most sincere and heartfelt rejoicing that you are arriving at so desired a consummation of so many earthly wishes. If any human being deserves success, and rest, and repose, after so many of life's battles have been so successfully fought, it is surely yourself. Receive, therefore, the kindest congratulations of one who under any or all changes of circumstances can never cease to be your friend.

Truly and sincerely yours, AMOS DEAN.

Selections from Letters to Her

A LETTER OF CHARLES L. BRACE.

NEW-YORK, February 20, 1852.

My dear Miss Lynch: I thought much of you yesterday and to-day while visiting your parishioners of the Wilson Industrial School. Mrs. Wilson has them in excellent training, and they look up to her as if she was a queen. I find our little German rag-pickers are the most hopeful subjects of the lot. They were really enthusiastic in what they told me of the sewing, and singing, and soup. Mrs. Wilson has succeeded, in some mysterious way, in cleaning their faces and untying their tongues. It all looks well so far, and the enterprise, with which you have been connected from the beginning, will go far in improving the condition of these poor children. What a treasure of a woman Mrs. Wilson is! You made a grand selection there! One of your protégés came to me,—the boy from Twelfth street,—and I promised him work. He looks like a very clever lad. We have a great work before us; if thoroughly carried out as we intend, it will be a grand reform. I am very happy, Miss Lynch, to think our acquaintance began in such an enterprise, and it looks now like a real basis.

I must tell you how very much I have enjoyed our acquaintance, and how much I hope it will become a long and sure friendship. It seems to me there is nothing we should thank God more for than a new friend who will help us to do what is better and nobler, and who truly feels with us. You have really done me good. I have new faith and courage in knowing you and being friend to such as you. I have not much to offer in the way of friendship, being made up of a very fair proportion of "human nature," except that I can say I am a sure friend for all weathers and changes, even if a rather faulty one. I do hope our friendship will prove to be a real one among all these shams, and be a pleasure and support to us both for many years. However, friendships are not made by words entirely. But, at least, you will take this as an expression of how much I value ours, and that I shall be glad to take from you, and give to you, the frankness and downrightness of a friend, feeling assured there will be no offense or distrust to either of us.

You may not place much value on my good wishes and hopes; for, no doubt, you have had quantities of them at various times, "*patés*" for the sentiment. Still, I cannot but think in our driving "Vanity Fair," we, none of us, find such a throng of true friends as to incommode us. And even you may bear one or two more, who will love and stand by you through all kinds of weather, of which I hope to be counted one. Now, dear friend, pardon my frankness, and believe me ever yours,

C. L. BRACE.

A NOTE OF CHARLES O'CONOR.

March 1, 1852.

My dear Miss Lynch: . . . I have many times experienced the pleasure of perusing occasional productions of your chaste and classic pen. This now has been renewed and increased by my becoming the possessor of your collection in one volume. It will always have a favored place with the few books not devoted to professional purposes which furnish my literary enjoyments; and I trust that the amiable and gifted authoress may long continue her contributions to our literature, and enjoy the respectful consideration she so richly merits. With many thanks, my dear Miss Lynch, I am yours sincerely,

CHARLES O'CONOR.

A NOTE OF MR. SAMUEL RUGGLES.

NEW-YORK, January 8, 1850.

My dear Miss Lynch: . . . I have just been reading some of your beautiful poems. They are indeed exquisite gems of genius, taste, and feeling. It might be invidious even to select from so much that is so desirable; but no one can fail to feel the tender and beautiful imagery the gifted author has thrown so gracefully into the "dark, unfathomed caves of ocean," nor the mingled grandeur and beauty, the exalted feeling, the truly celestial splendor of the glorious invocation "To the Sun." . . .

Most truly yours, SAMUEL RUGGLES.

A NOTE FROM GEO. TICKNOR.

BOSTON, MASS., October 23, 1860.

My dear Mrs. Botta: . . . I have been so much interested in your "Handbook of Literature." The portion relating to Italian literature I have read with great care and much interest. From the moment when I found that you said "Italian literature had risen or declined as the inspirations of Dante's genius have been more or less regarded," I felt that the true key-note had been struck, and I enjoyed all that followed. The other parts of the volume I have only turned over, but shall recur to them as I may have occasion.

Please offer my best regards to Mr. Botta. I remember our little acquaintance with great interest, and wish it might be renewed. . . . Believe me very cordially yours,

GEO. TICKNOR.

LETTERS OF FITZ-GREENE HALLECK.

GUILFORD, CONN., March, 1864.

Dear Mrs. Botta: The reason for the brevity of your note of the 28th grieves me sadly. Now that you are about to become one of Milton's

Ladies whose bright eyes
Rain influence, and judge the prize,

those bright eyes ought not to be doing penance for the mischief they have done to young hearts in their girlhood. Pray take quickly good care of them, for your own sake and for all our sakes.

I hope that their "influence" may be "rained" over all sorts of "Porte-Monnaie" at the "Fair," to its exceeding advantage; and am quite vexed — reprobate and immoral as I am — at our friend Mr. Bellows and his brother dissenters — especial favorites, you recollect, of the Reverend Joker Sidney Smith — for their denunciation of lotteries, thereby depriving you of the pleasure of awarding the prizes Milton names. My old-fashioned reverence for things sacred was shocked some time since by hearing a clergyman, when reminded that our Saviour had sanctioned wine and drinking by a miracle, say: "I admit the fact, but, were he now on earth, he would not dare to outrage public opinion to such a degree"; and now it seems that clergymen, claiming to be successors of the eleven apostles, pronounce their conduct in choosing a twelfth by lottery (see Acts, I Chap., 26 verse) an outrage upon the purity and piety of the party members of the New-York Legislature! Truly, as Horace Greeley says, quoting from Galileo, "The world moves!"

Truly yours, FITZ-GREENE HALLECK.

October 17, 1865.

My dear Mrs. Botta: Among the "winged words" (I am reading Lord Derby's "Homer") and winning words of yours that made our recent interview so pleasant to me, were those expressing your willingness to possess the inclosed portrait of mine. I trust that its beard, being more flowing and picturesque and Byrant-like than mine is since its last reaping, will have the honor to meet your generous and gracious approval.

When Madame Catalani, at Weimar, was proffered an introduction to Goethe, she innocently asked: "Who is *he?* What instrument does he play upon?" I find myself fast becoming as ignorant of books and of their authors as a dozen opera-singers, for until I saw (since seeing you) at Appleton's your very handsome husband's very handsome volume, I had no idea that he was an author, even in his own language, still less that he was so complete a master of ours as a glance over the volume so convincingly showed me. I look forward to great pleasure and profit from its perusal.

Why did you not, my dear lady, mention it to me the other day when we were talking about Dante? Why did you allow me to utter such superficial nonsense about his writings, translations, etc., when you were brimful of all his beautiful thoughts and still more beautiful expressions, and could have set me right when I was wrong, and made me knowing when I was ignorant? O woman! woman! how you must have laughed at me in both your sleeves!

I am not quite sure that I thanked you in voice, at the time you gave it, for your "Handbook." If I did, twice over can do no harm. I wish I had had access to such a work in my boyhood. It would have saved me from becoming tired of getting by heart all the quartos and octavos composing such a library as Charles Lamb says "no gentleman is without"—such works as Tom Campbell defines many of the Elizabethan dramas to be—a bucket of water containing a single glass of whisky. Your well-brewed and delicately flavored bowl of punch is worth them all.

Pray oblige me by saying that this inclosed has reached you, and that you are, as usual, "healthy, wealthy, and wise"; and believe me, dear Mrs. Botta, Truly yours,

FITZ-GREENE HALLECK.

April 13, 1867.

Dear Mrs. Botta: Since viewing very gratefully your twofold gift, the sonnet and the letter, I have passed a week in New-York. "Indeed!" you say, "and did not call on me, Mr. Halleck?"

Strike! my dear madam, but hear me!

A violent cold—my penance, I presume, for preferring a hot chop to a smoked herring during Lent—caused me during the whole week to be as deaf as any personage the most distinguished in that line of calamity in history, from Julius Cæsar to Miss Martineau, and consequently to be such a disagreeable and unendurable conversationist as you would walk a dozen miles to miss.

Therefore, in denying myself the pleasure of seeing you, I have done you a great kindness, and may justly claim your thanks for my self-sacrifice and your sympathy in the suffering it has caused me. As soon as I recover the possession of all my seven senses, I shall hasten once more to ring at your door.

In the mean time, should you be on your way across the water, I bid you and yours *bon voyage* out and home. I hope you will be delighted with Europe, and I know that when she knows you as well as I do, she will be delighted with you.

Pray, why should your dear mother (to whom please kindly remember me) be the obstacle you mention? Why does she not go with you? The change from shore to sea, and from sea to shore will add years to her life, and if she declines going, you know that the request, "Ye gods! annihilate both time and space, and make two lovers happy!" has been granted—may say per telegraph, "Good morning" to each other as punctually as you have ever done.

You have added a pure and lasting source of pleasure to Mr. Peabody's honorable consciousness of well doing, by the graceful sanction of your song, so briefly and beautifully anticipating the expression of "the thanks of millions yet to be." That you have made it a compliment to me is very kind on your part, and as it has reminded you of me and given me the lines and the letter, I thank you from my heart.

With my kindest regards to Mr. Botta and your good mother, believe me, dear lady, Very respectfully yours,

FITZ-GREENE HALLECK.

Selections from her Writings
in Prose and Poetry.

Prose

Leaves from the Diary of a Recluse [1]

January 1, 1838. To-day it occurred to me that I would keep a journal. The reason I have not done so before is because I have thought that where no events happened, as here, and where one's mind dwelt so uniformly as mine has done on a few general conclusions that have given me the darkest views of life, a journal would be a monotonous document. What can have led me into such clouds of dark thoughts? I shall never forget with what contempt I turned away from B——, who told me I should *outgrow* melancholy. But lately his words have often occurred to me, and I am half inclined to believe that melancholy is but another name for ill health — want of air and exercise. Ennobling thought, that all these immortal longings, these aspirations that neither earth nor heaven can satisfy, "this perpetual moaning of the soul for sympathy, like the sea-shell for the waters that should fill it"—that these should be the results of a fit of indigestion! No; it cannot be so. It is the struggle of the soul when she feels for the first time her fetters, as she wakes from the unconsciousness of childhood, bewildered with the mystery around her; aspiring, doubting, despairing, she at last falls, overcome with her own violence, and when she rises from the shock, it is with the subdued serenity of middle age.

I am often inclined to laugh at the inverted notions of things I used to have, but before a smile is formed tears get the start of it. "Reverence, O young, the delusions of that youth," says

1 This "Diary" was written by Mrs. Botta in the last period of her residence on Shelter Island, N. Y. It was published in "The Gift," a magazine of that time. It is now republished as a remarkable expression of her sentiments at that early age. See page 4.

Schiller. It is traitorous to our own hearts, when we alone have witnessed their agonies and known their indefinable desires, thus to turn the world's evidence, and join in the smile at their vain aspirations and fruitless struggles, and betray their weaknesses. No, my poor heart! never again will I jest with thy delusions or the tears it has cost thee to part with them. Little indeed hast thou found of sympathy or love in the world; and now that thou wouldst cast away the mantle of the Ideal as unfit for the blasts and frosts thou must encounter, and wouldst gird on thy shrinking form the protecting armor of Philosophy, though thou totterest with its weight, I would not bereave thee of thy last stronghold, the sympathy of thyself.

2d. I quite like journalizing. It will be company for me, and this is what I most need. To be thus "the cannibal of one's own thoughts" is horrible. To move among our fellow-beings, wrapt in ourselves, invisible, scanning the actions, compassing the petty motives, too often detecting other qualities than virtue: this drives us back upon ourselves, and teaches that

> There is no bond that mocks at Fate
> Like man's with his own heart.

Moore says, in his "Life of Sheridan," that the knowledge we acquire in maturity and from inclination, in contradistinction to that received through the medium of the *birch*, has about it a freshness the latter can never possess. This is my daily experience. Knowledge breaks upon me now like light upon the restored vision of the blind. I thank Fortune that I was such a paragon of idleness in my childhood. I am far from being free from it yet, however, though it is quite time. Twenty years of a life is sufficient for hibernation.

I am really pleased with this new acquaintance—myself. She is more companionable than I thought she would be, after being neglected for a lifetime. Not that I have had no thoughts, but they were shadowy from not being expressed in language. Why, then, have I never written before? I believe it is because life has seemed of too little importance to record even a feeling of its weariness. But that state has passed away. There is sublimity to me now in existence alone. To know that I am a part of this infinite, mysterious creation,—a conscious atom, capable of beholding the beauty and immensity of the universe,—this is indeed worth a life of suffering.

3d. It was my intention in commencing this journal to express some of the thoughts that have agitated me for the last two or three years. I have never given them utterance before—not because my heart was not aching to do so, but because I have never met those who cared what I thought, or who would understand me, perhaps, if I told them. Goethe says somewhere that he was possessed of a surplus of sentiment, and as he could do nothing until he had disposed of that, he wrote "Werther." And I have an accumulation of egotism that I must throw off here, or I shall not be able to proceed. The action of mind is always interesting to me, particularly when it is under the influence of strong emotions.

Until I was seventeen I was a mere child in thought and action. I think it was studying natural philosophy—albeit I studied sparingly—that first gave an impulse to my latent faculties. That was the "deep-felt ray" that loosened the avalanche of thought, which, rushing with rapidity and violence through my devoted head, left despair and desolation in its track, and stopped not in its mad career till it reached the very outposts of the universe, till it had boldly questioned time and eternity of their secrets, and nature of her Author. Then my mind—to drop the avalanche—stood still, overwhelmed with doubt and confusion: it had flown beyond its natural atmosphere, and could not breathe the rarefied ether that surrounded it; like the meteoric stones that by some strange convulsion are elevated almost without the sphere of the earth's attraction, but yet revolve with it until some other change once more precipitates them into its bosom; here have I been these three years in this unenviable state of betweenity, till now, suddenly and by some unknown cause, I find myself once more on a mental *terra firma*, and on the whole, if no wiser, I think rather better, for the jaunt. In this state of feeling of which I have been speaking, but for a few ties life would have been an intolerable burden. As it was, I often deliberated on the question of throwing it off. To me,

> Love, fame, ambition, avarice, were the same;
> Each idle, and all ill, and none the worst:
> For all were meteors of a different name,
> And death the sable smoke where vanished the flame.

To trace the cause of this state of mind, it would seem to have arisen from the intellect being suddenly excited to action, and then continuing to act without any regulator to its motion, so that it was tossed about like a boat without rudder or ballast on a stormy ocean. If I had then formed the habits of industry I now have, or had become more interested in study and society, I might have been spared much suffering. It is keeping aloof from the bustle and conflict of life, and looking at it through the cold medium of reason, that makes us chilled and indifferent; as often in a ball-room I have been an uninterested observer till I became at last an excited actor. He is wrong, then, who calls this indifference to life, and the consequent misery, in one who idealizes rather than acts, the effect of an overwrought imagination. It is no fancy; it is indeed the truth. All is vanity. But he errs, I admit, who dwells morbidly on it. There is somewhere in Bulwer's "Asmodeus at Large," the story of a youth who, thirsting for forbidden knowledge, would

> Lift the painted veil that men call life.

To escape from the horrible sights that his newly acquired power reveals to him, he flies to his mistress, but as he approaches her he discovers "no whole but a million of lives loathsome and awful." It had such an effect on me when I read it that I cannot think of it now without a shudder.

The external world is beautiful. Turn which way we will, to the heavens, the sea, the earth, we are "dazzled and drunk with beauty" ; to the graceful forms of animals, and our wonder is lost in admiration ; to our own species, to the soul-lit eye, the blushing cheek, and the intellectual brow, and our delight is deepened into love. Life itself is a pleasure — the power of motion in the invisible supporting air, and the thousand exquisite sensations we are so delicately constituted as to receive every moment, are in themselves sufficient to make existence almost rapturous; but woe to him who would penetrate those regions of darkness and doubt that lie beyond the natural boundaries of his mental vision. He is like that lover who, not satisfied that the cheek of his mistress blushes for him, would decompose it to its frightful elements, till, horror-stricken, he turns from the hideous sight. I have not then been acting or thinking falsely, but only foolishly. Henceforth, since there is a bright side to human life, let me keep my eyes steadily fixed on that, and, if possible, be blind to all else. With this page let there be an end to all horrors.

5th. Just finished Latrobe's "Travels in North America." He says, "No man can pass over it, from east to west, from north to south, without bringing away the impression that if on any part of his earthly creation the finger of God has drawn characters that would seem to indicate the seat of empire, surely it is there." The desire to travel has been a passion with me for years. If the body is always confined, the mind must remain so in some degree, despite reading and thinking. It convinces us that we are not indeed the center of the world, and that the sun shines on other lands and other races. Once, my ideas of the delights of traveling were more highly wrought, as my knowledge was more limited; but knowing the facts instead of the poetry has not diminished the desire.

It has always seemed to me that our country presented a noble field for a national poet. The elements of poetry are here, and want but the master hand to combine them. These elements are its immense extent, its varieties of climate and scenery, its noble rivers, its boundless prairies, its primeval forests, its aborigines, the sudden dawning of the continent like a radiant vision on the eyes of the Old World; and lastly, its present government and the glorious revolution that established it.

7th. Just read the "Court and Camp of Bonaparte," and I half regret it, for the writer with his faint praise has succeeded in belittling Napoleon, in my eyes at least, much more effectually than Scott, whose prejudice is so apparent that one sees at once that for him nothing good could come out of France. This other writer, instead of dazzling us with glimpses of Napoleon's comet-like career, gives us petty details that destroy the whole effect. The reading of it is like going behind the curtains at one of those dioramas, which are very beautiful if seen in the proper distance and light.

"Of all that flattered, followed, sought, and sued," how few adhered to the Emperor in his fall! What a bitter disappointment to a young and generous nature to find that the world is indeed made of such materials! I used to have a sort of poetic creed that it was selfish, cold, and ungrateful, but at the same time there was a latent hope that it might be poetry after all. It remained for experience, corroborated by history, to demonstrate its sad reality.

8th. To-day I read a book of travels, a poor thing enough, but interesting to me, as it describes

The scenes my earliest dreams have dwelt upon.

Can it be that my presentiments will never be realized, and that I shall die without seeing those lands, when I have envied even the waves that kiss their sunny shores?

The author seems to belong to that class of persons who are neither poets nor men of common sense. Poets often lack common sense, or rather see everything through a poetic haze, and nothing with vulgar eyes. For instance, Lamartine, in his "Pilgrimage to the Holy Land," while our own countryman was disputing with his guide about the bakshish, belaboring his donkey, or amusing himself with his servant Paul's personation of the disciple at Jerusalem, he was weeping in holy raptures, prostrated before the sacred relics. Lamartine was a poet without common sense—Stephens a man of common sense, without a spark of poetry. Both are delightful in this case; but I like best those characters which unite these qualities; and where they are united the best poets are produced,—that is, poets who delight all,—and Goethe says, "The poet deserves not the name when he only speaks out those few feelings that are his as an individual. Only when he can appropriate and tell the story of the world is he a poet." None but the most poetic minds read Shelley, while the most ordinary appreciate Byron. But I am getting into difficulty, for I really think Shelley the greater poet of the two—so I must think it over again.

To-day I have been so lonely! This loneliness I generally contrive to keep at bay by intense occupation of some kind—yet there are times when this fails and books offer no consolation—when I want a living, breathing, sympathizing friend. But Mashallah! as the Turks say. I am just reading "Constantinople and its Environs." As long as I do not travel, I have a strong desire ungratified, and this has something to do in producing happiness, I think. It has always seemed to me that perfect happiness and perfect misery were nearly allied, because both states are hopeless. I remember reading a story of two lovers who died of being perfectly happy—and, paradoxical as it seems, I fully believe such a thing might happen.

12th. The last volume of Smollett's continuation of Hume I finished last night. Thank heaven, it is read through! It appears to me that Hume is overrated. Though his history is good as a reference, and it may be a duty to read it, it is hardly a pleasure. He could not easily be more uninteresting.

14th. Read Burr's Memoirs. I recollect a little incident Mr. T—— told me of him. At some place where he visited there was a pretty child, of which he was very fond and often brought it presents. Caressing it one day the child playfully put her hand in Burr's pocket. Mr. T—— said he should never forget the look of scorn with which he cast the little girl from him; he never spoke to her again. Whatever may have been his faults, it is melancholy to see an old man like him walking among his fellow-men scorning and scorned. I have a fellow-feeling with misanthropes; that is, I can understand how a noble nature should turn from the mass of its fellow-creatures too often with pity or contempt; it should be pity, pity for their selfishness and petty malice—their stupidity, living in such a world of wonders, where every pebble and every blade of grass is a miracle and a mystery, yet living and dying with scarcely a thought above the sod that at length covers their dust. Yet, were we made to soar? May not genius be a disease? Oh, dear! it is dull talking to one's self—one wants contradiction sometimes.

20th. Since I wrote here last, I have stood by the death-bed of and followed to her narrow home my friend C——. O Heaven! what a scene!—to see the dread conqueror clasp in his embrace the form we have often caressed, and the cold damp earth heaped over the bosom that cherished high aspirations and warm affections! To-night I have been to the grave. One week ago I spoke to her, I held her hand, I kissed the cheek that daylight may never more look upon.

Answer me, burning stars of night,
Where is the spirit gone?

How strange that though I have often thought of death, and even meditated hastening it, I never till now knew the weight of mortality! Hereafter, let me live with the last hour before me. I have not loved my friends enough; I have been exacting of their love, and avaricious of my own. How mad, how insensible, I have been! I see myself in a new light,—an intellectual and moral being, by a mysterious destiny brought into existence, borne irresistibly along toward a gulf which I cannot fathom, and over whose depths hang clouds dark and impenetrable. Every moment hurries me along; and yet I ask not, I think not, I know not, to what.

21st. "The moon is beaming silver bright," the stars are looking down with a melancholy gaze; I have looked on them a moment since; they are the very same that inspired the fantasies of Plato and Pythagoras. There they shine with their pale, sad light, and Plato and Pythagoras are gone, and generations have vanished like the waves that have broken on the sea-shore. Myriads of eyes have looked on them, myriads of beings like myself have "lived, loved, and died," yet they are not changed. I look upon them to-night — a few more years and I shall see them not, but still they will shine on. What is humanity amidst such a universe, and what am I? The very trees under my window have lived longer than I can live, — my life, the very breath of heaven can destroy it. Races and generations are nothing; the mighty machine rolls on and sweeps them away. Father of light and life! thou alone knowest the conflicting thoughts that agitate my soul; give me a right spirit, and guide me in the way of truth; thou only canst know my desire for it. Make me submissive to thy decrees, and prepare me for whatever fate awaits me hereafter.

23d. This has been a wretched day to me. I have had another of those paroxysms of tears that I vainly thought had ceased forever. I thought their fountains were dry. Struggle on, brave spirit! thou dost buffet the billows right bravely. Storms of wild thoughts have rushed over thee; thou hast fed on the gall and wormwood of existence; "thou hast made idols and hast found them clay"; thou hast looked over the broad universe for one spot where thou mightest repose, but in vain — all is inhospitable, dark, and forbidding — back thou comest to thyself, weary, but finding no rest, yet thou dost struggle on; — courage, good heart! thy pilgrimage shall soon be over, and though no beam of brightness break through the gloom of the future, yet on the mercy of thy Creator thou mayest calmly repose.

24th. This has been a day of continued occupation, and all the thinking that I have done has been to wonder how I could possibly feel so wretchedly as I did yesterday. My occupation has been nothing less than overturning the garret and restoring it to order! As garrets and poets are often connected, perhaps there is something inspiring in the air of one. I feel so well I am ashamed. I have no more sympathy with what is written on my last page than a child. I have but one feeling, that of perfect health, with the liveliness that always gives me. I wonder how every one can look so doleful and mope about so,—and yesterday I was on the bed crying my eyes out half the day, in the most hopeless melancholy and despair. All this for breathing the air of the garret! But I shall have another day of rapture to-morrow, gathering paper, rags, emptying old bandboxes, and packing bundles. After that I suppose I shall sink again to the level of the second story and the companionship of musty books.

28th. Finished Guizot's "History of Civilization in Europe," a clear and concise view of its progress, speaking of which he says, "Thus man advances in the execution of a plan which he has not conceived, of which he is not aware, and comprehends by its results alone. Conceive a great machine, the design of which is centered in a single individual, though its various parts are intrusted to different workmen, strangers, and separated from each other; none of these understand the work as a whole, which he concurs in producing; and thus by the hand of man are the designs of Providence wrought out in the government of the world." Thus it has often appeared to me that we are the instruments of some great and unknown end. But I forbear to speculate.

I have been quite ill to-day from a blow received on my head yesterday by being unceremoniously thrown out of a sleigh and dashed against a fence, and but for my quilted bonnet, that honored member (my head) would have lost all sensibility to pains and aches. As I was riding home I amused myself with thinking how little force was wanting to have quieted me forever. Then I should have been unconscious. There would have been the same bustle, the preparing of coffin and shroud that there was here a few days since; they would have buried me, canvassed my merits and failings, wept a little, and there it would have ended. In the hearts of a few the shock would be great and lasting; but I have been so long separated from all I love that even were I to die, I should be scarcely a loss to them. Oh this waste of the affections! this hoarding of them up as the miser does his treasures, till they rot and rust! it is death — it is worse than death! To live in such a desert as this I must be made of "sterner stuff" than many. I do not forget my books: they indeed are all my consolation; but they are like the sun in this wintry day — it shines, it lights up the earth with a thousand beautiful hues, but it is distant, it is cold. It warms not, though it gives us light. How often my heart aches for a kind word, an approving smile, from some one who loves me. But, perhaps, this is weakness.

Feb. 1st. Read "Mary of Burgundy." The Lord of Hannut says, "Hidden within the bosom of this mortal clay is some fine essence, participating in the affections of the earthly thing it inhabits, but thirsting for knowledge beyond this world, and yearning for joys more pure and love more imperishable than the joy and love of this world can ever be."

I regret that I do not write here every day. When I think of all the thoughts that have passed over my mind like shadows across a mirror, and left as little trace, it is always with a feeling of regret, and yet why should that be cause for regret more than that the beautiful clouds will disappear, and the flowers and leaves? A beautiful thought is not more beautiful than a flower, yet we see myriads of them die without leaving a trace of their existence, and never sigh for them,— why should we for lost thoughts?

3d. I determined to write a page here, good or bad, every night, but last night I had no fire, and to-night I have no ideas.

I said to B—— to-day in my letter, that some years ago my imagination took the reins of my mind, and drove off after the manner of Phaeton, leaving the other faculties to come up at their lagging pace. Thinking of it again, I am sure it is so.

Poor C——, how soon I have forgotten her! I have often asked myself if I were willing to be as lightly thought of. I answer, yes. While I live I am avaricious of every breath of affection and love my friends can bestow, but after I have ceased to be conscious in the oblivion of the grave, or have passed into a higher and holier state, why should I demand the tears and vain regrets of those who loved me here? If there were still enjoyments in the world, why should I have their thoughts coffined with me?

But would I be forgotten? Oh, no! I would have my memory recalled like a strain of remembered music, like a pleasant landscape or a sunset, causing no sorrow when they disappear.

Hitherto I have always been unable to comprehend the desire, expressed so often and by so many, for posthumous fame; but to-day as I sat reading, the idea of my thoughts living in the minds of thousands when I existed no longer came across me with an emotion of sublimity I have rarely felt. This power to reach down, if I may say so, and connect one's self with the remotest posterity, is indeed a glorious immortality.

I am quite horrified to think how little I improve the time. Strange, that when these few flitting years are all that we possess, we squander them in such idle pursuits, with a world of science, art, and beauty before us to be explored! Would I could always remember that the moments are flying like arrows, and worlds cannot redeem one of them — that he is unworthy of life who has lived and made the world no better, and set fainting virtue no bright example.

6th. I often find that when I begin to express my thoughts they are quite new to me, or, before they are clothed in language, I cannot distinguish them. I suppose it is because I have never written them before now, and for the last year or two have not spoken them at all. My mind will collect materials, but it shrinks from the labor of putting them together — it will form the cocoons, but it does not like to spin and weave them into fabrics.

7th. Read "Attila." I like the character of Ildica. After the scenes of terror she passed through, the voice of her lover had no music for her, and she retired to the solitude of a convent, though no obstacle prevented her union. I can conceive it. When the events of our lives call out an unnatural energy, the moment we become conscious of a superhuman power to meet and battle with our fate, that moment life assumes a new aspect. Gifted with a strange power, breathing in a rarer spirit, we are forced against our wills above the passions and feelings whose slaves we once were, and doomed from our elevation to behold them diminish in magnitude and luster. Alas for that elevation! Alas for that human heart!

It is dreadful to think how I have wasted all my life. The next three months I mean to improve vigorously. The mind is acted on by laws like matter, and the more resistance we overcome the more we have the power of overcoming. If I were to measure the momentum of my mind, however, by the force required to put it in motion, it would be tremendous. It is idle to regret the past; the future I can control. But am I quite sure of that? How do I know that we are not made for a certain destiny, as a clock to strike so often? How this question of destiny haunts me! It is better to act than to speculate, however. I laugh outright often at the stupid wonder that overcomes me when I begin to think—but I oftener cry.

Commenced the "History of Rome." What a divine power is this of acquiring knowledge! Though I often ask myself, "What from this barren being do we reap?"—surely it is not so barren.

We should be thankful for the boon of existence, had we but this one faculty of acquiring knowledge—that is, as I happen to feel just now. Add to this the countless pleasures of eye and ear—of the affections and the senses—and who shall say he is miserable? What a beautiful bond of union is mind! How it carries us back and unites us with the great spirits of the past! Ages have trodden down their graves, worms have eaten their very dust; yet their thoughts live. Ethereal and imperishable, they float down the awful current of time, while empires and men are swallowed in its mysterious depths. And I, but a bubble on this mighty ocean—I can comprehend these thoughts, can sympathize and unite my own with them, can make them a part of me, and feel that they at least will be immortal.

8th. I have always delighted in that story of Bulwer's, in the "Pilgrims of the Rhine," called "The Life of Dreams," where a young German student succeeds in continuing a dream night after night, till at length it becomes the reality, and real life the dreaming state. Why, since the beings of the actual world are such, should we not betroth to ourselves the beings of the mind? Speak to them, they answer in our own tongue; love them, and the glowing page tells us eloquently that they would have loved us. Is love a dream or a reality? Once I believed in love, how devoutly! But was not this love of the imagination? I think it was. Yet it is the highest feeling of which our nature is capable. I say it is the love of the imagination, yet I know not that. We call it so, perhaps, because lovers are not often under its influence for a long time. They seem to discover that they have loved an ideal instead of a reality, and then they graduate their love accordingly. This every day's experience proves, but it does not, after all, disprove the existence of love. How much I have dreamed of love when I was younger and more poetical than I am now! I have looked on the dewdrops and seen them by some strange sympathy draw nearer and nearer, and mingle into one; I have seen floating blocks of inanimate matter, without any apparent cause, advance till they united; I have heard the strings of a guitar, when you spoke on the key to which it was attuned, thrill back a corresponding tone; I have watched the electric cloud whirling through space, stormy and dark, giving no brightness and uttering no voice till it met its sister cloud; and I turned in bitterness of soul to ask myself if amid all these sympathies of nature the human heart only was doomed to wander on its pilgrimage, desolate and alone And is it indeed so? Are all these aspirations and desires to be mocked by the *seeming* of love, as the mirage of the desert mocks the thirsty traveler with green spots and flowing streams? I have struggled against this conviction, but I feel that this love is too elevated for humanity. We may desire, but we cannot attain it. Earliest, brightest, and last of my delusions, I resign thee. I turn from thee as from a guiding star: pale, steady, and bright, thou hast beamed on my dark horizon, and now thou settest forever. As the idolater, knowing not the true God, lavishes his adoration on some object of his own creation, and invests it with the attributes of the Deity, Spirit of Love! even so have I worshiped thee. I have worshiped thee, and thou art but a phantom of my own mind. I renounce my idolatry. Sweet, radiant dream! throwing over life an ideal drapery, thou comest no more to me; the touch of reason has broken the spell that bound thee to me, and now thou departest forever.

March 9th. I am delighted with Gibbon. Though I have such a grand plan marked out for study, I cannot follow it up with half the perseverance I wish. Can I not throw off this torpor by exertion, as travelers keep awake in frozen regions, where to sleep is not to wake again? In this case sleep is death also. For what is it to live without the exercise of our powers, like toads that lie buried for years in rocks? I choose to come out, if it is only like the toad, to hop round a little, and take the air.

Spring has come again with her warm south winds, her loosened waters, and melting snows. What a perpetual miracle is this change of seasons! How they roll on and bear me with them! For some weeks I have not thought of death. Would it not be well to set apart a few minutes every day to reflect on it?

11th. With such a delightful course of study before me, how can I weary as I do? It must be that I have no natural fondness for it, but have been driven to it by circumstances. I have long known that I must not place my hopes of happiness in others. Death follows in the rear of the unfaithful, and snatches up the few that remain to us. And how melancholy a thing is this change! There has been a friend that we loved, with whose heart our own accorded, and like well-tuned instruments they gave not a discordant note. We part—years intervene—we meet again, but oh! with what sinking of heart, to find that we are strangers! Different scenes and thoughts have turned the currents that ran so smoothly together, and they mingle no longer. That is a bitter and melancholy hour, more bitter and melancholy than death itself; for if death takes those we love, their memory remains fresh and beautiful, and on that we can repose. But the estranged, the cold, the changed!—it were well if we could blot out their memory. As I was saying, then, our friends die and change, we ourselves grow old, and as the vigor of our youth decays, and the flowers of our spring wither, some objects must supply their place; and where shall we find them if not in our own minds? and what shall these objects be if not the cultivation of taste and the acquisition of knowledge? These make us independent of time and place. Like the camel in the parched desert, we bear within us the fountain to supply the wants of our solitary pilgrimage. Thus refreshed and invigorated, we patiently travel on, while those around us languish beneath the storm, or die of the feverish thirst. One might ask, "Will not this course make you selfish, by putting you above the necessity of sympathy?" No; not more than is necessary. Why, when we find nothing to lean upon, should we not support ourselves? I have been too dependent. Like the harp that responds to every breeze, so has my inmost soul vibrated to every adverse breath of unkindness, injustice, and change. Is it not time, then, that the instrument were new strung, and the chords made of sterner stuff? Since the midsummer of my life is departing, let it bear with it like the summer of earth its perishing flowers. Bright, beautiful aspirations of my youth! yearnings for that love a God only can satisfy,—for that sympathy that earth will never give!—"radiant and white-robed dreams," ye leave me now forever! Go with the youth that cherished you and the tears that flowed at your coming.

12th. I find myself even now, with all my improvements, often debating whether this mortal coil is in truth a desirable appendage. A sudden weariness of life comes over me, and

I could lie down like a tired child,
And weep away a life of care.

But I know this is wrong. I know that it is better to live. We are endowed with beautiful sympathies and divine faculties: we can love and pity; we can think and imagine, and paint those imaginings in words and colors; we can perceive the harmony and beauty of the world about us,—and is not this worth living for? And on the arch that history builds over the gulf of the past, we can wander back to remote antiquity and trace the nations of our kind while they sleep under the weight of centuries. "What are our woes and sufferance?" What if the world is unkind, our friends indifferent, and our affections water but the desert? Nature is true. In the calmness of the sunshine, in the terror of the storm, in the beauty of the insect and the flower, in the mysteries of the stars, and in the action of her unchanging laws, does she not alike reveal herself beautiful to our gaze and worthy of our contemplation? Then come those "beings of the mind" that people the visions of the poet and minister to those finer wants of our nature that reality overlooks. Then there is the power of doing good to those around us. With such objects before you, will you call life a burden when a few brief years at most will deprive you of it? Let me then lay aside this morbid sensibility, and pass at once from the dreaming and sentimental girl to the active, resolute, and high-souled woman, chastened and subdued by thought and adversity.

To-day I finished the reign of Diocletian. Is it not strange that history presents but two instances that I recollect, of men wearied with the glitter of a throne voluntarily descending from their elevation? When Maximian remonstrated, Diocletian replied: "You would not wonder if you could see my cabbages grow."

Is it not a proof that we are low in the scale of being, this fact that anything like greatness of mind, nobility, or generosity strikes us as something so strange? The world gazes in as much astonishment to see a man perform a really generous action as if he had suddenly mounted in the air on wings. It must be a low state of existence when the beautiful, the holy, and the elevated excite such emotions of novelty, rather than that which is base, cowardly, and low. The latter surround us like the air we breathe. Show us the contrary, and we wonder and praise: praise a good action!—praise virtue!—praise a man because he has done just as he should do!

13th. A lost day.

14th. Almost as bad. I fail to keep constantly before my mind the idea of the shortness of life and the certainty that I must die. How every disappointment and petty vexation is swallowed up in that awful truth! What a panacea for all ills! How cheerful, how happy, I am after thinking of it! It gives my thoughts a freedom they never had before, and my mind a calm and delightful elevation. I say it does this when I think of it, and I was just wondering why it is so little in my thoughts. Perhaps the reason is that it is unnatural to one of my years and temperament. Hitherto I have rebelled,—now I submit. Since life was so fair I was disappointed that it was not paradise. I have overlooked the actual good, and clamored for the imaginary.

15th. Despite philosophy and everything else, there have been two or three hours to-day when life was almost insupportable. Suddenly the fit passed off, and left me as light-hearted as it found me. How many thousand times has this sickness come over me, and I have wept till my tears were exhausted! It is a strange state, this abandonment of despair! Friends, foes, art, nature, the beautiful, the deformed, all disappear in the blackness that enshrouds me. Indifference to life, death, heaven, and hell takes the place of my warm affections and lively perceptions. Formerly I felt this often, but of late more rarely. As I have said before, it is not imagination, but truth, that produces this effect, and the error is in allowing ourselves to think upon that which maddens and overwhelms us. As in crossing some awful precipice the only safety is in fixing your eyes on some distant and motionless object, neglecting which, you are precipitated into the abyss, so in passing through life, if the soul is diverted from heaven and repulsed from earth, concentrated in herself, and intent on her slender foothold, she reels with fearful giddiness, and, perhaps, in madness plunges into the gulf of the unknown future.

Another week is gone irrevocably! — how strange that it should startle us no more! Silently and steadily the days glide along, stealing from us our youth, digging our graves, and hastening our footsteps toward them, and we, fools that we are, heed not the swift-winged messengers. Ye fleeting hours, particles of this existence that is wasting so rapidly away, shall I permit ye to depart with no record that ye have passed over a being like myself, when, like the south wind that sweeps over the flowers, thy wings should be laden?

16th. To-day I have read over some old letters,

> Relics of love and life's enchanted spring,

and thought of my old friends, the dead and the changed; for change or death has them nearly all. I held in my hand words traced on the most perishable material, yet even they had survived the hearts that dictated, the hands that transcribed them. I read over the gushing and glowing thoughts of those who are now as changed and cold to me as I to them, but whom I once met delighted and delighting. Bitter, melancholy truth, that neither love nor friendship endures! Time sweeps over and buries all, as the clouds of sand sweep over the plains of Egypt, burying her magnificent monuments, and gradually entombing the pyramids themselves. As the excavator among these relics removes the sand and soil, and stands in the presence of the past, so I have to-day communed with these specters of love and friendship.

I wish to write here every day, for I think when I have nothing to say, it is evidence that the day has been wasted, and who is so rich that he can afford to lose a day?

To-day I have painted. What delightful arts are painting and poetry! — with the one we can delineate the forms, and with the other the emotions, of beauty.

17th. I have just been reading two or three of Hazlitt's essays, where he expresses my feelings almost in my own words.

How delightful thus to meet with a soul that responds to mine, though thousands of miles intervene between the countries of our birth, and beyond rises the impassible barrier of the grave!

As I was walking along on the shore to-day, I found myself musing on a notorious instance of unkindness, and asking myself, "What have you to expect from such a world?"— which I think was a very silly question. Of course I have nothing to expect. And do I ask a reward for whatever good I might chance to do, in the shape of kindness or gratitude? Are my virtues to be sold even at such prices? Then are they paltry indeed. No; I have nothing to sell. Whatever good I can do should be done freely, without hope or reward. If I would live aright, self-sacrifice is the first lesson I must learn. What a low motive for being good, the hope of a reward! And even if it were not a low motive it would be a very useless one, inasmuch as the reward is seldom forthcoming. The greatest Benefactor of the race, men crucified. Let me endeavor to imitate his divine humility and love, and his utter abnegation of self.

I continue to read Gibbon. When I think of those massacres of thousands, each one of whom was a creature like myself, and follow the gradual but irresistible march of ages as they move on, bearing down empires and trampling on humanity as on dust, how do I shrink into nothingness! Often after reading history a mental giddiness comes over me, and the world and the things in it seem gliding like a moving panorama before me, as, after sailing a long time, when we stop, the room takes the motion of the boat.

. . . .

25th. This is our first spring day. How delightful it has been! and yet there is always something melancholy in this season — to me "the saddest of the year." I just now returned from an hour's sitting on the rock by the shore, watching the sunset: surely none could be more lovely, Italian or any other. I leaned my head back and half closed my eyes; the clouds seemed like islands in some land of enchantment (islands in land!), and while I sat watching, one after another faded, till at last "they were gone and all was gray." B——'s idea of perfect happiness is floating on a cloud with the one we love. Dreamy enough, yet I could not give a better definition of happiness. There must be moments in love that would atone for a life of misery,—that first consciousness of its presence when

> We feel that we adore,
>   To such refined excess,
> That though the heart would break with more,
>   It could not live with less.

To feel this must be to feel the concentrated poetry of existence. In the desert of life, love is the oasis that we pine to reach — that reaching, we weep to part from, and to which we still turn back with longing, lingering look.

As the time approaches for me to leave this place, I grow so impatient that it seems to me the next fortnight will never pass. How two years of solitude and study have changed me! How gay I was once! How subdued and sedate I am now! Those that have known me before will scarcely recognize me now. In thinking over the list of my early friends, how many have gone to their last repose! — only a few weeks since, H——, among others. She was my earliest friend. How many giddy hours I have frolicked away with her! — yet the last time we met, how cold was our meeting, how tearless our parting! We had grown strangers.

April 7th. To-morrow I shall leave this "abomination of desolation" forever. It will cost me some pain to do so, notwithstanding it has scarcely afforded me a happy moment for the last two years that I have vegetated here. Perhaps I shall be like the old prisoner released from the Bastile, who went back and begged to die there.

This is the last page of my journal: I close this and my exile together.

Notes on History

History is the record of the collected experience of man in all ages. One writer defines it to be "Philosophy teaching by example"; another, "A vast collection of social and moral experiments, that mankind make involuntarily and often very expensively upon themselves." Accepting these definitions, it would seem almost inexplicable that the study of history should be so neglected, were it not proverbial that we are reluctant to avail ourselves of the experience of others, which, as Goethe says, "is even like the stern lights of a ship, and sheds no light on the path before us." With the exception of a few scholars among us, whose lives are devoted to the pursuit of letters, the knowledge of history is extremely limited. Isolated names and facts, the faint glimmerings of school-boy days, may indeed linger in the mind; Marathon, Thermopylæ, Alexander, Cæsar, Charlemagne, and Alfred may be familiar names to the ear, and yet the events and eras in the world's history, the great spirits who have created them, their relative connection with one another and with our own time, remain a sealed book. History, to be comprehended, must be taken as a whole. As in looking at some grand historical picture, if we would take in the scope and design of the artist, we must first regard the work in its general outlines and effect, rather than in detached limbs, figures, or groups, which, however worthy of our attention in themselves, lose their force and meaning when separated from their natural connections.

Guizot, in his "History of Civilization," speaking of its progress, says: "Thus man advances in the execution of a plan which he has not conceived, of which he is not aware, and which he comprehends by its results alone. Conceive a great machine, the design of which is centered in a single individual, though its various parts are intrusted to different workmen, strangers, and separated from one another, none of these understand the work as a whole, which he concurs in producing; and thus, by the hand of man, are the designs of Providence wrought out in the government of the world." If this be true, as it must be,—if Providence directs the great events that it is the office of the historian to describe; if God dictates what he writes,—it is certainly worthy of our profound study and regard. Nature has been called "the newly uttered word of God." History is not less the continually uttered word of God. And to seek the interpretation of this revelation is one of the highest offices of the human mind. But in another view, history is the very alphabet and key of all knowledge: the preliminary step in literature; the foundation without which no permanent superstructure can be raised. And to obtain a general knowledge of the great events and characters over five or six thousand years of recorded history, is in reality a far less difficult achievement than is commonly supposed; and this should be the work of the first years of education. This general knowledge would prepare the mind for the reception of details, and for the assimilation of whatever nutriment it might derive from them. As the mass of people are educated, and as they read, the beautiful and unbroken succession of cause and effect, which lies at the foundation of all historical development, is overlooked; and yet no study of history can be efficient without the investigation of the succession of causes and effects.

This investigation is the principal object of the philosophy of history, of which the Italian Vico was the founder. By tracing this principle through the evolution of Roman law, he establishes the doctrine of a natural law in historic processes. Human society is based on these fundamental conditions: 1st. Worship, or the belief in divine power; marriage, or the restraint of the passions; and sepulchral rites, or the belief in immortality. 2d. Society has three great periods, the theocratic, the heroic, and the humane.

Whatever may have been man's primal state, when history

first finds him, he is civilized, skilled in arts, governed by laws, living in cities, worshiping in temples. The science of history is concerned only with man's conditions by social and civil organizations, which constitute the State, through which come liberty and right. Hence Rome becomes the theme of history, in which civil society is realized progress. By surveying the past and present of society, we see such evidence of development as will warrant us in assuming that progress is the aim and purpose of history. But what is progress? To this, various answers have been given. According to Hegel, progress has three stages, dividing the world's history into three epochs: the period of the Oriental nations, when only one was allowed to be free; that of Greek and Roman civilization, when freedom was accorded to many; and lastly, the period of the Germanic nations, when freedom is seen to be the rightful property of all. A more comprehensive term would be: progress in social organization, in which liberty is one of many elements; progress toward a state in which nationalities shall no more divide mankind; when the human family shall unite in one organic whole, a state embracing the greatest freedom of the individual with the greatest compactness of social union, seeming to all to be of the greatest possible advantage in their connection with one another. In this view, every epoch of human history is a new stage of social development, and every historic evolution exposing the inadequacy of each former state, inaugurates a new society, and is no exception to the universal law that nothing grows without the opposition of contrary elements. Regarded from one point of view, war, which occupies so large a shàre in the annals of the world, is a great moral evil. But there are holy wars of ideas, principles, and religions. Besides the antagonism of contrary elements, society is further conditioned by a principle of alternation within itself which makes the historic development of humanity to follow a spiral direction rather than an advancement on a straight line. Hence that development is realized through a series of revolutions which now speed, now retard, the progress of mankind. It was on this law that the immigrations and emigrations developed, colonizing Asia Minor, Palestine, Greece, Italy, and made the northern tribes descend into Italy to destroy the Roman Empire in its declining age; and it is this identical law that regulates the modern migrating epoch now in progress from the Old World to the New. Thus, by conflict, alternation, contradictions, and spiral revolutions, humanity advances not simultaneously in all its faculties, but in one or another, often retrograding in some parts, but always advancing on the whole toward an end which cannot yet be predicted. . . .

In studying history we see at once that great and unrecorded events had already taken place in the prehistoric period, when, in the imperfect light of the Oriental era, the historic scene is first revealed to us. Through ages languages had been formed, races separated, states established, and laws, customs, religions, and arts, had already attained maturity. From this remote antiquity to the eighth century before the Christian era, the separated members of the historic family remained in an isolated condition, each preparing apart its contribution to the common development of the race. And as these nations of southwestern Asia maintained their independently different elements of civilization, one by one they fell before the attacks of the vigorous mountain races, whose descent inspired these luxurious and oppressive nations with terror, and whose course they were powerless to resist. But above this desolation and despair of the nations were heard the voices of the Hebrew prophets, who, alone, saw with the eyes of prophecy what we now see inductively,—the great law of historic progress.

The first attempt at centralization is manifested in the Assyrian Empire, which centered at Nineveh, and the second in the Chaldean, of which Babylon was the center, differing little from the preceding, except in its increasing extent. On the ruins of these, Cyrus laid the foundations of the Persian Empire, which was to last through twelve centuries, and which brought to the civilization of the Semitic race all the peculiarities of the Aryan stock; and from the fusion of these races a new, and a far higher and richer, civilization was evolved. Later, when Darius, threatened with the Scythian hordes from the west and north, crossed the Hellespont with his army of eight hundred thousand men, arrayed in all the splendor of the Persian equipment, we witness one of the first grand steps in the march of Empire. This expedition resulted in the conquest of Macedonia and Thrace; and leaving a part of his army to complete his victory, Darius returned to his capital at Susa and attempted to organize and consolidate his vast dominions, extending from the Caspian Sea to the cataracts of the Nile, and from beyond the Indus to the shores of the Ægean Sea. He divided them into provinces, built post-roads, and established the first rude outlines of Empire.

This period was the commencement of the fifth century B. C., and was signalized by the development of a new element, the Spirit of Freedom, hitherto unknown in history. The Ionian colonies of Greece, which had been conquered by Crœsus and had fallen with the Lydian monarchy before the Persian arms, now raised in revolt, and pillaged and burned the ancient and beautiful city of Sardis. This little band, aided by the Athenians, met the whole force of the Persian army, and, although they were defeated, the indignation of Darius that they should have retarded him was not appeased, and he appointed an officer to stand at his table and each day to remind him of his vow to avenge this insult. His next encounter with the Greeks, on the plains of Marathon, was a battle which remains memorable in the annals of history. It had been known for ages in the East that there existed in Europe states that exchanged their productions for those of that country; and the prophets allude to the people of the isles "laying aside their broidered robes and uttering lamentations for the destruction of the great city" (Tyre). Before the age of Herodotus we have no Greek history. But suddenly, at the close of the Persian war, the Greeks appear before us in all the perfection of their splendid civilization. There is, however, one great monument of the prehistorical age which gives us a vivid picture of their earlier life, differing essentially from the character in which they first appear in history. It represents them in the heroic age before the arts had been perfected. What the sculptures on the grottoes of Beni-Hassan are to the history of Egypt, and the inscriptions on the walls of Persepolis to the Persians, the Homeric poems are to the history of Greece. . . .

Notes on Poetry

Some poems of our day seem to be the wailings of spirits that have looked appalled on the realities of life,—on its friendships that change, on its love that becomes indifference, on the hollowness of fame, and on death, the certain and awful consummation of this life-tragedy. This is one view of life, but it is not the highest nor the truest; nevertheless it is a view that we must take in our ascent to a higher and better one. That glow of youthful feeling which paints life as a pastime and a revel, is not more false than the despair which succeeds it, when the world seems a charnel-house, and life a funeral pageant. The valley from which we set forth on our pilgrimage lies bathed in sunlight around us; flowers bloom under our feet with their dew unexhaled and their perfume unwasted; farther on, dark clouds gloom heavily over us, and their lightning flashes cast a lurid glare over all things; but upward and onward the eternal stars shed their cloudless beams, and God and Heaven are above us. Not brilliant and rapturous, not hopeless and joyless, but solemn and sublime is the pilgrimage of a human soul. It would seem that all subjective poetry must be desponding in its tone, and that whatever may be the nature of the outward life, no one who draws from the inward of his experience will sport in gaiety of composition. The authors who have written most of themselves are those whose works are the most melancholy. Rousseau, the most subjective of late writers, is deeply melancholy, and Byron's poetry is that of the individual himself. It is

> Even as a broken mirror, which the glass
> In every fragment multiplies, and makes
> A thousand images of one that was
> The same.

And that image was himself.

Objective authors, on the contrary, are those who are inspired by the beauties of nature. Chaucer is as buoyant in cheerfulness as in fancy, and he deals mostly with outward life. A like tendency in literature might be traced, we apprehend, from the age of Chaucer down to that of Byron. But it does not follow that we have the individual life either in the one case or the other. Rabelais was a solemn spirit, and Sterne was through life an unhappy man. Cowper, who has throughout written cheerfully, was predisposed to gloomy insanity, and more than once attempted his own life. The cause of this distinction must be that subjective writers, taking small account of those passing sensations of which life is in a great measure composed, fall back upon the boundless and enduring soul which no sensations can fill; and life in this aspect must always be disconsolate. The opposite tendency may be equally one-sided, but it is not disheartening. Outward existence draws men from the sources of their sorrows, and they lose the sense of individuality in sympathy or interest. It is well, then, to paint life as it appears to our hopes or to our despair; and as there is nothing absolute in our condition, relatively, the painting will be true to the reality. The highest genius is that which gives us a comprehensive and total humanity.

In our later poetry, these two marked and different tendencies are apparent, one personal, and the other impersonal; one which breathes out from the individual existence, and the other which lives in the imaginative and the ideal. Byron is the highest example of the one; Shelley of the other. Poetry would be complete in the union of these two; in the actuality of Byron enlarged and elevated by the grandeur of Shelley, or the spirituality of Shelley made incarnate in the force and passion of Byron. Should any one arise having affinity with our times, to unite these separate tendencies, he will be the true and great poet of the age. No era has been when mightier poetic elements existed than in the present; but they are chaotic, and await the brooding of some great spirit to give them form and utterance. Whether such a spirit will arise from the worn-out monarchies of the Old World or the free governments of the New, is a point yet to be determined. Miss Martineau, in her "Society in America," after speaking of witnessing the process of world-making, both natural and conventional, in this country, says: "Some genius will yet arise. The expectants take a wail here and a flourish there to be the music; but the hour has not yet struck, the leader has not yet come to his place, to strike those chords that must echo over the world."

Mrs. Hemans, one of the most beautiful and gifted spirits of the age, is the poet of sentiment rather than of passion; and the same may be said of almost all the female writers of the present day. To express the poetry of passion, a certain force is necessary that few women possess. To give expression to the perception of objective beauty or the beauty of sentiment, is by no means a rare power, and requires far less force of original genius than the expression of the poetry of passion. The artist, in the one case, fashions the statue, perfect, it may be, in its proportions, and beautiful in its repose; in the other, like Pygmalion, he wrestles with the gods till he inspires his creation with the Promethean fire.

I have no doubt that America is destined to produce a literature worthy of herself: startling almost as the first dawning of the continent on the eyes of the Old World. She commenced her career at once; not as nations have done, in the past. Fettered by no antiquity, borne down by no hereditary aristocracy, humanity here takes a new stand. With the recognition, if not the practice, of great principles for the foundation of government; with a magnificent country, whose shores are washed by the two great oceans, whose lakes are seas, whose rivers the most majestic that water the earth, whose commerce whitens every sea, whose railroads and canals, like great arteries, intersect its whole surface, and bear life and activity to its remotest corner,—here it would seem the human mind is destined to develop its highest powers. The materials for a great national literature are not yet exhausted. There are sublime moral truths that as yet have found no utterance in any literature, but which, when spoken in the trumpet tones of eloquence and poetry, must vibrate through the universal heart of humanity. The great end of all literature has been to idealize the actual. The new and higher literature must aim at the realization of the ideal. As yet there has been properly no Christian literature. The sublime truths of the New Testament, the "Peace on earth and good-will to men" that was sung by angel voices over the plains of Judea, have wakened no echoes in Christendom; nor could they ever in those countries where the divine rights of the many were sacrificed to the one or to the few. A new theater, a new world, was necessary to the development of those great truths, and here, if ever, they must be realized. Every age has had its poets, but the present age opens a new era in the history of the race; political and religious freedom have been born, and they require stronger nutriment than poetry: they demand philanthropy. A nation has arisen and, as if by divine inspiration, declared the fraternity and equality of man; and though the prophet has belied his utterance, that utterance has gone forth and cannot be recalled. Christianity, truth, justice, demand its fulfilment— not, indeed, as France demanded it, with the sword and the guillotine; but by a power mightier than they, by the omnipotent spirit of love, of Christian love—that sees in God a common Father, and in his image recognizes a Brother. Our country has been the first to declare these truths; she should be the first to put them in practice. If it be true, as they have asserted who have scanned closely the annals of the race, that each nation as it rises from the bosom of the sea of time and like a mighty billow rolls onward and breaks, has a mission to accomplish, an element of humanity to develop, as the Greek nation developed the love of beauty, the Romans the love of country,—the idea our country is destined to realize must be the love of man. This mission she is slowly, imperceptibly it may be, but it seems to us surely, accomplishing. And one proof of this is found in the fact that we as a people much prefer the work that appeals merely to the love of beauty, the work which addresses itself to the whole higher nature, that deepens our reverence for God and man, removes us from that insignificant center—self, around which we too often revolve, unites us to the great brotherhood of men, and attracts us to that sublime orbit whose center is God.

Notes on American Civilization[1]

A LATE distinguished critic of ourselves and our institutions, while admitting that the United States have solved the social and political problem with remarkable success, goes on to examine what is done here toward solving the human problem. He defines civilization to be the humanization of man in society; he says that the several elements or powers that go to build up a complete human life are the power of conduct, of beauty, of social life and manners, and the power of intellect and knowledge, and that we are perfectly civilized only when all these elements are recognized and satisfied. But the term civilization as used in the loosest way by most people, narrows down to a demand for the comforts and conveniences of life, and to their being within reach of persons of limited means. This he does not believe constitutes civilization. What human nature demands in a high and satisfying civilization is best described by the word *interesting*. Do not tell me only of the magnitude of your industry and commerce, of the beneficence of your institutions, your freedom, your equality, of the great and growing number of your churches, schools, libraries, and newspapers; tell me if the civilization, which is the grand name you give to all this development, is *interesting*. He says: The aspiration toward a harmony of things which every-day reality denies us, the rich and cultivated classes attempt to realize by the splendor and refinement of high life, and the interest which this attempt awakens in the classes not rich or cultivated, to whom the life of the great in castles and palaces appears as a pageant and a fairy tale, bears witness to a like imaginative strain in them tending after the elevated and the beautiful. The great

[1] A paper read before the "Wednesday Afternoon Club."

sources of the interesting are distinction and beauty; and he goes on to say that the landscape here is not interesting, and the climate harsh and in extremes. The cities have hardly anything to please a traveler with a natural sense for beauty, and of the really beautiful in art or literature very little has been produced; that no people in whom a sense of beauty or fitness was great could have invented or could tolerate the hideous names ending in *ville,* and the jumble of unnatural and inappropriate names everywhere. As to distinction, everything is against it in America, and against the sense of elevation to be gained through admiring and respecting. "In short," he continues, "in what concerns the solving of the political and social problem, they see clear and think straight; in what concerns the higher civilization, they live in a fool's paradise."

Pascal has said that "the succession of men in all ages must be regarded as one man who lives always and learns continually," but to understand his condition at any one period, we must look at him as a whole. It is impossible to judge aright the history or civilization of any one country, in its widest sense, without a knowledge of its development and progress from the beginning, as well as that of all other countries, and of its relation to them—as in a great historical picture we grasp the scope and design of the artist not by the study of a single figure or group, but by regarding the work as a whole. Before, then, we consider the question of American civilization, let us give a glance at the conditions which have produced it. Let us follow the history of the race from its infancy in the remote east, in its successive migrations through the despotisms of Asia and Egypt, the civilizations of Greece and Rome, their fall before the barbarous hordes of the north, the reconstruction of Europe, and, in the middle ages, to the discovery and settlement of a new continent under new conditions. We may then ask, if through all these various changes humanity has not been steadily advancing, whether, in all the varying phenomena and apparent confusion that the history of the race presents, there is not a principle of order, an unchanging law, underlying, that reduces it to a complete, harmonious, organic whole?—whether, as in the world of matter, the race is moving on in a vast uninterrupted evolution from lower to higher conditions, and what position our country holds in this onward march toward a more perfect unity, and a broader freedom, under the organizing power of that Providence

> That out of evil still educes good,
> And better thence again and better still
> In infinite progression ?

Before the middle of the last century, no attempt had been made to reduce the facts of universal history to a science. The brilliant historians of Greece and Rome were annalists who narrated the events of the past, or of their own age, in picturesque language and flowing periods ; but their works were narratives only, from which they made no attempt to deduce conclusions or generalizations. Vico, an Italian, who died in 1774, is regarded as the founder of the science of history. His theory was drawn from the history of Rome, which he made the typical history of mankind, and the periods corresponding to youth, manhood, decrepitude, and death were the cycles through which he believed nations were destined to pass. But the science of to-day opens a wider vista, and shows us that national decay and death are followed by resurrection in higher forms.

Passing over the prehistoric age, when man dwelt in caves and clothed himself in the skin of animals, to which he was nearly allied, we come to the earliest civilizations of which we have any knowledge, those of Asia and of Egypt ; and here we find the vast majority of the populations utterly degraded, with no community of interests, no national feeling, and no aspiration, apparently, for a higher state. They were separated into castes as impassable as the line that divides the various species of the animal kingdom, and under the absolute dominion of one ruler, whose will was law. In India, three fourths of the population were slaves. If one of this class presumed to occupy the same seat as his superiors, he was exiled or ignominiously punished ; if he spoke of them with contempt, his mouth was burned ; if he sat on the same carpet, he was maimed for life. If he listened to the reading of the sacred books, boiling oil was poured into his ears; if he committed them to memory, he was killed. The penalty for murdering him was the same as for killing a cat or a dog. He was forbidden to accumulate wealth, and doomed to abject eternal slavery.

In Egypt, too, everything tended to favor the higher caste and to depress the lower. The laborer was not allowed to change his employment nor to possess land; he was a beast of burden compelled to unremitting and unrequited toil. The erection of those stupendous and useless structures that are still wonders of the world, are proofs of the tyranny of the rulers and the slavery of the people.

Passing on to the Greek nation we find that they never rose to the conception even of national unity; while within the restricted limits of their great cities, and amidst the jealousies and rivalries that distracted them, they went through the several phases of monarchy, oligarchy, and so-called democracy. Three fourths of the population were slaves; liberty with them was not that of the individual, but of the caste or of the nation; power was chiefly confined to the great families, who claimed descent from the heroes and to act under their authority. Woman in Sparta was brutalized by the laws, and Athens in her great age condemned her to confinement and obscurity. With all the special gifts with which they were endowed in literature and in the arts, the religious ideals of the Greeks found embodiment in a host of divinities whose attributes and characteristics were among the lowest that degrade humanity.

The Romans, in the time of their highest culture, slaughtered the generals of their enemies, after dragging them in triumph behind their chariots; and their prisoners of war were thrown to the beasts of the circus—"butchered to make a Roman holiday." Under the laws, the father had absolute power over his children; he could sell them as slaves, abandon them to wild beasts, or inflict the punishment of death with his own hand. In marriage, the wife was not considered a person; and over her, the husband had the power of life and death. Slaves could be tortured and killed for the amusement of their masters, while the old were left to die of hunger and exposure.

With the introduction of Christianity, a new ideal was presented to the human race — the Fatherhood of God and the brotherhood of man; and while above the turbulence and disorder of the time this still small voice was heard, its benign accents bearing the message of love and brotherhood were little heeded, and are even yet far from being realized. The Roman Empire at length reached such a vast extent and became so thoroughly corrupt that it fell an easy prey to the vigorous barbarians of the north. Then followed the dark ages, centuries in which society seemed to be disintegrating and dissolving, and civilization to be disappearing. About the year 1000 the belief was general that the end of the world was at hand. Western Europe, where Rome had left the impress of her civilization in the construction of roads, towns, and cities, had become overgrown with forests, with only here and there a convent or a struggling town. Intercommunication had almost ceased in it, by the ordeal of fire; and boiling water took the place of appeals to the law, which seemed almost abolished, and crime and disorder everywhere prevailed.

Then followed the feudal system, under which everything belonged to the king or to the lord, and individual freedom and political rights were unknown. By a law called *Le droit du Seigneur*, when a peasant chose his bride the lord had the first right to her virginity. The desire for marriage and the wish to leave descendants to inherit their miseries, became almost extinct. Human ingenuity was taxed to its utmost to invent instruments of torture: impaling, tearing to pieces, breaking on the wheel, the rack, burying alive, were among the devices to test the degree of agony the human frame could endure. While the writers of fiction have thrown a poetic haze over this period, it was in reality a system in which abject slavery formed the lowest grade and irresponsible tyranny the highest.

Even as late as the seventeenth century, the charming Mme. de Sévigné relates with approval that a tax of 10,000 crowns had been imposed upon the city of Rennes, which, if not paid, was to be doubled in twenty-four hours and collected by the soldiers, who had cleared houses and streets of their occupants, and forbidden any one, under pain of death, to receive the evicted people; so that old men, children, and women near confinement were wandering round, crying, without food or shelter. "Day before yesterday," she writes, "a fiddler was broken on the wheel for getting up a dance and stealing some stamped paper. He was quartered after death, and his limbs exposed in the four corners of the city. Sixty citizens have been thrown into prison, and to-morrow begins the business of punishing them. This province sets a fine example to others, teaching them above all to respect their governors."

The fifteenth century marked a great era in the history of humanity. Constantinople, the last stronghold of the Eastern Empire, long besieged by the Turks, fell before them, and Greek learning and art took refuge in Western Europe. The invention of printing came upon the darkness of the middle ages like the sun on a polar night. Literature, before confined to manuscripts the possession of the learned few, and so precious that a book was sometimes accepted as the ransom for a city, was suddenly spread abroad; the human mind was stirred with new impulses, and new vistas were opened, along which it rapidly advanced. Toward the close of this memorable century, the discovery of a new world suddenly broke upon mankind; and following upon these great events came the Reformation, proclaiming the right of private judgment in religious belief, breaking the bonds of ecclesiastical domination, and opening the way for a still further advance. But while we recognize the law of progress, it must be observed that the law is also imperative that progress must be through conflict. This has never been more forcibly illustrated than in the results of the Reformation. For more than a century the great principle it asserted was combated by the most cruel and destructive wars that have devastated Europe, laying waste cities, towns, and villages, and giving up men, women, and children to fire and sword. But the sword of the Spirit is mightier than any material weapon; ideas are the invisible, invincible forces that rule the world; and when in great and master minds

> Thought by thought is piled till
>   Some great truth
> Is loosened, and the nations echo round
> Shaken to their roots,

it is vain to seek again to bind or to imprison it. It has become the property of the race; years may pass, but, like the planted seed, it will germinate sooner or later and bear flower and fruit.

From the Reformation we come to the period called modern times. The nations of Europe had emerged from the barbarism of the dark ages; new languages had been refined and perfected, literature took form, settled governments were established, and society assumed a new aspect. The principles of religious and individual liberty asserting themselves in England, brought Charles I. to trial, condemnation, and the scaffold; then, crossing the Atlantic, they found their habitation in the New World, there to lay the foundations of a government on ideas never before proclaimed.

After the Reformation had asserted the right of private judgment, the next great phase in the expression of the idea was the Declaration of Independence, that the object of governments was to secure the rights of the people, from whom alone it derives its powers; and when it becomes destructive of these ends, it is the right of the people to alter or to abolish it. These great principles here expressed for the first time in the history of the world, gave free scope to the individual soul to grow and to expand in accordance with the laws of its being; and to the state composed of souls so developed, to govern themselves. These principles constitute the foundation-stone of American civilization.

From this glance over the past, it seems undeniable that the great current of events has moved steadily on, and that this advance has been in the direction of unity and freedom; slowly it may be, like the glacier, but as surely, as irresistibly.

The civilization of a country is to be judged by the material, moral, and intellectual condition of its people, the liberality of its government, the diffusion of education, and the position it accords to woman, compared with other nations in the past or in the present age.

But civilization in America is a fact apart; as we have seen, it has no parallel among the nations which have preceded and whose accumulated experience it inherited. It was "the heir of all the ages." Beginning in the light of the seventeenth century, it had no period of barbarism to pass through; possessing a continent extending from the tropics to the Arctic circle, washed on the east and on the west by the two great oceans, with every variety of climate, scenery, and soil, with no hereditary rulers, no traditions of birth or of caste,—humanity here makes a new departure. Half a century ago, an English traveler writing of this country says: "No man can pass over it from east to west, from north to south, without bringing away the impression that, if on any portion of his earthly creation the finger of God has drawn characters that would seem to indicate the seat of empire, surely it is there."

Gladstone says of it: "It has a natural base for the greatest continuous empire ever established by man"; and of the Constitution of the United States, "It is the most wonderful work ever struck off by the hand of man." Adam Smith, in his "Wealth of Nations," predicts the transfer of empire from Europe to America. De Tocqueville says that "since prehistoric times populations have moved westward as if driven by the mighty hand of God. The world's scepter, as we have seen, passed from Asia to Greece, from Greece to Italy, from Italy to Britain, and is now passing to the great West."

This vast area, traversed in all directions by railways and waterways, has a soil so fertile that its productions might fill the granaries of the world, and yet seven eighths of the arable land is uncultivated. Half the gold and silver supply of the world is furnished by its mines, and its mining industries are greater than those of all continental Europe, Asia, Africa, South America, and the British colonies, while the larger part of the mineral wealth of the country is undeveloped, and thousands of square miles are unbroken. From 1870 to 1880 the wealth of the nation increased 175 per cent.

The charge is brought against our people that they have an inordinate love of money, and that they follow this pursuit to the exclusion of all nobler passions and tastes. But even if this is true, the desire for pecuniary independence is a legitimate and worthy one. Without it the mind is degraded by sordid cares and the higher powers are paralyzed. Wealth gives to its possessor the power to alleviate suffering, to enlarge his experience, and to multiply his resources; it places at his command the treasures of art and taste, and all the elements that go to make up the fullest and most perfect life. With all the enormous wealth of our country spread out before them, and all the facilities for acquiring it, it would be indeed extraordinary if the people refused to avail themselves of it.

Besides the desire for pecuniary independence, there is also in the heart of man an equally strong desire for the possession of some portion of the soil for a literal foothold on the globe, which assures him a certain dignity of position. While in most other and older countries this acquisition is unattainable except for those possessed of large means, here a vast domain invites free occupation and ownership. The half-brutalized European peasant, whose progenitors toiled for generations on a master's estate, poorly clothed, poorly fed, poorly paid,—here finds free and fertile lands to reward his labor, free schools to educate his children, free institutions to make men and women of them.

The condition of Europe to-day is that of a vast military camp, garrisoned by millions of soldiers armed with the most destructive weapons of war ever known, suspiciously watching one another, their rulers listening with breathless interest to the utterances of the young Kaiser, who proudly calls himself the "War-King," and who, at the head of his enormous and well-drilled forces, is a constant menace to the nations about him. These millions of armed men are taken from the peaceful pursuits of life, and forced into wars for territorial aggrandizement, or other causes, in which they can have no personal interest.

The army of the United States consists only of a few thousand volunteer troops, for the protection of our western frontier. And yet when the moment came that found the institutions of the country in danger, the citizens eagerly answered the call, for each had a personal interest in the issue; and when the danger was over, and four millions of slaves were made men and citizens, the Grand Army of the Republic left its million brothers "dead on the field of honor," and vanished like a morning mist. The citizen soldier had returned to his peaceful occupations, and changed his sword and spear into the plowshare and pruning-hook.

In the history of the world the names of a few military heroes and conquerors stand out in bold relief: Alexander, who sighed for more worlds to conquer; Cæsar, who strove to overthrow the liberties of Rome; Napoleon, who overran Europe, and who wrote to Talma, "Come to Erfurt and you shall play before a pit full of kings"; Washington, who led a struggling people through the gloomy way of our Revolution to independence and nationality; Lincoln, commander-in-chief of one of the great armies of the world, whose memorable words on the battle-field of Gettysburg were spoken "with malice toward none, with charity to all." As civilization advances, and as war comes to be regarded in its true light as a relic of barbarism, it is not too much to say of these names that "the last shall be first."

The sense of individuality, of personality, which American civilization has developed was unknown to the ancient world, and is almost impossible in those countries where the system of caste prevails, where men live and die in the rank in which they were born, where there is little or no sense of common humanity, where a hereditary aristocracy has ruled for ages and entailed upon all below it an inherent sense of inferiority that could only be obliterated by some terrible crisis like the French Revolution. This sense of equality and individuality leads often, doubtless, to a self-assertion not consistent with good manners, but which, after all, is less offensive than the assumption of superiority on the one side, or the expression of groveling servility on the other, which is invariably found when the class below is struggling up and the class above crushing it down. A recognition of the rights of others, and a courteous consideration of them, is the groundwork of all good manners; and since these principles lie also at the foundation of our government, there seems every reason why we should look for a higher type of manners here than has existed elsewhere.

From the beginning, the founders of our government regarded education, moral and intellectual, as the first essential for a free people; and as the log-cabins rose in the wilderness, side by side rose the church and school-house, and from that time they have kept abreast with the advancing tide of population. With no interference from the government, with absolute religious toleration, the churches supported by the voluntary contributions of their members to-day number more than 300,000; the free public schools are estimated to be 180,000, maintained at an annual expense of $93,000,000, while 20,000 free schools are educating more than a million of the freed slaves; 25,000 school libraries contain 45,000,000 books, more than all the public libraries of Europe combined; and $90,000,000 are annually spent in the purchase of books, against $80,000,000 spent in England. The new Encyclopedia Britannica in its original edition and in the several American reproductions found 108,000 subscribers in the United States.

We are charged with having no literature and no native art. In the struggle for existence that followed the settlement of the new country, the conditions for the development of either were wholly wanting, and it may be admitted that as yet we take a subordinate place in these respects among those nations that have had a thousand years to mature; but, as the increasing wealth of the country affords the means of gratifying taste and the leisure to enjoy it, we may safely say that works of genius will be produced and appreciated.

Our civilization is still in the formative period; it is a growth which in time will have its full development. While other nations have reached their culminating point in the ages that have passed, America is bound to obtain quite as satisfactory results in the days that are to come.

Literature is the expression of national life, and a new national life will demand a corresponding new expression. If poetry consists in the glorification of war, in the expression of national or personal ambition, or in the delineation of man as he is or as he has been, we may not perhaps look for a nobler literature than the world now possesses. But if, as some believe, the high office of the poet is not to idealize the world as it is, but to proclaim that the ideal is the real, the true and only real, then there will dawn on humanity the splendor of a new day. De Tocqueville, in his "Democracy in America," says in reference to our literature: "While the principle of democracy has dried up most of the old springs of poetry, it has disclosed new ones. The idea of progression, of indefinite perfectability, belongs to a democratic people. They care little for what has been, but their imagination of what will be, opens the widest range to the genius of the poet and to visions of the ideal: the march of a great people across the continent, subduing nature and peopling its solitudes. While the life of the nation is unpoetical, the underlying thought is full of poetry. Hitherto, incidents in the life of a nation or an individual have formed the subjects of the great epics; but the destinies of mankind will be the theme of the future. Looking at the human race as one great whole, its destinies regulated by the same design, they recognize in each individual traces of that universal and eternal plan on which God rules our race. Passions and ideas will be the subject of poetry rather than persons and achievements,—man seen for a moment on the verge of two abysses and disappearing. Poetry will not be fed with legends or old traditions—the poet will not people the universe with supernatural beings in whom he and his readers have ceased to believe, nor coldly personify virtues and vices; but the destinies of mankind, man himself in the presence of nature and of God, with his passions, his doubts, his propensities, and his wretchedness, will afford new and vast themes for poetry."

Among many other charges, our foreign critics accuse us of national conceit, of boasting loudly of our country and of its institutions; but if the sketch here presented of the nations which have preceded us in history is correctly drawn, if our country has elements of civilization they did not possess, elements that tend to advance the human race to a higher level than it has ever before reached,—why should we affect not to know it, or knowing, seem to undervalue it? There are, however, two standards of comparison, the relative and the absolute; and while under the first we may be justified in our national pride, comparing our civilization with that absolute, ideal state, by which is meant the state we can all conceive as possible, and which we are as yet so immeasurably far from reaching, our attitude is one of profound humility. Looking forward to this state, the narrow bounds of patriotism give way to the thought of that time when all nations will form one people, when order and beauty will be evolved out of disorder and deformity, when war will cease, and poverty and crime disappear. This state, which the ancient poets believed had existed in the dawn of the world, they called the golden age — the Christian looks forward to it in the far-off future as the Millennium, and the science of to-day sees its approach in the operation of those immutable laws that held the planets in their courses ages before those laws were formulated by the genius of Copernicus, Kepler, and Newton.

Under all the exceptional conditions that have attended the establishment of American civilization, it would be extraordinary if they had not made a distinct mark on the inhabitants. It is a fact in physiology, animal as well as human, that the admixture of races under favorable circumstances produces superior vanities,—a fact easily verified in our national experience. The great apostle of evolution says: "The wonderful progress of the United States, as well as the character of the people, are the result of natural selection; for the more energetic, restless, and courageous men from all parts of Europe have emigrated to that great country, and have there succeeded best." Herbert Spencer says: "From biological reasons it is to be inferred that the eventual mixture of the allied varieties of the Aryan race forming the population, will produce a more powerful type of man than has hitherto existed, a type more plastic, more adaptable, more capable of undergoing the modifications needful for complete social life. I think, whatever difficulties they may have to surmount, whatever tribulations they may have to pass through, the Americans may reasonably look forward to a time when they will have produced a civilization grander than the world has ever known."

In this consummation an important factor is found in the condition of woman. Nowhere in the world, past or present, has she the freedom, the respect, and the condition of equality that she has here. To quote again from De Tocqueville: "In Europe, a certain degree of contempt lurks in the flattery men lavish upon women; although affecting to be her slave, it is clearly seen that they never consider her their equal; here she is raised, morally and intellectually, as far as possible to the level of men." A drudge in the savage state, a slave or a toy in the semi-civilized, and elsewhere always an inferior, here she is raised to her true position and dignity. Woman, endowed with a more complex organization, finer instincts, a higher emotional nature, a deductive reason, is the crown and flower of humanity. She is the mother of men. It is proverbial that great men are born of great mothers, and when woman comes to understand the power and extent of her influence for good or evil — that the education of a child, as some one has said, begins a hundred years before birth; that she *must* transmit her own characteristics to succeeding generations — she will understand how great is the part assigned her in the advancement of the race; the exercise of political power, which is sure to come soon, will dwindle in importance, and she will regard the responsibilities laid upon her with reverence and awe. Philosophers tell us that nothing is destroyed, that every particle of matter has its place and its importance, that the destruction of the smallest atom would destroy the equilibrium of the universe. If, then, the atom has its place and its function, how much more is this true of the individual, however limited his sphere or capacity? This thought gives new value and dignity to the humblest life, and awakens the aspiration to aid in the great onward movement. In the words of Mill, "The destiny of humanity is onward. The advance of each individual enters as an organic element, advancing and exalting the race. Better approximations shall be made, finer realizations, nearer approaches to the infinite goal. In ages better than ours, generations shall be happier born, with clearer brain and purer blood, to whom our words shall seem childish and coarse, our conceptions dim and crude; who shall see where we but grope, shall walk and leap where we but totter and fall. The great atonement and reconciliation prepared from the foundation of the world, shall be wrought out, and life become absolute realization. But it shall be by the same method of approach, all things seen in relation, lower transcended and cast aside for higher; attainment, surrender, pursuit, repose, reality, revelation, seen, unseen, blending, dividing, ascending, flowing, soaring onward without end."

A Journey to Niagara Falls

From my experience, and from my limited observation of human nature, I have come to the conclusion that when either the masculine or feminine mind once becomes possessed with an idea, and with the desire to translate this idea into action, however absurd and fantastic it may appear to others, the only effectual mode of treatment, as in the case of certain diseases, is to let nature take its course, and to allow the idea to become a fact of experience. When, for instance, an ambitious youth becomes what is called stage-struck, or affected with a passion for the sea, solitary confinement and low diet only aggravate the disease, which will be generally found to terminate in a quiet departure from the paternal roof some morning before the family are stirring. When an individual becomes thus affected, the mode of treatment we suggest, which might be called the "method of nature," has a twofold advantage. The patient may be convinced of his folly, and the adviser may indulge in that most satisfactory phrase in our language, "I told you so!" As to advice, the text of Scripture, "It is more blessed to give than to receive," will in this be found to be of universal application and adoption; and the most that can be expected of those who disregard it, and follow the "inner light," to use one of the cant phrases of the day for self-will, is, that they confess on being convinced, and to the "I told you so," reply "You were right." In this category I now place myself, and proceed with my confession.

The idea with which I became infected was that of taking a journey on foot; and here I am forced into an acknowledgment that I would willingly forego, were I not sure of betraying myself should I attempt to withhold it—and this acknowledgment, dear reader, is this: I belong to the gentler sex. It is a little singular that while it is so common for women to wish, with Desdemona, that Heaven had made them men, men on the contrary seem to be always entirely self-satisfied, and never wish to change places with us. The idea of a pedestrian excursion in search of the picturesque was first proposed in a pleasant circle among whom were several artists and amateurs, who were in the habit of meeting frequently. "Charming!"—"delightful!"—was heard on all sides; but when the moment came for putting the idea into execution, it was found that only two had given it serious thought; my friend Mr. Cushman the artist and myself alone remained firm in the resolution of making the attempt. I had heard of William and Mary Howitt making the tour of Germany on foot, and of the pedestrian capabilities of English ladies in general; and wishing to emulate them, as well as being pleased with the novelty of such an enterprise, we decided to make the experiment. After due deliberation, it was finally agreed that our destination should be Niagara, and that we should take the canal at Schenectady, by which we could walk or rest, as we chose, or give up walking entirely, should we find it necessary. My dear mother, finding expostulation vain, at last consented to this arrangement, and to making one of the party, for the purpose of matronizing me; though, being in delicate health, she could not anticipate any of the pleasure we promised ourselves from the exercise of walking. I should premise here that Mr. Cushman and myself are believers in the water cure, and the positive benefit we both expected to derive from this change of ordinary habits was proportioned to our faith in the system. As the time appointed for our departure drew near, we found it very difficult to obtain any information beyond what was put forth in a flaming advertisement in the papers, announcing that passengers for Buffalo could obtain tickets at the office in this city, which would take them the whole distance from here to Buffalo in fine packet-boats, duly pictured in the paper as attached to horses galloping at full speed, for the astonishingly small sum of four dollars! To the less unsophisticated there would have been something suspicious in this extraordinary cheapness; but innocent of any thought of imposition, we set forth. Our passage-tickets up the river destined us to the steamboat *Belle*, and Mr. Cushman being a stranger here, and I not aware that this was not one of the first-class of our unrivaled North River boats, we accordingly drove to the wharf where she was lying. I would not say anything derogatory to the character of the *Belle*, but Ma, who has an eye for neatness and a taste for agreeable surroundings, at first strenuously refused to proceed by that means of conveyance; but it was doubtful if we could reach the other boat in time, and being convinced that worse was to come in the "hereafter," we concluded to make this first step in our descent to packet-boat traveling. On reaching the depot at Schenectady we were beset by a *banditti*, apparently, though known by the name of "runners," whose office was to secure passengers for the various boats to whose interests they were attached. This process is very like that employed to entrap certain animals—by stunning them first, and capturing them afterward; for they actually so confound the unwary traveler who finds himself the bone of contention among them, by their abuse of one another, their noise and their impertinence, that he falls an easy victim to the boldest, and is quietly led off, glad to escape. Thus we found ourselves and our luggage finally bestowed in a nice and comfortable-looking boat, just ready to set out, when Mr. Cushman accidentally showing the passage-ticket we had procured at the New-York office, and which we had been assured would take us on any boat on the canal, the captain denied any knowledge of such an office, or such an agency, and refused to take us at all, without full fare being paid over again. Highly indignant, we immediately left the boat and ordered our effects to be sent after us. The captain, equally indignant at not having secured us, managed to remove his boat to some distance from the bank, to which he then pitched our trunks with all the momentum that could be brought to bear upon them. The banditti rushed upon us again, and commenced vociferating louder than ever. Mr. Cushman was pale with suppressed rage, and Ma with agitation, while I was not a little excited and infinitely amused. At length the captain of a new boat, just starting, agreed to take us for the ticket we had paid for, though we were afterward convinced that it was of no value to him, and that we had been grossly imposed upon at the office in New-York; in short, we were actually embarked, and advancing toward Niagara at the enormous velocity of three miles an hour. I was amused to observe Ma looking cautiously around for a seat, and taking her handkerchief to dust before occupying it, while I immediately doffed my civilized costume, exchanging my Middleton gaiters for a pair of "seven-league boots" bought for the occasion, and my traveling-dress for a morning-gown *passée*. Thus adapted to my circumstances, I felt equal to any emergency, and looked, as Mr. Cushman said, "the genius of the place." At the close of the first day we had accomplished twelve miles on foot, coming on board the boat at frequent intervals to rest; and at night we were prepared to enjoy a profound repose, "cabined, cribbed, as we were."

A day on board a canal-boat may be described, but language is wholly inadequate to convey any idea of a night; it is one of those passages in life that must be experienced to be understood. I will only say, therefore, that after our vigorous exercise we slept even there as soundly as the seven sleepers, though our slumbers were less protracted, as we usually rose as the first streak of dawn appeared; and after a walk of five or six miles, returned to the boat in time for breakfast, with appetites that would have given great uneasiness to the captain had not our meals, luckily for him, been an extra charge. The scenery through which the canal passed was in general tame and uninteresting, but there were passages of exquisite beauty; and in the alchemy of sunset, the gray light and the repose of early morning, or seen beneath the veil of silver moonlight, the commonest woods and hills were picturesque and beautiful. The scenery near the village of Little Falls, in the valley of the Mohawk, abounds in bold and striking features, and was more romantic than any through which we passed. But wherever there is the expanse of sky above and of field and wood below, though they may not be disposed with reference to pictorial effect, yet the true lover of nature will find there beauty and companionship. Communion with Nature, even in her most unattractive form, brings us nearer to her great Author than the contemplation of the most magnificent works of man. They ally us to our kind,—we participate in their aspirations and their triumphs,—and the bond of our common nature is drawn more closely, while with Nature nothing intervenes between us and her Author. A German poet has called Nature "the freshly uttered word of God!" and whenever we are with her, that word, if we listen, becomes audible, and to the reverent ear speaks messages of love, of consolation, and of hope.

As we approached Salina, we were sufficiently in advance of the boat to stop and examine the salt works, where thousands of barrels are every year manufactured. Immense flats are covered with reservoirs ten or twelve feet square, which are supplied with water from the salt springs, the evaporation of which leaves a deposit of delicate white crystals, which is afterward refined and barreled for exportation. The second and third days of our journey we advanced twenty miles each day on foot, without experiencing any other than that healthy and pleasant fatigue which makes repose so delightful, and which is so different from the exhaustion and lassitude one feels after a walk through Broadway. At noon on the fourth day we found ourselves at Fairport, a small town eighteen miles from Rochester by the canal, but ten only by the stage road. We had already walked ten miles since morning, and this distance would finish the day so roundly that we determined to undertake it, though the afternoon was warmer than any we had experienced on our route. The country was hilly, and sandy, and without shade, and we found it much more difficult to walk ten miles without resting, for we had previously taken frequent intervals of repose; and for the first time my companion began to flag, and my own elasticity to give way. By way of stimulating our failing energies, I began reciting, and went through all the stirring poetry I could call to mind from "Lochiel's Warning" and the "Battle of Hohenlinden" to "Macaulay's Roman Ballads." When at length we reached the suburbs of Rochester—the novelty of our descent upon a strange town—our own costume and travel-worn appearance, the fancy that we might be taken for wandering minstrels or strolling players, altogether so appealed to our sense of the quixotic and the ludicrous, that it was some time before we could command the requisite dignity to make the grand *entrée*. We found the boat had not yet arrived, and so we occupied the interval in looking about the city, for we were by this time in the condition of the famous cork leg; we had walked until it became less fatiguing to continue than to stop. Since I am at the confessional, I may say here, that had I followed the advice of my companion, or listened to my own better judgment, we should have taken some conveyance on the road when we found our walk becoming too long for our strength; but experience, though often so dear, is worth all that we pay for it. On rejoining our *compagnons de voyage,* I began to feel the effect of my over-exertion, which manifested itself not in muscular fatigue, but in excessive nervous excitability; my brain seemed to be describing spiral curves, my hands trembled, and occasionally a frightful sensation of departing consciousness stole over me, all of which was greatly aggravated by my efforts at concealing it from the watchful eye of my mother. I privately begged Mr. Cushman to procure a phial of laudanum before we left the wharf, and the dose that I took, with a view of composing my disordered nerves, only added to the difficulty, so that after a sleepless night, I rose the next morning positively ill.

I could, of course, expect no sympathy from our fellow-travelers, who were, I am sure, not a little gratified to witness the fulfilment of their reiterated prophecies, and to behold me reaping the reward of my foolhardiness; and the compliments, prescriptions, and advice, with which it is usual on such occasions to overwhelm the invalid, were wholly omitted in my case. The truth is, I was unpopular, notwithstanding my attempts to be kind and conciliating. There is something in the unloving glance of the human eye peculiarly painful to me, and which I would always, if possible, avert, even in the case of the humblest individual, but here I was wholly unsuccessful. My presumption in daring to act differently from them in any particular, even the simple one of walking a few miles, was an unpardonable offense, and not to be tolerated. Public opinion was as powerful a ruler here as elsewhere. I was particularly unfortunate in drawing upon myself the disapprobation of the two chambermaids, who governed with despotic rule; and who, being exceedingly intimate with the others, seemed to delight in making me the scapegoat of all their ill-humor. From the first I had treated them with uniform kindness and consideration, which seemed only to exasperate them still more, by leaving them without the shadow of excuse for their impertinence. The captain would have discharged them forthwith, I am certain, had I represented to him their conduct in its true light, for he seemed exceedingly desirous of making our journey as agreeable as circumstances would permit. I preferred, however, to let things take their course, and to study human nature under this new aspect, though it certainly was a most unattractive one. I had always been a firm believer in the law of love, and convinced that love alone was omnipotent to overcome hatred and malignity; but my observations on this occasion led me to different conclusions—to the belief that there are cases where power must take precedence of love, and despotism of magnanimity and generosity; and that there are inferior natures on whom these higher virtues are lost, and who must be controlled by the force of superiority. One of these two damsels who presided over the feminine department of the boat had one night planted her mattress, and herself upon it, directly under the shelf upon which I was to sleep, so that it was impossible for me to approach it without almost stepping upon her. As there was sufficient space beyond, I civilly requested her to move, and as she deigned no answer, I repeated the request, accompanied by some remonstrance and expostulation, when she finally turned to me, and said with a look and tone the impudence of which was inimitable: *"You 'd better go to bed!"* I was absent so frequently from the boat, and thus beyond their spiritual spheres for the greater part of the time; I had thrown myself so entirely into the discomforts about me, and had so resolved to enjoy them, that the two chambermaids *rampant*, instead of being a source of annoyance, added not a little to my amusement. It was a curious study to see what they would do next.

I like to test my capacity for endurance, and if one can survive five days' sojourn on a canal-boat, without having lost temper or spirits, he may endure anything he will be likely to encounter afterward. However, much of my buoyancy was doubtless the result of my extraordinary muscular exertion in the pure air, and the entire change of my ordinary habits; I seemed to have returned to primitive and savage life, and almost dreaded to come back to civilization and brick walls. I like also to reduce my wants to the lowest terms, to see how little is absolutely essential, and how much can be dispensed with without causing positive unhappiness. It is a kind of experiment, however, that is not likely to become very popular, though in my own case I have found it extremely beneficial; and as the constrained and painful attitudes that professional dancers subject themselves to in the laborious practice they daily go through, will give them command of muscle and grace of movement, so this voluntary penance prepares one for the thousand annoyances of daily life. It acts on the same principle as a cold bath in the morning, which, though it requires some courage to go through with, yet fortifies one against the chills and changes of the succeeding day.

On the morning of the fifth day we reached Buffalo, and with my canal-costume I laid aside the high spirits and the wild gaiety with which I had worn it. Having slept the night before between an open door and window, I woke with a violent cold, which, added to my previous indisposition, rendered me quite tame and manageable.

The genii of the boat, the two fair chambermaids, manifestly changed their bearing as their reign drew near its close, and became as officious and servile as they had before been disagreeable; but as it usually happens with tyrants, their repentance came too late, and they would have left a far better impression on my mind if they had held out to the last as they had begun. On reaching the hotel at Buffalo, with its airy rooms, its veritable mattresses, and abundant water, the delight we experienced was sufficient to compensate for our late deprivations in those luxuries, had we had no other compensation. In continued enjoyment we cease to appreciate the blessings that overwhelm us, and we ought to dispense with them occasionally for the mere luxury of higher appreciation.

At Buffalo we took the steamboat for Niagara, which landed us two or three miles above the Falls. As we were nearing our destination, Mr. Cushman threw out the comfortable suggestion that we were now in the current of that arrowy stream, and that if any of the machinery were to give out, or the boat in any way to become disabled, we should, inevitably, not only go to the Falls, but over them. This fact was so obvious, that although we felt no positive fear, yet we had a more pleasant sense of security when we were once more on *terra firma*. We arrived at the Cataract House, after our long journey, in rather a subdued state of feeling. Our spirits seemed to have effervesced, and left us in the condition of champagne that has stood uncorked over night. I had visited the Falls once before, and the impression they had left upon me was vividly retained. My sense of the ideal, the sublime, the infinite, had been filled, and tears had been the only power of expression left to me; and now for many months I had felt an intense longing to renew these emotions, and to feel myself once more lifted for a moment beyond the present and the actual. My two companions had never visited the Falls before, and so I was entitled to their experience in addition to my own. But there was among us all an ominous want of enthusiasm that argued ill for any original manifestations of feeling, and the paramount thought of creature comfort apparent was shocking in the extreme. Ma and Cushman were suffering the consequences of their fatigue; and I with my cold and illness felt as incapable of emotion of any kind as if I had been turned by machinery from one of the trees in our path. We made an attempt to see the Falls before the dinner-hour, but after advancing a short distance we seated ourselves on a rustic bench, and unanimously confessed ourselves unfit to proceed. In the course of a few hours, however, they rallied and came up to the high-water mark of enthusiasm; but the effect on me was altogether painful, giving me the idea of vastness and terror only. At night, when I attempted to sleep, these impressions returned with such force that I awoke distressed and terrified. I seemed to stand on the bank of some frightful precipice, of which Niagara was only a miniature, and over whirlpools black and deep as the bottomless pit. The roar of the rapids and the Falls strengthened the illusion of my fancy, and after two nights spent in these chaotic and awful scenes I could endure it no longer, and the third day we took the cars for Lewiston, with the intention of returning the *natural* way, or, in other words, by railroad. Our journey was varied by no incidents or accidents; after dining at Troy, and walking about that pleasant little city, we took the cars for Greenbush, opposite Albany, from whence a ferry-boat was to convey us over the Hudson to take the evening boat. On this ferry-boat we were safely deposited, and waited impatiently for the officiating Charon to set out, for at least three-quarters of an hour. To our repeated intimations that we should be too late for the boat, he only replied: "You will be in time." The cause of this detention must forever remain among other unsolved mysteries; and the effect was that when we at last reached the wharf at Albany, finding no carriages, we were hurrying along with all possible speed, bag and baggage following us, when several voices saluted us with: "She 's off!" "The boat has just left!" Truth obliges me to confess that for a moment my patience and temper gave way; but a conviction of the utter absurdity of railing, or doing anything but quietly submitting to this mysterious dispensation, finally prevailed, and we took our way to the Delavan House, three silent and crestfallen individuals.

Newport Forty Years Ago

From the middle of July until the first of September, Newport is at its flood-tide of gaiety and fashion. All parts of the Union, all classes of men, women, and children, all peculiarities of individual character, have their full representation, and studies abound. It is a general remark that persons learn more of one another from traveling together for a short time, than from long and intimate acquaintance in the routine of ordinary life; and this remark applies with equal force to a temporary sojourn at a watering-place. Thrown off their accustomed track, seen in the light of new circumstances, people daguerreotype themselves when they are least aware of it, and at moments when they think least of sitting for their portraits, which, of course, are not always from the most favorable points of view, and therefore, to me, not the most pleasant.

A lady, not long ago, assured me that the White Mountains were becoming more fashionable every year, and I was about to repeat her remark with regard to Newport, which really seems every year to become a more favorite resort. Ornamental cottages, built in the most perfect taste, are springing up in various parts of the island, and for three or four months in the year they are the residences of some of the most distinguished families in the country, while the transient visitors who come to Newport for a few weeks or days number many thousands. The beach is unrivaled in its hardness and beauty, above all, in its safety, and from ten to twelve o'clock in the morning it presents a most lively and exciting scene. The bathing costume, which is frightfully unbecoming, is fortunately an effectual disguise, and the gay groups that issue from the bathing-cars, and bound with white feet over the sparkling sands to "wanton with the breakers," seem like unknown genii from the coral caves. A gentleman remarked to me, in view of those who came dripping from the foam of the sea, that hereafter he renounced his belief in the old Greek fable of the origin of Venus. In the afternoon, the scene on the beach is scarcely less animated. Its smooth, hard surface forms a most delightful drive, and splendid equipages, and vehicles of all descriptions, equestrians and pedestrians, give it great variety and life. Unlike most other watering-places, however, the attractions of Newport are entirely independent of the thousands who annually seek health or pleasure in its delicious air and its white-crested waves. Notwithstanding the almost entire absence of trees, the scenery of the island is remarkably picturesque. The undulating fields are covered with luxuriant grain, the cows and sheep feed upon the hills, the cliffs rise dark and frowning upon the shore, meeting unmoved the impotent fury of the angry waves, and around lies the all-embracing sea, restless as the heart of man, mysterious as its desires, and boundless as its aspirations. Aquidneck, the Indian name of the island, which signifies the Isle of Peace, seems particularly well adapted to this beautiful spot.

Hail, pleasant isle! as freshly shine to-day
The sky, the beach, the breaker, and the bay,
As when, slow curling o'er the oak-wood's green,
Miantonomo's council-smoke was seen.
And in these waters bathed their locks of jet,
Thy dusky daughters — old Metaunamet!
Though gone thy ancient name — thine ancient race —
Not yet is fled the genius of the place.
Though the pale settler's ax, and war's rude hand,
Have felled the sylvan monarchs of the land —
And though a skeleton, the sycamore
Moans in the wind and finds his leaves no more —
Though the light deer no more thy green sward tread,
And many a song of olden days is fled —
Yet there 's a glory haunts thy sapphire sky,
Thy emerald slope and swell, not soon shall die.

So sings the poet who has made his home here, and whose sweet notes reach us from time to time, like the mysterious music of Pascagoula, which he has so well described.

Newport was formerly the residence of many Jews; and the Jewish burial-ground, with its classic entrance, sculptured with the inverted torch, is a prominent feature of the town. The synagogue, however, has been closed for some time. The Redwood Library here was one of the earliest founded and best selected in the country; and although it was greatly injured by the English while the island was in their possession during the Revolutionary War, even now the scholar may devote himself, with great advantage, to its dusty volumes. Not far from the town is Tonomy or Tammany Hill, which was strongly fortified by the English, and the form and boundaries of the old intrenchments are yet visible. The name is a vulgar abbreviation of Wonnumetonomy, who was the resident sachem or governor of the island at the time it was purchased by the first settlers, and whose wigwam was situated here. The Aquidnecks, or original natives of the island, were conquered by the Narragansetts some time before the settlement of Plymouth, and remained tributaries to them until the white inhabitants took possession of it. Newport is rich in romantic and historic associations. A few miles from town is Vaucluse, a most lovely villa, built some years since by an English gentleman of fortune, who gave it this name from the real or fancied resemblance of his woes to those of Petrarch. His, however, were not "*melodious* tears," and, consequently, he has not "given himself to fame."

Beyond what is called the Second Beach, is a vast chasm in the rock, known as Purgatory. Within this gloomy abyss the water is said to be fathomless, and the spectator is thrilled with horror as he gazes over the black depths that seem yawning to engulf him, and where the sea howls like some angry monster. One legend attached to this place is, that through it the great Adversary, once upon a time, returned to the infernal regions, and a more appropriate place for his exit could not be conceived. It is also celebrated as the scene of a lover's leap. The tradition runs thus: A beautiful and capricious heiress, rambling on the cliffs with her lover, demanded, as a test of his devotion, that he should leap across the abyss. He accomplished the feat, but it placed between the lovers a chasm far wider than that of Purgatory; for from the bank he had miraculously gained, the lover made his particular parting compliments to the lady. A singular incident is recorded in the early history of Newport, which comes down well authenticated, and which loses none of its interest from the seventy or eighty years that have elapsed since it occurred, and which have failed to throw any light on the mystery. The farmers and fishermen one morning discovered a vessel under full sail, with her colors flying, making rapidly toward the shore, which, at that point, was considered inaccessible. The inhabitants gathered in crowds upon the beach, expecting every moment to witness the destruction of the vessel, which seemed guided by unseen hands, and which, gliding between the rocks and billows, at last reached the shore in perfect safety. No one appearing on the deck, she was boarded. Coffee was found boiling on the fire, and everything seemed to be prepared for the breakfast of the crew; but with the exception of a dog, no living thing appeared on board of her. There had been no storm on the coast, the vessel was in good condition, and to this day there has been no satisfactory conjecture as to the fate of its crew.

Two or three miles from Newport is the house built by the celebrated Berkeley, and occupied by him during his residence in this country, and to which he gave the name of Whitehall. It is a modest, unpretending cottage, standing some distance from the road, and beneath a hill which commands an extensive prospect of the island and the ocean. The reason he gave for not choosing this site in preference to the one he did was that the view, constantly before him, would have given him far less pleasure than the occasional enjoyment of it, stopping, as he always did, on the summit of the hill when he left or returned to his house. His object in coming to this country, as is well known, was to found a college at Bermuda, for the education of the original "native Americans." The English government had made a large appropriation for this object, and Berkeley embarked, in the year 1728, with a corps of scientific and literary men. Having lost their way for some time in a dense fog, when it dispersed they found themselves in Narragansett Bay. On landing,

Berkeley determined to make this island the seat of his institution. After waiting patiently for two years to receive the promised appropriation, he was finally obliged to return, and to abandon his benevolent scheme. Not far from the house he occupied are the hanging rocks, gigantic masses which overlook the sea, and in one of the clefts or alcoves of which he composed his "Minute Philosopher." On my recent visit to the house, the worthy farmer who is its present owner told me that he had great difficulty in keeping the old mansion in repair; that he had had serious thoughts of tearing it down, but a gentleman came there one day, a "furriner," who said that the man that tore down that house ought to be *hung*, upon which he decided to reconsider the case. Berkeley, on his departure, presented to Yale College the house and farm, consisting of one hundred acres, together with a library of a thousand volumes. The organ of Trinity Church, still in use, is also his gift.

The English had possession of the island three years, from the commencement of the Revolutionary War to the autumn of 1779. During this time they cut and consumed all the ornamental and forest trees, with many of the valuable orchards; and, contrary to the usages of civilized nations, they carried away the town records.

Newport, even at this period, was the chosen resort of the opulent and educated; and in colonial importance second only to Boston. Many of its inhabitants were from the aristocratic families of England, and it was regarded as the center of fashion, refinement, and taste. In the summer of 1780, the French fleet and an army of six thousand men arrived at Newport, under the command of Admiral de Ternay and Count de Rochambeau, and many are the pictures which remain in the imaginations of the daughters and granddaughters of the beauties of that day, of the dinners, balls, and fêtes in honor of our gay and gallant allies. The admiral died soon after his arrival in Newport, and his remains still repose in Trinity churchyard, beneath the monument of black marble once inscribed in letters of gold, which was sent over by his unfortunate king.

On the northwest side of the island stands the house which

was occupied as the headquarters of the English commander, General Prescott. The harbor was filled with the enemy's ships, and the island with their troops; but Colonel Barton, of Providence, formed the bold resolution of capturing the general. A dark night was chosen for the enterprise; and with a few volunteers the gallant colonel embarked in a small boat, and with muffled oars they noiselessly made their way to the shore. They reached the general's house, silenced the sentinels at the door, surprised the general in his bed, and giving him only time to put on his small clothes, without shoes, coat, or chapeau, they assisted him very rapidly through the rye-fields that lay between them and the water; and while the drowsy sentinels of the English fleet cried "All 's well!" they passed under their bows, and safely regained the opposite shore. The general, taken thus ingloriously, lingered in confinement until he was exchanged for a prisoner of equal rank.

Newport has been the birthplace and residence of many distinguished men. General Greene resided here for many years with his family, and the mansion he occupied is still pointed out. The gallant Perry was born and educated here, and a monument, erected by the State, marks the place of his repose. The eminent Dr. Stiles, afterward president of Yale College, was for many years pastor of the Congregational Church in Newport; as was also the venerable Dr. Hopkins, the founder of the Hopkinsian sect. The Rev. Arthur Brown, afterward president of Trinity College, Dublin, was born and educated here. The lamented Dr. Channing was also a native of this island. He thus describes the influence of its scenery, in his own chastened and earnest eloquence:

> In this town I pursued my theological studies. I had no professor to guide me, but I had two noble places of study — one was yonder beautiful edifice now frequented as a public library, the other was the beach, the roar of which has so often mingled with the worship of this place — my daily resort; dear to me in the sunshine, still more attractive in the storm. Seldom do I visit it now without thinking of the work which there, in the sight of that beauty, in the sound of those waves, was carried on in my soul. No spôt on earth has helped to form me so much

as that beach. There I lifted up my voice in prayer amid the tempest; there, softened by beauty, I poured out my soul in thanksgiving and contrite confessions. There, in reverential sympathy with the mighty power around me, I became conscious of the power within. There, struggling thoughts and motives broke forth, as if moved to utterance by Nature's eloquence of winds and waves. There began a happiness surpassing all worldly pleasures, all gifts of fortune — the happiness of communing with the works of God.

Nor are the arts without their representatives. Stewart, Malbone, Allston, were either natives or residents of the island. It is said of Malbone, whose exquisite miniatures are so valued, and whose celebrated work, "The Hours," is still the pride of his native town, that going to London for the purpose of improving in his profession, he was presented to West, who, after examining some of his miniatures, inquired for what purpose he had come to England; and when Malbone replied, to perfect himself in the art of painting, he answered: "Sir, you can go home again; for a man who can paint such pictures as these need not come to England for instruction." It is pleasant to know that the reputation of Newport, as far as the fine arts are concerned, is not likely to degenerate. Stagg, a most promising and successful young painter, already approaches Malbone very nearly in excellence of coloring and delicacy and force of expression. The late Baron of Kinsale was a native of Newport. In the early part of the eighteenth century, his father, the younger brother of the Baron of Kinsale, emigrated to America for some private reasons, and fixed his residence at Newport. He came with small means of support, which being exhausted, he was obliged to become a day-laborer in order to obtain subsistence. It is probable that he married here, though from the destruction of the records it is impossible to determine. His eldest son was bound an apprentice on board a merchantman belonging to this port, and was serving in the forecastle when the news of his uncle's death reached him. By this event he became Premier Baron of Ireland, with the hereditary privilege of wearing his hat in the royal presence. He retained a strong attachment to his native land; and no Rhode Islander, to his knowledge, approached within fifty miles of his residence without receiving an invitation to his hospitable mansion; and the worthy captain to whom he was apprenticed, received from him annually a cask of wine until the period of his death.

Any sketch of Newport which did not include a particular account of the Old Stone Mill would be like the play with the part of *Hamlet* left out. This singular edifice has excited more curiosity, interest, and speculation than any other remaining in our country. Although it may have been used as a windmill, there is every probability that it was erected for some other purpose; and various are the conjectures as to what this purpose might have been. No similar structure is to be met with in any section of the country. Had the English found it here, it would seem that they would have made some allusion to it; and had it been erected subsequently, so singular a piece of architecture could scarcely have failed to excite a passing notice. The most reasonable suppositions with regard to this relic of another age are that it was either of ante-Columbian origin and built by the Northmen during their visit to this new world, which it is now generally admitted that they made, or it was erected for a fort by traders who might have visited the island previous to its settlement in 1638. A particular description of this structure has been transmitted to the Royal Society of Antiquarians at Copenhagen: and from this, Professor Rafn, one of the most learned antiquarians of Europe, in an article of great ability, has aimed to prove its Scandinavian origin, and to identify it with similar edifices erected in the north of Europe previous to the twelfth century. He says: "There is no mistaking, in this instance, the style in which the more ancient stone edifices of the North were constructed, which belongs to the Roman or ante-Gothic architecture, and which, especially after the time of Charlemagne, diffused itself from Italy over the whole of the north and west of Europe, where it continued to predominate until the close of the twelfth century; that style which some authors have, from one of its most striking characteristics, called the round-arch style, which in England is denominated the Saxon, and sometimes the Norman, architecture. From the characteristics of the ancient structure of Newport, I am persuaded that all who are familiar with old Northern architecture, will concur that this building was erected at a period not later than the twelfth century." The learned professor next brings forward three ancient edifices in Denmark belonging to this period, and also a structure among the ruins of Mellifont Abbey, which in the general principles of their construction bear a strong resemblance to the Old Mill. He goes on to prove that Bishop Eric made a voyage to the shores of Narragansett Bay in the early part of the twelfth century, and that while there he probably erected the building in question, as a portion of a church or monastery. He supposes that after the thirteenth century the Northmen gradually intermixed with the aborigines, as was the case at a later period in Greenland, and that they lost all traces of the civilization they had inherited from their ancestors, and the connection with the mother-country was forgotten.

Washington City Forty Years Ago

As a nation, we are generally, and with truth, considered a vain rather than a proud people, morbidly sensitive to the opinions and criticisms of our European neighbors; the distinction between vanity and pride being, that while the one restlessly desires and seeks the good opinion of the world, the other is satisfied with the consciousness of deserving it. But, more than elsewhere, at our seat of government, the true American finds his national vanity elevated into national pride. It is true he may miss the magnificence of European capitals, the conventional elegance of European courts; but he walks through the wide avenues and the spacious edifices of Washington with a feeling of possession and ownership that could be felt in no other country, although he may not claim the title-deeds to an acre of the broad lands of which it is the center. When he enters the legislative halls, where the talent of the country, from Maine to California, is assembled, to execute the will of that body of which he forms a part, that hackneyed phrase, "the sovereign people," assumes a new significance—a majesty that reflects directly upon himself, and he feels a new consciousness of the dignity of his manhood and of the responsibility of his position as an American citizen. And well he may; for in our country a new field opens, and humanity here takes a new stand, fettered by no antiquity, borne down by no hereditary aristocracy. While other nations have gradually emerged from barbarism, ours has begun her career in the meridian sun of European civilization. With the broadest principles of freedom for the foundation of our government—with a people springing from the fusion of many races, and whose energies are as inexhaustible as the resources of the country they inhabit,—it would seem that here the human mind is destined to develop its highest powers, and that, while on one side its influence will roll back upon the tottering monarchies of Europe, on the other its advancing tide of freedom and civilization will stretch across the Pacific to the shores of Asia, and pour upon them its fertilizing flood. What the Roman Empire was to the ancient world, our republic seems destined to become to the modern; and well may the American citizen emulate the Roman in his patriotism; well then may he be proud, for with so noble a country national pride is neither a weakness nor a fault.

The capital of our country is often singularly misjudged—both by foreigners, who contrast it with the centralized capitals of Europe, and by ourselves, to whom its "magnificent distances" seem to imply an absence of the enterprise and commerce which constitute the life of all our other cities. But the great founders of our republic wisely designed it only for the political center of the country, to be far removed from the disturbing influences that agitate great capitals abroad; and growing, as it necessarily must, only by the reflected growth of the whole country, it may be considered a type of the Union in the grandeur of its plan and the incompleteness with which it is as yet carried out. In Pennsylvania Avenue, which is the main artery of the city, and crowded with continuous blocks of buildings, only fifty years ago the sportsman started the partridge and woodcock from a swamp overgrown with underbrush; and the fifty years to come will doubtless make far greater changes in the external aspect of the city. Like America, Washington must be judged only by looking to its future—the great future which we of this generation are destined to see only with prophetic eyes.

It is a singular circumstance that on the ground now occupied by the city of Washington, the neighboring Indian tribes formerly met to deliberate, and here the flame of their council-fires ascended as they unsheathed their war-knives or smoked the pipe of peace. It is also an historical fact that as early as 1663 the city was laid out and called Rome, and the little stream that flows at the foot of Capitol Hill still retains its classical appellation of "the Tiber."

When the seat of government was removed to Washington in

the year 1800, only one wing of the Capitol was built, and the whole surface of the city was covered with trees; yet the discerning eye could not fail to mark its great natural advantages of position, climate, and scenery, and to admire the wisdom that selected it for the capital of our republic. Now, while each year adds to its stability by new structures and noble monuments, it adds also to its historical associations, and renders less probable the sacrilegious idea of its removal.

Standing on the shore of the broad and beautiful Potomac (or "River of Swans," as the name signifies in the original), surrounded by an amphitheater of hills, luxuriant with every variety of foliage, there are many points from which Washington presents the most picturesque views, and its sites for suburban villas are unsurpassed even by those on the banks of the Hudson.

About six miles from the city is Riversdale, the seat of Charles Calvert, Esq., the lineal descendant of Lord Baltimore; and nearer is Kalorama, built by Joel Barlow, after his return from France in the year 1805. Here he completed and first gave to the world his "Columbiad," at that time the most elegant volume that had ever issued from the American press, and now the only American poem that aspires to the dignity of an epic. Here also he devoted himself to the collection of materials for a history of the United States—a department in which he would doubtless have been more successful, having himself been an actor in the scenes of the Revolution; but in the midst of these pursuits he was appointed minister to France, and died, as is well known, on his way to visit the Emperor. His house at Kalorama, the grounds he laid out, and the trees he planted, remain a pleasing monument to his memory.

Arlington, the seat of G. W. P. Custis, Esq., occupies an elevation of about three hundred feet above the river, on the Virginia side, and commands a view of Washington, Georgetown, and the whole surrounding country. Mr. Custis himself, the last survivor of the family of Washington, seems to form a connecting-link between the past and present. It is an event in one's life to have seen and spoken with a man who, seated at the feet of Washington, has listened to his voice as it spoke to him in the familiar tones of family intercourse, and whose mind is stored with incidents and anecdotes of the great men of that great age. Mr. Custis has great dramatic power in conversation; and in describing so vividly the scenes and actions that have made our history illustrious, he carries us back to them more nearly than any written narrative, even by himself, could do. The plate of Washington, and many curious and interesting relics, are in the possession of Mr. Custis. Among them is a picture, designed and executed by the wife of the first ambassador from Holland, and presented by her to General Washington. The scene represents the cave of the Fates, who are weaving the thread of the hero's destiny. As Atropos approaches with her fatal scissors, Immortality descends, and seizing the thread, bears it away to distant ages. The lines accompanying this ingenious design, also by the same lady, are the following:

In vain the Sisters ply their busy care,
To reel off years from Glory's deathless heir:
Frail things may pass — his fame can never die,
Rescued from fate by Immortality.

Mr. Custis has also in his possession a model of the Bastile, carved from one of the stones, after its destruction, and sent a present to Washington by Lafayette; and accompanying it was the veritable key of the Bastile, which still hangs in the hall at Mount Vernon, calling up, in the sanctuary of freedom, dark pictures of the mystery, the crime, and the suffering that it locked in the cells and dungeons of that stronghold of tyranny.

Many anecdotes told by Mr. Custis, of Washington and of his father and mother, seemed almost to bring us into their august presence. Of the theory that the character of the child depends mainly on that of the mother, the history of Washington affords a striking illustration; and who shall say that if more American women made his mother the model of their lives, their sons would not more resemble hers? The mingled reverence and love with which she inspired all who came within the sphere of her influence, the blended dignity and grace of her manner, the firm will and the mild expression of it,—above all, that elevation and nobility of character, that circumstances could no more give than they could take away,—the possession of all these qualities rendered her fit to be the mother of such a son. Having been separated from her during the whole period of the war, after the surrender at Yorktown, he hastened to join her at Fredericksburg. She received him with that calm approval that expressed no surprise at his splendid career, but which conveyed the far higher praise of his having only fulfilled her expectations. Lafayette said of the mother of Washington, that she belonged to the Roman matrons of the best days of the republic. On his first presentation to her, he found her in her morning-dress attending the flowers in her garden; but with the air of one conscious that her dignity did not depend on her garments, she advanced to meet him, and said: "Marquis, I wish not to pay you the poor compliment of making my toilet before I bid you welcome to my house."

The public buildings, of course, constitute one of the most important external features of Washington; and it is to be regretted, as much on the score of convenience as of effect, that they are so scattered and often on such ill-chosen sites. Through a wholly mistaken economy, the Capitol and almost all the public edifices are built of a sandstone found in the vicinity, which is incapable of resisting the action of the atmosphere, and the cost of the paint required to preserve it equals that of erecting new walls every thirty years. The error has been at last perceived, and the wings to the Patent Office, and the additions to the Capitol now being erected, are of pure white marble.

As the public taste improves, more liberal ideas direct the legislation which has hitherto seemed to reverse the principle that prevailed in the republics of Greece and Rome, where, according to Gibbon, "the modest simplicity of private houses announced the equal condition of freemen; while the sovereignty of the people was represented in the majestic edifices destined for public use." One of our own writers on this subject says: "With us it is the people alone whose sovereignty is constant and unchangeable. But what manifestation have we of their power, written in that eternal alphabet of stone and marble, which has preserved the memory of Egyptian kings and Roman emperors? Where are the resplendent temples in which their representatives make the laws and their judges administer them? Where are the magnificent halls in which their youth are instructed under the tutelary care of the State? Where the spacious galleries of art maintained by the public treasure for the public good? Where are the parks as spacious as those of London, the fountains as superb as those of Versailles? Are kings to have their pleasure-grounds and palaces, and not the people theirs also?" Before many years have passed away these questions may be in some measure answered; and we may point to the Capitol enlarged and beautified, to the National Park, and to the Monument, higher than the pyramids, as at least more in accordance with the dignity of the nation, and more worthy of its capital.

The Capitol of the United States stands on an eminence, about one mile east of the Potomac, overlooking the whole surrounding country. The corner-stone was laid in the presence of General Washington, in the year 1793. The building was suspended during the War of 1812, at which time both wings were destroyed by the enemy; and it was not entirely completed until 1827. The length of the building is three hundred and fifty-two feet, and it covers an area of one and a half acres. The columns of the eastern front compose a portico of one hundred and sixty feet in length, surmounted by a tympanum embellished with a colossal group of statuary, designed by John Quincy Adams, then President, and offered by him after forty designs had been rejected. It represents the Genius of America, attended by Justice and Hope, bearing the scroll of the Constitution. Two statues, nine feet in height, representing Peace and War, stand in the niches on either side of the entrance. The east and west fronts both lead to the Rotunda, which occupies the whole center of the building, and is nearly one hundred feet in height, and of the same diameter. The panels of this magnificent hall are appropriated to historical paintings, and four sculptures in bas-relief, which were executed by pupils of Canova. The paintings by Colonel Trumbull are remarkable for their historical accuracy. The artist, as is well known, was aide-de-camp to

General Washington, and afterward deputy adjutant-general under General Gates. He early resolved to cultivate his talents for painting in order that he might become the delineator of the heroic scenes in which he took part. After the close of the war he continued his studies abroad; and on his return, he visited various parts of the country from New Hampshire to Carolina, and completed his collection of portraits and views of places. In 1816 Congress passed a resolution authorizing him to paint the four pictures that adorn the walls of the Rotunda, and which are the Declaration of Independence, the Surrender of Burgoyne, the Surrender of Cornwallis, and the Resignation of Washington. The heads in these pictures are mostly from life. There are besides these, three other pictures: the Embarkation of the Pilgrims, by Weir; the Baptism of Pocahontas, by Chapman; and the Landing of Columbus, by Vanderlyn.

The House of Representatives, occupying the south wing of the Capitol, has the distinction of being the most badly constructed hall for public speaking known in any country. At certain points, a whisper scarcely audible to the ear into which it is breathed, is distinctly heard at some remote extremity, while, at others, the voice of the loudest speaker seems lost in vacuum. Political and other secrets are thus discovered, and eloquence is often wasted on the empty air. The hall is built in the form of the ancient Grecian theater, with the dome, which is sixty feet in height, supported by columns of variegated marble. Above the speaker's chair is a colossal figure of Liberty, and in front and immediately over the entrance is a beautiful statue in marble, representing History, in a winged car, traversing the globe, on which are figured the signs of the zodiac, and the wheel of the car constitutes the face of a clock. The whole design is full of significance, the visible personification of a great truth. While the hours roll on, History, in her winged car, is indeed there to record the thoughts that are uttered, and to bear them over the world that listens for them anxiously, but with hope and faith.

The Senate Chamber, which is in the north wing of the Capitol, is poor and meager in design, and although in some respects similar to the House of Representatives, is of much smaller dimensions. The galleries are accessible only through dark and narrow passages, and are wholly destitute of elegance, comfort, and ventilation. Beneath the Senate Chamber is the Supreme Court room, an apartment entirely inappropriate to the dignity of this high tribunal. The Congressional Library, consisting of fifty thousand volumes, recently destroyed by fire, occupied the western front of the main body of the Capitol, and afforded one of the most pleasant resorts in the city. The first library, selected under the direction of Mr. Gallatin and others, was burned by the English during the late war. Mr. Jefferson's library, afterward purchased, formed the nucleus of the one lately destroyed, and his arrangement of the books was still preserved. Among the many valuable works, there were few that cannot be replaced; but the new books and the new apartments, like new friends, will lack the charm of association, and thus fail wholly to supply the places of the old ones.

The proposed addition to the Capitol is to be in the form of wings, north and south, projecting both east and west beyond the main building and connected with it by corridors, the three other sides of the wing being surrounded by a colonnade of a corresponding style of architecture. The new House of Representatives and Senate Chamber are each to be in the form of a parallelogram, which has been found best adapted to halls for public speaking. The work is under the direction of Mr. Walters, an able architect, and when completed, the whole building will cover four acres and a quarter. At present, the Capitol is inclosed within an area of forty acres. In the center of the space, on the eastern side, stands the colossal statue of Washington, by Greenough. This is a magnificent work of art, and not unworthy of any age. It is purely classical in its design, and hence it finds little favor with the strict admirers of modern art. The figure, which is in a sitting posture, if erect would be twelve feet in height, and is represented as holding a Roman sword in one hand, and pointing upward with the other. The design is not intended to commemorate any single action, but to express in marble the energy, the fortitude, the integrity, and the devotion of which the character of Washington was the embodiment and realization. The other sculptures of the Capitol have been executed by foreign artists; but the names of Greenough, of Powers, of Crawford, of Mills, and a long list of others, both in painting and sculpture, indicate that the day has gone by when we must depend on Europe for our works of art.

As wealth, intelligence, and refinement become more and more diffused among the people, they demand a more liberal expenditure from their representatives, as is seen by the large appropriations made at the last session of Congress for the enlargement of the Capitol and the extension of the public grounds. The grounds about the Capitol, disproportionate to its original size, would still less accord with its increased dimensions. The open waste, therefore, lying between the Capitol, the President's house, and the Potomac, is about to be converted into a National Park upon a plan proposed by Mr. Downing, to whom we already owe such a national debt of gratitude for the taste and elegance he has introduced into the architecture of country residences. His name is synonymous, not only in this country, but abroad, with whatever is tasteful, beautiful, and correct in landscape gardening and rural architecture, and the country can have no better guarantee of the excellency of the plan than to know that he conceived and is to execute it.[1] The area contains about one hundred and fifty acres, and the principal entrance is to be through a superb marble gateway, in the form of a triumphal arch, which is to stand at the western side of Pennsylvania Avenue, and which will form one of the most striking features that meet the eye of a stranger on entering the city. From this entrance a series of carriage-drives, forty feet wide, crossing the canal by a suspension bridge, will lead, in gracefully curved lines, beneath lofty shade-trees, through the whole park to the gate at the other ex-

[1] Since this paragraph was written a frightful calamity, so fresh in the minds of the community that it need not be designated, has deprived the country of the invaluable services of Mr. Downing. Standing, as he did, alone in his profession, without a rival or a competitor, his death, at the early age of thirty-seven, has left a vacancy that we seek in vain to fill. Although so young, he has exerted an unbounded influence on the public taste, and there is scarcely a town or village in our country that has not some monument of his genius.

tremity. The carriage-drive, going and returning, will give a circuit of between five and six miles. The park will include within its area both the Washington Monument and the Smithsonian Institution, which, with its fountains, pavilion, and summer-houses, will give it an architectural and picturesque interest apart from its sylvan and rural beauties. Besides the most effective groupings of trees and shrubs, the smooth lawns, embowered walks, and artificial lakes, Mr. Downing proposes to introduce another and higher feature in the National Park ; this is an *arboretum*, or scientific collection of trees, forming a kind of boundary plantation to the whole area, where will be at least one specimen of all the trees and shrubs that will grow in the climate of Washington. It is especially his intention to plant specimens of every American tree that belongs to our widely extended sylva ; and each, marked with its popular and scientific name, and the part of the country from which it has been obtained, will thus be made to convey instruction in a form as novel as it is agreeable. To enliven the winter landscape, the park will be largely planted with evergreens. The transformation of this marshy and desolate waste into a National Park has been already begun, but it will probably not be completed for four or five years to come — even with all the aid that the advanced science of the day affords for preparing the soil and transplanting nearly full-grown trees.

After the Capitol, the next object of attention is the President's mansion ; and to not a few of our aspiring fellow-citizens it has even a higher interest. It is about one mile west of the Capitol, forty or fifty feet above the level of the Potomac, which spreads out its calm waters before the southern front. The east room, the principal apartment, is magnificent in its proportions, and, like other parts of the house, is not wanting in mere furniture; for the entire absence of all works of art and taste gives to the whole house more the air of a great hotel than the residence of the chief magistrate of a nation where painting and sculpture are beginning to be appreciated and encouraged. The only work of statuary to be seen here is a bust placed conspicuously in the entrance hall, but whom it is intended to immortalize no one appears to know. Our legislators do not apparently remember that it is the arts, not less than the arms, the laws, and the institutions of a country, that make it illustrious. Phidias and Praxiteles have added a luster to the glory of Greece not less than Solon, Lycurgus, and Aristotle, and the creations of Da Vinci, Michelangelo, and Raphael would, of themselves, make Italy immortal, had she no other remembrances of the past. Take from her the splendor that the arts shed upon her, and her glory would be departed. The discomforts of the White House at that period are described in the following extracts from letters written by Mrs. John Adams, the wife of the President of that name:

MRS. ADAMS TO MRS. SMITH.

WASHINGTON, November 2d, 1800.

In the city are buildings enough, if they were compact and finished, to accommodate Congress and those attached to it; but as they are, I see no great comfort for them. The river, which runs up to Alexandria, is in full view of my window, and I see the vessels as they pass and repass. The house is upon a grand and superb scale, requiring about thirty servants to attend and keep the apartments in proper order, and perform the ordinary business of the house and stables; an establishment very well proportioned to the President's salary. The lighting of the apartments, from the kitchen to the parlors and chambers, is a tax indeed; and the fires we are obliged to keep, to secure us from daily agues, is another very cheering comfort. To assist us in this great castle, and render less attendance necessary, bells are wholly wanting, not one single one being hung through the whole house, and promises are all you can obtain. This is so great an inconvenience, that I know not what to do or how to do. The ladies from Georgetown and in the city have many of them visited me. Yesterday I returned fifteen visits; but such a place as Georgetown appears! Why, our Milton is beautiful. But no comparisons;—if they will put me up some bells, and let me have wood enough to keep fires, I design to be pleased. I could content myself almost anywhere three months; but surrounded with forests, can you believe that wood is not to be had, because people cannot be found to cut and cart it! Briesler entered into a contract with a man to supply him with wood. A small part, a few cords only, has he been able to get. Most of that was expended to dry the walls of the house before we came in, and yesterday the old man told him it was impossible for him to procure more cut and carted. He has had recourse to coals; but we cannot get grates made and set. We have indeed come into a "new country."

You must keep this to yourself, and, when asked how I like it, say that I write you the situation is beautiful, which is true. The house is made habitable, but there is not a single apartment finished, and all withinside, except the plastering, has been done since Briesler came. We have not the least fence, or yard, or other convenience without; and the great unfinished audience-room I make a drying-room of, to hang up the clothes in. The principal stairs are not up, and will not be this winter. Six chambers are made comfortable; two are occupied by the President and Mr. Shaw; two lower rooms, one for a common parlor, and one for a levee room. Up-stairs there is the oval room, which is designed for the drawing-room, and has the crimson furniture in it. It is a very handsome room now; but when completed, it will be beautiful. If the twelve years in which this place has been considered as the future seat of government, had been improved as they would have been if in New England, very many of the inconveniences would have been removed. It is a beautiful spot, capable of every improvement, and the more I view it, the more I am delighted with it.

MRS. ADAMS TO MRS. SMITH.

WASHINGTON, November 21, 1800.

. . . Two articles we are much distressed for; one is bells, but the more important one is wood. Yet we are surrounded with trees. No arrangement has been made yet, but promises never performed, to supply the new-comers with fuel. Of the promises, Briesler had received his full share. He had procured nine cords of wood; between six and seven of that was kindly burnt up to dry the walls of the house, which ought to have been done by the commissioners, but which, if left to them, would have remained undone to this day. Congress poured in, but shiver, shiver. No woodcutters or carters to be had at any rate. We are now, through the first clerk in the Treasury office, indebted to a Pennsylvania wagon to bring us one cord and a half of wood, which is all we have for this house, where twelve fires are constantly required, and where, we are told, the roads will soon be so bad that it cannot be drawn. Briesler procured two hundred bushels of coals, or we must have suffered. This is the situation of almost every person. The public officers have sent to Philadelphia for woodcutters and wagons. . . . The ladies are impatient for a drawing-room; I have no looking-glasses but dwarfs for this house; nor a twentieth part lamps enough to light it.

In the open square, opposite the President's house, is about to be placed the equestrian statue of Jackson, in bronze. This work is remarkable not only for its excellence, but from the fact that it is the first piece of statuary of any magnitude in this material that has ever been cast in this country. The artist, Mr. Mills of Charleston, previously known only as the sculptor of a bust of Mr. Calhoun, and some others, when applied to by the committee to furnish a model for this work, declined to do so, feeling himself incompetent to the task, having never even seen an equestrian statue. But, haunted by the idea, he commenced the design, and after some months of labor, submitted a model to the committee, which was at once adopted. It was said by all connoisseurs that it would be impossible to cast such a statue in this country, and the price offered by the committee did not warrant its being done abroad. Mr. Mills, nothing daunted by the difficulties in his way, with true American enterprise and energy, set about removing them. He remembered that when a boy he had seen a heavy iron chain melted when by accident exposed to the heat of a coal-pit, and on this suggestion he constructed a furnace, and found it entirely successful. With less than half a cord of pine-wood he melted sixteen hundred pounds of metal. Leaving his valuable invention to be perfected at some future time, he has gone on with his work, which is now nearly completed. The whole group is entirely sustained by the two legs of the horse upon which it rests, an experiment which has never before been tried in any similar work. The figure of Jackson, in this statue, if erect, would be eight feet in height, and the whole is cast of the bronze of condemned cannon. This production of Mr. Mills, executed under so many disadvantages, as well as many other works of our native artists, indicate that a talent for sculpture is one of the peculiar gifts of our countrymen, and that the time is not far distant when our public edifices and squares will be peopled by these bronze and marble resemblances of our great and good, which, though mute, will yet speak and awaken in the youth of our country a purer patriotism and a higher virtue.

The Departments of State and of War, near the President's house, are wholly unworthy of notice in any architectural point of view, and not being fireproof, they wait only the accident of being burned down, as the other departments have successively been, with all their valuable records, in order to be substantially rebuilt. For the members of the Cabinet the government has as yet provided no residences, and as the private houses of Washington are generally very small, they afford the most inadequate accommodations for the entertainments these officers are expected by the public to give, and convey the idea of national poverty not at all belonging to the country. But what Congress had failed to do, the public spirit of a citizen of Washington is about to effect. Mr. Corcoran, the banker, so well known for his extensive charities and his liberal patronage of the arts, has proposed to build a certain number of residences for members of the Cabinet, in keeping with the dignity of the office, and to transfer them to the government at their actual cost. Should this proposal be accepted, this very desirable work will be soon accomplished, and the time seems to have come when it cannot longer be delayed. Every year Washington is becoming more an intellectual and scientific, as well as a political, center, and its improvement and embellishment is now an object of national interest.

The Treasury, notwithstanding its architectural faults and its unfavorable position, from its extent and the beauty of its Ionic columns, had an imposing air, which has been wholly destroyed by the paint with which it has recently been defaced, which, instead of being of a uniform shade, is of three distinct and inappropriate colors.

The General Post-office is a spacious and well-proportioned edifice of white marble, in the Italian style of architecture, and the Patent Office, in the Grecian Doric, is unsurpassed by any of the public buildings. Here are deposited all the models for which patents have been granted, the original Declaration of Independence, the camp-chest and a part of the wardrobe of Washington, the gifts presented to our naval and civil officers by foreign powers, pictures, busts, Indian portraits, the collections of the National Institute, and all the treasures of the exploring expedition under Commodore Wilkes.

The National Observatory, recently established, and now under the able superintendence of Lieutenant Maury, is not less creditable to the country in a scientific point of view than useful for the attainment of astronomical information. Besides the various instruments for determining the latitude and longitude of the stars, there is a large transit instrument which, in connection with the magnetic telegraph, will afford the readiest means of ascertaining the exact longitude of any point, thus greatly increasing the accuracy of geographical knowledge. The principal object of interest, however, to the unscientific observer is the great equatorial telescope, arranged under the dome of the building, which moves with the slightest force, and enables the observer to turn the instrument in any direction. In one apartment of the Observatory all the chronometers are tested that supply our national vessels, and their exactness, when ready for use, has done much to render navigation more secure. A small equatorial instrument is mounted in the open air, and two comet-seekers are kept constantly employed in clear weather, watching for the approach of these wandering eccentricities. A meteorological register is kept with great minuteness and accuracy, and everything relating to astronomical science receives its full share of attention.

About one mile from the Capitol, on the eastern branch of the Potomac, is the Navy Yard, probably the most complete and extensive in the United States. Here chains and anchors are made for the largest ships, and a foundry has lately been erected for the heaviest castings necessary for government use. The Arsenal is at the junction of the eastern branch with the Potomac, surrounded on three sides by water. Here are foundries, workshops, magazines, laboratories, and everything necessary to the preparation of the implements and munitions of war.

Not far from the Navy Yard is the Congressional Burying Ground, where are many monuments inscribed with names familiar to us on the page of history. Over the remains of every member of Congress is erected a plain white monument of peculiar form, and every year they dot more thickly the green foliage of this beautiful spot. This cemetery is indebted to nature only for its picturesque beauty, and art will have much to accomplish before it will compare with Mount Auburn, Greenwood, or the beautiful cemetery on the heights of Georgetown, which has just been completed at a cost of fifty thousand dollars, and presented to the city by Mr. Corcoran. This lovely dell is wooded with native forest-trees and laid out with great skill and taste; an entrance lodge and a small stone chapel add much to its beauty.

Near the Capitol is the office of the Coast Survey, one of the most important of the government works. The project for the survey of our thirty thousand miles of coast, which has been in operation since 1832, is probably more perfectly organized than that of any other country. The object is to form accurate maps of our extended seaboard, to ascertain the latitude and longitude of the principal points, the topography of the country parallel to the coast, the nature of the bottom of the sea accessible to the sounding-line, the position of bars, harbors, and channels, the direction and depth of currents, the declination of the magnetic needle, and every particular connected with the improvement of navigation and the defense of the coast. Upon their observations the most correct geographical maps are constructed. The charts exhibit the foundation of the bottom of the sea, specimens of which are collected, and which not only serve as indications to the navigator, but are also of great interest to the naturalist, as they are found to contain organisms of great variety and minuteness, showing that at different depths of the sea, as on land, distinct species have their places assigned them. The development of the laws which govern the distribution of these infusoria, by which an elevation or depression, however gradual, may be detected, will be found of great importance to the geologist. The charts of the Coast Survey, invaluable to our commerce, are copied by an ingenious application of the electrotype to the original plate, which remains almost unimpaired, and immediately furnished to the public at a low cost. Among other discoveries that have signalized the progress of the Coast Survey, is that of a new channel, more straight and deep, into the harbor of New-York; sunken rocks have been indicated, the Gulf Stream, that remarkable phenomenon of our continent, has been explored, and new investigations made on a point of great scientific interest, the determination of a degree of latitude on different parallels, and deducing from this the figure of the earth. These and other observations have given to experimental science an impulse it has never before received; and, under the able superintendence of Professor Bache, whose eminent attainments and discoveries have enabled him to introduce improvements into every department of the work, it is still going on with energy and success, creditable alike to himself and his corps, and useful to the government and the nation at large. Our revenue, as is well known, is derived mostly from merchant ships, and the loss of the duties upon four of them would actually cover the whole amount of the yearly appropriation for the Coast Survey, to say nothing of the loss of life, or the loss of time by ships having no accurate charts, being obliged to wait for pilots.

In 1829, James Smithson, Esq., a descendant of the Duke of Northumberland, died, leaving to the United States the sum of more than half a million of dollars, to found, under the name of the Smithsonian Institution, an establishment for the increase and diffusion of knowledge among men. Mr. Smithson was a gentleman of retired and studious habits, who devoted his attention to the sciences, particularly that of chemistry, and among his personal effects preserved at the Patent Office are many small vessels for experiments upon the most minute scale, one of the subjects of his analysis having been a "lady's tear." By a law enacted in 1846, the President, Cabinet, and some other officers of the government, to have perpetual succession constitute the Smithsonian Institution, the immediate superintendence being given to a secretary. By the authority of these officers, constituting the Board, a picturesque and stately pile has been erected, of red freestone, in the Norman or Romanesque style of architecture, comprising a library, lecture-room, museum, laboratories, and galleries of art. Its length is four hundred and fifty feet, and its breadth one hundred and forty. The office of the secretary is to take charge of the property of the Institution, to superintend its literary and scientific operations, and to give an annual report to the regents. By a skilful management of the funds, the original amount not only remains unimpaired, but is considerably augmented, and the regents have resolved to divide the income into two equal portions, one to be devoted to the encouragement of original research, and the other to the foundation of a library, museum, and gallery of art. Under the first head several valuable works have already appeared, or are now in press, and the library numbers about ten thousand volumes. The gallery of art contains the choicest collection of engravings and books on art in the country, comprising some of the best works of nearly every engraver of celebrity, such as the engravings of Albert Dürer, the etchings of Claude Lorraine, Rembrandt, and others.

Professor Henry, who holds a position of the highest eminence in the scientific world, has filled the office of secretary of the Institution since its establishment, and it is gratifying to know that it could not be more ably filled. In his profound researches on the subject of electro-magnetism, he was the first to develop the principle of immense magnetic force, and to apply it to the moving of a machine. In his experiments on the transmission of electrical currents through long wires, he pointed out the applicability of the result to the telegraph, and the publication of these papers in this country and in Europe was the immediate precursor of the invention of the present system of telegraphing. Professor Henry has constructed a thermal telescope, by which the heat of bodies may be made perceptible at the distance of miles, and he has discovered that two rays of heat may be so combined as to produce a diminution of temperature or comparative cold. His experiments on the phosphorogenic emanation of the sun, or that which produces the glow of the diamond in the dark, after its exposure to the solar rays, and on the heat of the spots on the sun, are of the highest interest.

Professor Jewett, the assistant secretary of the Institution, has in his last report submitted to the Board of Regents a plan for forming a general catalogue of American libraries, which promises to lead to very important results. As most libraries are constantly increasing, the continual rearranging and reprinting of the catalogues becomes at last, even in our national establishments, an intolerable burden, and all the large libraries of Europe have been driven to the necessity of printing none at all. Professor Jewett proposes to stereotype all titles separately, and to preserve the plates in alphabetical order, so as readily to insert additional titles in their proper order. By these means the great cost of republication—that of composition, revision, and correction of the press—would be avoided, and difficulties that have discouraged librarians, and involved such enormous expenses, would be overcome. The importance of the Smithsonian Institution in the center of our country, and the benefits it will confer, have not yet been truly estimated. Science, literature, and art will concentrate here; and in the enlightened encouragement they will receive, they will diffuse their radiance over the whole length and breadth of the land, and the political center of our country will thus become, as it should be, the seat of learning and the arts. It is a significant fact that a descendant of one of the most renowned families in England should have chosen this country as the field wherein his great idea should germinate and expand, and it was in a prophetic spirit that he has somewhere expressed his belief that his name would be remembered when that of the Percys was forgotten. Their conquests were on the field of battle; those won by his munificence will be in the regions of thought, of wisdom, and of beauty: their victories were for one generation; his will be for all time.

About midway between the Capitol and the President's house stands the national monument erected to the memory of Washington. As yet it has reached the elevation of only about one hundred feet. It is to be constructed of granite encased in marble, and the height is to be six hundred feet. The base is to consist of a grand circular temple, two hundred and fifty feet in diameter and one hundred in height, from which springs the obelisk, seventy feet square at the base, and five hundred in height. The spacious gallery of the rotunda at the base of the column is designed to be the Westminster Abbey, or the National Pantheon, to contain statues of the heroes of the Revolution, and pictures to commemorate their victories, while the space beneath is intended as a place of burial for those whom the nation may honor by an interment here; and in the center of the monument are to be placed the remains of Washington. Each State has been invited to furnish a block of native marble with the name and arms of the State inscribed upon it. The temple base, in the plan of the monument, has been objected to by artists and architects, and it is possible that the design may be somewhat modified. The whole cost of this structure, it is estimated, will not much exceed one million of dollars, and this is to be collected by the voluntary gift of the people for the erection of the noblest monument ever raised by the gratitude of man. It will exceed the Pyramids in height, as it will far transcend them and all the monuments of antiquity in the moral grandeur of the sentiment that rears it, and the character it commemorates. The Hon. Robert C. Winthrop, in his address on the laying of the corner-stone, in 1848, says: "Build it to the skies, you cannot outreach the loftiness of his principles; found it upon the massive and eternal rock, you cannot make it more enduring than his fame; construct it of the peerless Parian marble, you cannot make it purer than his life; exhaust upon it the rules and principles of ancient and modern art, you cannot make it more proportionate than his character." At present there are some fears expressed that the contributions will not be sufficient to carry on the work, and that to another generation will belong the glory of completing it.

About fourteen miles from Washington, washed by the waters of the Potomac, is Mount Vernon, the Mecca of the New World; a spot of profound interest not only to every American, but strangers from all parts of the world turn aside to visit the hallowed ground, and ships from foreign lands reverently lower their flags as they pass by. The shadow of the departed whose ashes repose here seems to lie on all around; a spirit whispers in every breeze, and a spell is written on every leaf. The house itself is a vestige of former days, and its wainscoted halls, its spacious and hospitable dining-hall, the library, and every object within and around is instinct with the noblest associations. Here is the bust of Washington, cast from the living model by Houdon in 1785, and although smaller than those usually seen of Washington, it is by far the most majestic head that art has preserved.

Mount Vernon was built by the elder brother of Washington, and named by him after Admiral Vernon, under whom he had served. It is beautifully situated on the banks of the Potomac, the lawn before it sloping gradually down to the river, the bank of which is densely wooded with venerable trees, except an occasional opening, where, through the green vistas, the broad and shining river is seen flowing beneath. Not many rods from the house is the tomb in which stands the sarcophagus containing the remains of Washington. It is simple and almost without inscription; but the inscription is written on the hearts of his countrymen, and "We read his history in a nation's eyes."

The society of the city of Washington has peculiar features which distinguish it from that of any other in the Union. It is certain that, whatever the political institutions of our country may be, its social organization is far from being democratic. Every town and village has its exclusive circle, composed of those who from wealth, family, or fashion assume, with more or less absurdity, to be the aristocracy of the place. At Washington, on the contrary, the President and officers of the government, holding their positions directly from the people, owe, even to the humblest of them, a certain allegiance, and it is the tacit admission of this that gives to the society of the capital such entire freedom from all constraint and formality, and renders it the only truly and practically democratic city, not only in the Union, but in the world. In the capitals of other countries the stranger is impressed only with the power and the majesty of the government, everywhere forced upon him by the pomp and circumstance with which it surrounds itself, and the deference it demands; while in that of our own he feels only the sovereignty of the people, of whom the government is absolutely and literally the servant. In other cities in our own country, "the best society," as it is called, and often justly, is hedged round by so many conventionalities that it is almost inaccessible to those who are without its charmed circle; but here, the President and Cabinet open their doors to all, and all meet on the same social plane; not that distinctions are not felt here more, perhaps, than elsewhere, but the distance with which one towers above another is the result of native superiority alone, and not of artificial props. As a natural consequence, character soon finds its level, and receives its just appreciation. The fact that one is a governor, a judge, a millionaire, or a leader of fashion, at home, where these qualifications give him standing, avails him nothing here, and he inevitably falls into the place which nature, and not adventitious circumstance, assigns him. It is found that this peculiar atmosphere of Washington affects astonishingly all who come under its influence; and the magnate of the town or city, at home so unapproachable and so tenacious of his position, here, finding how little his factitious advantages avail him, suddenly becomes affable, genial, and courteous to all. Hundreds of people, not only members of the government, but temporary residents, thus brought together from all parts of the Union, and tried by this new standard, cannot fail to compose a society of the most striking and original elements, and incomparably superior to any other that our country affords. In this social collision, sectional prejudices wear off, and the East and West, the South and North, thus brought into closer intimacy, become cemented by more enduring ties. As "the king never dies," so the government never ceases, but it is constantly changing its officers, and it is this perpetual change that gives to Washington all the gaiety and abandon of a great watering-place, without its accompanying frivolity.

Another characteristic feature of social life in Washington is, that here men and women take their proper places as leaders of society, while in our country generally, it is mostly given up to the young and unmarried of both sexes, the fathers often absenting themselves entirely, and the mothers merely fulfilling the duty of matronizing their daughters. This circumstance alone would give a higher tone to society here, even if it were not, as it is, composed of the most brilliant talent in the country.

The President's reception, or levee, which takes place one evening of every week during the season, is open to all, and the President and the ladies of his family, after receiving their guests, mingle with them in the drawing-room. In this promiscuous assemblage we meet with representatives from every class of society and every State in the Union, with foreigners titled and untitled, citizens distinguished and undistinguished, and with characters, manners, and toilets equally diverse. In such a gathering one can scarcely fail to find amusement and interest. The hours of reception are limited from eight to ten o'clock, and no refreshments are offered, the chief magistrate thus setting an example of true republican simplicity. The members of the Cabinet also receive in the same general and unostentatious manner, although they are expected by the public to give other and more substantial entertainments, such as dinners and evening parties, and otherwise to maintain the dignity of the office in a manner not at all warranted by the salary; and hence, without an income independent of that, a man can scarcely afford to accept a seat in the Cabinet, however he might desire the honor.

The resident foreign diplomatic corps constitutes another interesting element in the society of Washington. Adopting the maxim of doing in Rome as the Romans do, they open their doors with little exclusiveness, and their entertainments are always the most brilliant of the season.

In conclusion, it may be repeated that it is only here that the great principles upon which our government is founded are fully and practically carried out in social life. Like the high officers of state, the high places of society are open to all; and while the government has solved the great political problem, and demonstrated that men are competent to govern themselves, society has solved the great social problem, and shown that there is no natural or necessary alliance between democracy and vulgarity.

Poetry[1]

INDIAN SUMMER

O SWEET, sad autumn of the waning year,
  Though in thy bowers the roses all lie dead,
  And from thy woods the song of birds has fled,
And winter, stern and cold, is hovering near;
Yet from thy presence breathes a holy calm.
  The fervid heats, the lightning storms, all past,
  A tender light o'er earth and sky is cast,
And all thy solemn voices chant a psalm.
Oh, Indian Summer, autumn of the soul,
  That no returning Spring shall visit more,
  Though all thy rose-hued morning dreams are o'er,
And phantoms dread stand threat'ning at the goal,
  Yet are these days dear as e'en Summer knew;
  These Sibylline leaves of life, so precious, since so few.

TO THE UNKNOWN BUILDER OF THE CATHEDRAL OF COLOGNE

UNKNOWN great Master! whose creative thought
  Is here inscribed, though from Fame's shining scroll
Thy name is lost, this wondrous dome is fraught
  With the expression of thy reverent soul.

[1] The last edition of Mrs. Botta's poems was published in 1881 by G. P. Putnam's Sons.

Immortal, in each curve and line inwrought;
  As in the vast, harmonious, perfect whole:
We see buttress, tower, and pinnacle that reach
  In forests of great columns, towering high,
With deep grooved arches interlacing each,
  Lift their bold outlines dark against the sky.
It rises like a vision in mid-air, indeed
  A temple meet for a divine abode;
The embodied symbol of man's highest creed;
  A symphony in stone; a thought of God.

TO CAPTAIN WEST, OF THE STEAMER ATLANTIC[1]

The gathering clouds around us lower,
  The tempest wildly raves,
But fearlessly our noble ship
  The angry ocean braves,
And buoyant as a sea-bird rides
  The crested mountain waves.

The gale, the storm, the night may come,
  No fear disturbs the breast;
Our ship is strong,—our Captain brave,—
  And we securely rest.
Long life to him and all his Line!
  Health to the gallant West!

Pilgrims to many lands are we,
  And now our travel o'er
Once more beneath the Stars and Stripes
  We near our native shore;
And since we parted from it last
  Who does not love it more?

1 This poem was written on her return from Europe in 1853.

Anne C. L. Botta

Adieu, new friends and old, adieu!
  May every wandering breeze
That meets you on the Voyage of Life
  Be far less rude than these
That our good ship has met so well
  Upon the wintry seas.

LINES TO ——

I THANK thee — not for that kind deed alone,
  Though deep within my heart the record lies,
Engraved with those few pleasant memories,
  That like stray sunbeams on my life have shone:
I thank thee most for this — that when belief
  In human worth was darkening into doubt,—
As one by one, I marked with bitter grief
  Those I had reverenced with a faith devout
Turn recreant back upon their heavenward way
  And sink before me into common clay;
That thou dost come my faith to reassure,
  My wavering trust in goodness to restore,
And bid my fainting hope take wing once more.

SPRINGTIME

OVER the valleys and over the mountains,
  Borne on the wings of the south wind I come;
Breaking the ice-chains, unloosing the fountains,
  Waking all Nature to beauty and bloom.

Flowers from the green turf in myriads are springing;
  Zephyrs are faint with the perfume they bear;
While the voices of Earth, Air, and Ocean are singing,
  Hail to the springtime! the youth of the year!

Oh, gather my rosebuds and sport in my bowers,
  Children of Earth, while my footsteps I stay.
Wreathe with your garlands my vanishing hours,
  Which like life's sunny springtime are passing away.

TO GEORGE PEABODY[1]

No Eastern tale, no annals of the past,
    Of Greece or Rome, deeds such as thine relate,
    Deeds kings and emperors might emulate,
That o'er thy native land new luster cast;
The land that opens all her wide domain
    To the oppressed of every name and zone,
    And with a spirit generous as thine own,
Pours forth the gifts her boundless stores contain;
The land that shall embalm thy memory
    In love and honor, while long ages hence
    The bounteous stream of thy beneficence,
Bearing along to millions yet to be
    Tributes of light and love, its course shall run,
    Still widening as it flows, like the broad Amazon!

TO LAMARTINE

A POET led me once, in chains of flowers,
  A pilgrimage beneath the Orient skies;
And there I dreamed I walked in Eden's bowers,
  And breathed the odorous airs of Paradise.

He touched his harp, and when he sang of Love,
  Then all my heart was to the poet given;
For his sweet tones seemed echoes from above;—
  Strains that breathed less of Earth than Heaven.

1 This sonnet was read at the banquet given by the citizens of New-York to the great American philanthropist on March 22, 1867.

But when in majesty I saw him stand
  The sacred shrine of Liberty to guard;
The destinies of France within his hand,—
  Then in the hero I forgot the bard.

Poet and hero, thus alternately,
  Would claim my homage, each with equal art.
Allegiance I to neither could deny,
  So each by turns shared my divided heart.

TO FITZ-GREENE HALLECK

I see the sons of genius rise
  The nobles of our land,
And foremost in the gathering ranks
  I see the poet-band.
That priesthood of the Beautiful
  To whom alone 't is given
To lift our spirits from the dust,
  Back to their native heaven.
But there is one among the throng
  Not passed his manhood's prime,
The laurel-wreath upon his brow
  Has greener grown with time;
And in his eye yet glows the light
  Of the celestial fire,
But cast beside him on the earth
  Is his neglected lyre.
The lyre whose high heroic notes
  A thousand hearts have stirred
Lies mute — the skilful hand no more
  Awakes one slumbering chord.
O poet, rouse thee from thy dreams!
  Wake from the voiceless slumbers,
And once again give to the breeze
  The music of thy numbers.

Sing! for our country claims her bards,
She listens for thy strains;
Sing! for upon our jarring earth
Too much of discord reigns.

TO PETER COOPER

THE Pyramids of Egypt, even to-day
The wonder of the world, stupendous stand
In their material greatness, and defy
Alike relentless Time and Libyan sand.
But what great thought through those grim structures smiles?
What Aspiration reared those wondrous piles?
None,—save that kings, forgotten long ago,
Might leave their worthless dust to waste below.
This Shrine thou 'st reared to Science and to Art
A nobler Thought than Egypt dreamed contains,
And every stone speaks of a regal heart
Benignant as the Nile to desert plains,
When all the arid waste it overflows,
And the parched shores grow green, and blossom as the rose.

NIGHTFALL IN HUNGARIA

As when the sun in darkness sets,
And night falls on the earth,
Along the azure fields above
The stars of heaven come forth;

So, when the sun of Liberty
Grows dim to mortal eyes,
From out the gloom, like radiant stars,
The world's true heroes rise.

Anne C. L. Botta

The men of human destiny,
  Whom glorious dreams inspire;
High-priests of Freedom, in whose souls
  Is shrined the sacred fire.

The fire that through the wilderness,
  In steadfast luster gleams,
That on the future dim and dark,
  Sheds its effulgent beams.

Thus, O Hungaria! through the night
  That wraps thee in its gloom,
Light from one burning soul streams forth,
  A torch above thy tomb.

Thy tomb! oh no—the moldering shroud
  The worm awhile must wear,
Ere, from its confines springing forth,
  He wings the upper air.

Thy tomb! then from its door ere long,
  The stone shall roll away;
Thou shalt come forth, and once again
  Greet the new-risen day.

That day, that prayed and waited for
  So long, shall surely rise,
As surely as to-morrow's sun
  Again shall greet our eyes.

What though, before the shade evoked,
  The coward heart has quailed,
And when the hour, the moment came,
  The recreant arm has failed?

What though the apostate wields the sword
With fratricidal hand,
And the last Romans wander forth
In exile o'er the land?

What though suspended o'er thee hangs
The Austrian's glittering steel;
What though thy heart is crushed beneath
The imperial Cossack's heel?

Not to the swift is given the race,
The battle to the strong;
Up to the listening ear of God
Is borne the mighty wrong.

From him the mandate has gone forth,
The Giant Power must fall;
Oh, prophet! read'st thou not the doom,
The writing on the wall?

The slaves of power, the sword, the scourge,
The scaffold, and the chain,
Awhile may claim their hecatombs
Of hero-martyrs slain.

But they that war with Tyranny
Still mightier weapons bear;
Winged, arrowy thoughts, that pierce like light,
Impalpable as air.

Thoughts that strike through the triple mail,
That spread, and burn, and glow,
More quenchless than that fire the Greek
Rained on his Moslem foe.

Anne C. L. Botta

Rest, rest in peace, heroic shades!
Whose blood like water ran;
For every crimson drop ye shed
Shall rise an armed man.

Rest, rest in peace, heroic hearts!
Who wander still on earth;
Thoughts, your immortal messengers,
Are on their mission forth.

The pioneers of Liberty,
Invincible they throng;
They scale and undermine the towers
And battlements of wrong.

Speak! sages, poets, patriots, speak!
And the dark pile shall fall,
As at the prophet's trumpet blast
Once fell the city's wall.

TO CHARLES BUTLER[1]

THUS, one by one, dear friend, the years flow by,
That bear us onward to the silent land.
And one by one, around us falling lie,
The loved ones we have walked with, hand in hand.

And thus, the hour comes swiftly, surely on;
I see its shadow darkly toward us creep,
When one shall go, and one be left alone,
To bear life's chain, alone to wait and weep.

[1] For other poems dedicated to Mr. Butler see pages 12, 143.

How sad, how dark, did not the heavenly stars,
  Twin stars of Faith, and Hope, rise on our way,
To shed their luster through our prison-bars,
  To light our path on to eternal day !

That day that knows no cloud, no change, no night,
  Where tears, and pain, and sorrow, enter never,
Where the beloved on earth again unite,
  Where one in God, they part no more forever.

TO THE SAME

THY patron, good St. Valentine,
  Who lived so long ago,
Watched only over happy hearts,
  As all true lovers know.
But thou, born on his natal day,
  A truer saint I find ;
While he alone the happy loved,
  Thou lovest all thy kind.

Through all the sorrows, woes, and ills of life,
  That cloud our earthly road,
Serene through discord, danger, storm, and strife,
  Thou seem'st to walk with God.
And so thy gracious presence ever sheds
  A light as from above—
A light that all thy being overspreads
  With Faith, and Hope, and Love.

LIBERTY TO IRELAND

A NATION'S birthday breaks in glory ;
  Songs from her hills and valleys rise,
And myriad hearts thrill to the story
  Of Freedom's wars and victories.

When God's right arm alone was o'er her,
  And in his name the patriot band,
  With sacred blood baptized the land,
And England's Lion crouched before her,
  Sons of the Emerald Isle!
  She bids you rend the chain,
And tell the haughty ocean queen
  Ye, too, are free-born men.

Long had the world looked on in sorrow
  As Erin's sunburst set in night.
Joy, joy! there breaks a glorious morrow;
  Behold a beam of morning light!
A ray of hope, her night redeeming!
  And she greets it, though there lower
  England's scaffold, England's tower;
And though hireling swords are gleaming,
  Wild shouts on every breeze
  Come swelling o'er the sea:
Hark! 't is her starving millions' cry:
  "Give Ireland Liberty!"

TO EMMA

I look within those deep, dark, lustrous eyes,
And there I read thy heart's sweet mysteries;
There, like those lakes that mirror earth and sky,
The lights and shadows of the future lie.
For thee ambition has no clarion call;
Thou 'lt seek no home in court, or princely hall,
Where folly reigns, and the world's votaries throng
To wile the hours with mirth, and dance, and song.
Nor wilt thou seek to blazon high thy name,
As woman may, upon the scroll of Fame.

But there 's an empire o'er which thou wouldst reign,
Yet should thy subjects wear no despot's chain.
It is the empire of the Heart. It shall be thine,
And o'er it thou shalt reign by "right divine."

TO ANNA

For thee, the Sibyl in the future sees
A lovely cottage hidden by the trees;—
Round its white porch are trained the clustering vines;
Beneath its roof perpetual summer shines—
The heart's sweet summer that shall take its dyes
From the clear sunshine of thine azure eyes.
The nightingale shall sing thee to thy dreams;
The lark shall wake thee with morn's earliest beams;
The flocks and herds shall own thy gentle care;
All living things thy kind regard shall share.
And as thou wanderest midst the lovely scene,
The flowers shall claim thee for their fairy queen.
And here, where Nature wears her loveliest spell,
Shalt thou, her fairest work, serenely dwell;
Far from the world's "ignoble strife" and care,
With some loved spirit "for thy minister,"
Thy life like some fair stream shall glide away,
And thou shalt sleep, to wake in the Eternal Day.

TO NETTIE

Now has the spring her treasures all unbound,
  The earth has put her wedding-garment on,
And, robed in light, with flowers and verdure crowned,
  Comes forth in joy to meet the bridegroom sun.

Anne C. L. Botta

Thou, too, in thy young life's first bloom and pride,
  Joyous as spring, fresh as the morning air,
Fair as the flowers of May, comest forth a bride,
  And bowest thy head, Love's golden chain to wear.

Were mine the power, thy course of life should be
  Serene and tranquil as the summer sky.
No wintry blast should rudely visit thee,
  No tear of sorrow ever dim thine eye.

And when that hour should come, as come it must,
  And thy long summer day draw to its close,
Filled with immortal hope and heavenly trust
  Thou like the sun shouldst sink to thy repose.

Vain wish, for cloudless skies, life without tears!
  A wiser, higher power controls thy fate.
Sorrow and joy are each his ministers;
  And each alike on human footsteps wait.

Seek then his aid who was a man of grief,
  Who bore the cross and won a crown for thee,
And thou shalt walk the troubled sea of life,
  As once he walked the Sea of Galilee.

ON RECEIVING A PICTURE OF AN ITALIAN COUNTESS

Oh lovely semblance of a lovelier face!
  Upon thy classic contour as I gaze,
My eager thought flies through dividing space;
  And to the living picture tribute pays.

I see that brow with thought and goodness crowned,
  I see those eyes with deep affection shine;
I hear the language from those sweet lips sound,
  By poets made immortal and divine.

I would that I might follow my free thought,
  And see this gentle stranger face to face;
For such fair spirits I have ever sought,
  And such would ever hold in my embrace.

TO JULIETTE ON HER WEDDING-DAY

WHEN our first parents were from Eden driven
  To wander exiled in this world of care,
  Hope changed to fear, and memory to despair;
But once, to their posterity 't is given
  The vision of that blissful home to share:
  Whene'er two wedded souls as one are bound,
  Then the lost Paradise again is found;
But trifles light as air this dream dispel,
   And drive the hapless mortals forth disowned,
In the cold air of common life to dwell.
To-day for thee, these dreamland gates are riven;
  Enter, and in its charmèd precincts stay
  Till thy sweet life at last shall pass away,
And thou shalt find it is not far to Heaven.

TO JULIETTE'S TWINS

DEAR Catherine, and David too,
How very sweet it was of you
To telegraph that you were here,
New-lighted on this lower sphere.
That though unlooked for, both had come,
To bring into the earthly home
The light and joy of Paradise
That shine from your four infant eyes.

Anne C. L. Botta

Your excellent and learned papa,
Your beautiful and sweet mama,
Must be most charmed to call you theirs;
Although you bring new fears and cares.
Perhaps at night you 'll cry and roar,
And they must wake, and walk the floor.
You 'll have the measles and the mumps,
The whooping-cough, the rash, the dumps.

And all those things, so troublesome,
That mortal children suffer from.
Dear little pilgrims, just begun
In this wide world life's race to run
Upon life's rough and thorny road,
Fresh from the fashioning hand of God;
Speed on the course, and win the prize,
The prize most worthy in his eyes.

TO MISS EDITH M. THOMAS

YOUR Pegasus, Edith, is hitched to a star,
While mine drags along a Sixth Avenue car;
Yours bears you away to the far empyrean,
Mine carries me down through the quarters plebeian.
Now, soaring aloft, you stop at Antares,
Call it home, that 's the place for Penates and Lares;
Or back to old Greece with her heroes and gods,
You get up a flirtation in sonnets and odes.
(Though they hailed from Olympus, that classical spot,
These "old parties," confess, were a pretty bad lot.)
Then with dear Mother Nature you make very free
To fathom her secrets of bird, flower, and tree;
To live with her ever on intimate terms,
A freedom on your part, she always confirms,
Although so exclusive she is with the rest of us,
Never giving her password or key to the best of us.

But you have them both, and can seek at your pleasure
Her most secret haunts, her most precious treasure;
And she calls you in accents as winning and mild,
As some fond old grandmother calls a pet child.
The round of my Pegasus lies through the town;
He travels and travels, now up, and now down;
I pull on the strap, and he willingly stops,
And leaves me to visit the markets and shops.
(My car, you perceive, is the bobtail variety
So little admired by the press and society.)
But wherever we go he signally fails
To lift me above the street levels and rails.
So you see that our steeds are not matched for a race,
And with all best endeavors can never keep pace.

THE BRIDES OF INDRA

Lo, 't is Indra! he who kindles, God of celestial fire;
Who lights the thoughts of man with the flame of wild desire.
Have you watched the changeful sky, crimson, amethyst, and gold?
'T is his mantle, and the stars shine from every beaming fold.
He rides the snow-white elephant, lashed from the pale sea-foam.
From his hand the rushing thunderbolt, the arrowy lightning come.
Have you heard the shrieking east-wind when the trees were rent and strown,
And the white salt dust of the sea in the face of heaven was blown?
It is the wrath of Indra; and the sunlight is his smile.
When the clouds expire in raindrops, then Indra weeps the while.
In his beauty, none like him the earth or heaven have had:
With the wistful passion of a man, and the splendor of a god,
He has thrilled the earth's dark places, a supernal flash of fire,
He has sounded all the depths of guilt, and sorrow, and desire.

Now sinking in the struggle, now exalted soaring high,
The dark, wild heart of man strives with his divinity,
God of sunlight, God of storm, still the world his voice obeys,
And the sea of human passion, his mighty power still sways,

On its threshold, looking out on the changing world of life,
With its movement and its crowd, its uproar and its strife,
Stood a group of lovely maidens, charmed and dazzled by the glare.
The gaze of Indra fell upon them, and beholding them so fair
He loved them. Flashing earthward in a form of fire he came,
Kissed their lips, and then he left them, with blanched cheeks, and eyes aflame.
And they knew a god thus thrilled them ; and had sought his home again
Ere they tasted aught of love, save its first and sudden pain.
Then they, with vague desire, in their innocence went forth ;
Seeking what, or whom, they knew not, they wandered o'er the earth ;
And Love, who only breathes in the clearer, upper air,
Led them to the hilly land, where the stars were shining near.
And there, though far beyond them, looking down from cloudless skies,
They saw the great god Indra, with outstretched arms and passionate eyes.
Then their hearts sank faint within them ; fain was each one to turn back.
But the soul within had found its wings, and bore them rushing o'er the track,
In a superhuman ecstasy, along the dizzy space,
Till the arms of Indra clasped them in the fire of his embrace.
All unconscious of the bitter cost to those to whom 't is given
Thus to awaken the desire of the ardent sun of heaven,
With quivering lips and beating hearts was the sacrifice achieved,
And the sorrowful great gift — the love of Indra — they received.
Bear me witness, O ye mortals, by the kiss of fire refined,
How closely do the rapture and the anguish intertwine!

I know not which is greatest, for the bliss and suffering strain—
Strain alike, and all too fiercely, on the human heart and brain.
Yet who would cage his soul, when the mighty sun-god came
To thrill his being through, to draw his spirit forth in flame?
But the maidens, knowing naught of an Immortal's love,
Against the crown that Indra laid upon them, wildly, vainly strove;
Though it wrapped them in a glory, their young brows it scorched and tore,
And its golden hues the life-blood of the wearers crimsoned o'er.
"We are faint," they cried, "and weary; from our cheeks the blood has fled;
Our eyes are tired with beauty; in our souls the youth is dead;
The light is but a splendid pain; and, drooping, worn, and rent
With this eternal rapture, our weary hearts are spent;
We turn away in anguish, exhausted and oppressed.
From this fever of our lives, give us rest, give us rest."
They mourned thus until, at length, by resistless impulse led,
From the mountain of Méru, the brides of Indra fled;
Fled and sought those shadowy valleys where the stream of time flows by
Only measured by the seasons; and the mortal dwellers die
Of the slowly creeping years—not of sin, or shame, or wrong;
Not because they have lived too much, but because they 've lived too long.

Oh, what a pleasant land was that! Surely there might peace be found.
A sweet slumberous repose softly lay on all around.
No extreme of heat or cold, excess of light or depth of gloom,
Ever broke the wondrous calm of that wilderness of bloom.
And the hearts of those that dwelt there, emotion ne'er could move,
Or wake the slumbering ecstasies of hate, despair, or love.
Ever young and ever lovely were the women of that land,
And the men who ruled its councils were both courteous and bland.

No labor there was needed, no hardened hand of toil,
For all the heart could ask for sprang spontaneous from the soil.
Old age, disease, and poverty, and suffering could not stay,
For a dark and terrible river ever hurried them away,
As it poured its troubled waters through the shining land of gold,
Washing all its peaceful borders, muttering fiercely, as it rolled,
Words of menace and despair through its sinister black flood,
Which the smiling people on its banks heard, but never
understood.
Wretched, flying, worn, and weary, to this luxurious land
Hither came these hapless wanderers, the fugitive fair band.
Their strange beauty and their wanness, born of passions here
unknown
To the passionless who dwelt here, touched their hearts and
they were won —
Touched their hearts with sweet compassion for each lovely
fugitive,
And they cried, "Oh, stay here with us ; we 'll share with you,
while we live."

. . . .

Now pale, and with lustrous eyes, wandering daily side by side,
The once beloved of Indra in loneliness abide ;
No friendly voices greet them as, dejected and apart,
They pass the idle throng, slow of step and sad at heart.
Each morning wakes anew a gnawing, fierce desire,
That the evening, in despair and in misery, sees expire;
And a curse pursues them ever like an avenging ghost–
The curse that haunts and maddens, of a glory won and lost.

VIVA ITALIA!

Italia, in thy bleeding heart
  I thought e'en hope was dead;
That from thy scarred and prostrate form
  The spark of life had fled.

I thought, as memory's sunset glow
  Its radiance o'er thee cast,
That all thy glory and thy fame
  Were buried in the past.

Twice Mistress of the world, I thought
  Thy star had set in gloom;
That all thy shrines and monuments
  Were but thy spirit's tomb—

The mausoleum of the world,
  Where Art her spoils might keep;
Where pilgrims from all shrines might come,
  To wonder and to weep.

But from thy deathlike slumber now,
  In joy I see thee wake;
And over thy long shrouded sky
  Behold the morning break.

Along the Alps and Apennines
  Runs an electric thrill;
A golden splendor lights once more
  Each storied vale and hill.

And hopes, bright as thy sunny skies,
  Are o'er thy future cast;
The future that upon thee beams,
  As glorious as thy past.

Finis coronat opus

www.ingramcontent.com/pod-product-compliance
Lightning Source LLC
LaVergne TN
LVHW020926110826
845150LV00004B/782
* 9 7 8 1 4 2 5 5 5 3 1 3 5 *